INSIGHT GUIDE

FINLAND

Discovery CHANNEL

D0319334

PUBLICATIONS
Langenscheidt Publishing Group

ABOUT THIS BOOK

Editorial

Project Editor
Zoë Ross
Managing Editor
Huw Hennessy
Editorial Director
Brian Bell

Distribution

UK & Ireland
GeoCenter International Ltd
The Viables Centre , Harrow Way
Basingstoke, Hants RG22 4BJ
Fax: (44) 1256-817988

United States
Langenscheidt Publishers, Inc.
46–35 54th Road, Maspeth, NY 11378
Fax: (718) 784-0640

Canada
Prologue Inc.
1650 Lionel Bertrand Blvd., Boisbriand
Québec, Canada J7H 1N7
Tel: (450) 434-0306. Fax: (450) 434-2627

Australia & New Zealand
Hema Maps Pty. Ltd.
24 Allgas Street, Slacks Creek 4127
Brisbane, Australia
Tel: (61) 7 3290 0322. Fax: (61) 7 3290 0478

Worldwide
**Apa Publications GmbH & Co.
Verlag KG (Singapore branch)**
38 Joo Koon Road, Singapore 628990
Tel: (65) 865-1600. Fax: (65) 861-6438

Printing

Insight Print Services (Pte) Ltd
38 Joo Koon Road, Singapore 628990
Tel: (65) 865-1600. Fax: (65) 861-6438

©2000 Apa Publications GmbH & Co.
Verlag KG (Singapore branch)
All Rights Reserved

First Edition 1992
Third Edition 2000

CONTACTING THE EDITORS
Although every effort is made to
provide accurate information, we
live in a fast-changing world and
would appreciate it if readers
would call our attention to any
errors or outdated information
that may occur by writing to us:
**Insight Guides, P.O. Box 7910,
London SE1 1WE, England.
Fax: (44 20) 7403-0290.
insight@apaguide.demon.co.uk**

This guidebook combines the
interests and enthusiasms of
two of the world's best known information providers: Insight Guides,
whose titles have set the standard
for visual travel guides since 1970,
and Discovery Channel, the world's
premier source of nonfiction televi-
sion programming.

The editors of Insight Guides provide both practical advice and
general understanding about a destination's history, culture, institutions and people. Discovery
Channel and its Web site,
www.discovery.com, help millions of viewers explore their
world from the comfort of
their own home and also
encourage them to explore
it first hand.

This fully updated new
edition of *Insight: Finland*
is carefully structured to convey an
understanding of Finland and its culture as well as to guide readers
through its sights and activities:

◆ The **Features** section, indicated
by a yellow bar at the top of each
page, covers the history and culture
of the country in a series of
informative essays.

◆ The main **Places** section,
indicated by a blue bar, is a complete guide to all the sights and
areas worth visiting. Places of particular interest are coordinated
by number with the maps.

◆ The **Travel Tips** listings
section, with an orange bar
at the top of each page,
provides a handy point of
reference for information
on travel within Finland,
hotels, shops, restau-
rants and more.

EXPLORE YOUR WORLD
Discovery
CHANNEL

The contributors
This edition of *Insight: Finland* was revised by **Zoë Ross**, a London-based editor, supervised by managing editor **Huw Hennessy** at Insight Guides. The book has been completely updated with the invaluable help of a number of specialists.

The Places section and the Features essays on Finnish culture, as well as the Travel Tips were all updated by **Markus Lehtipuu**, an experienced, Helsinki-based writer who has contributed to a number of travel guides on Finland and many other countries around the world, both in English and in his native Finnish. **Timothy Bird** is a British writer living in Helsinki and a specialist on all things Finnish: he updated the history chapters for this guide, as well as the essays on architecture and design, and music and film.

The current edition builds on the excellent foundations created by the editors and writers of previous editions of the book, most notably **Doreen Taylor-Wilkie**, editor of the original *Insight: Finland* and its companion guides to Norway, Sweden and Denmark. **Kristina Woolnough**, who contributed to the original guide, acted as consultant on this current edition, using her vast knowledge of the country gained through 25 years of visiting the home of her Finnish-speaking Peruvian husband. She also wrote the Defence of Greenness chapter.

James Lewis wrote about Finland's history from the very beginnings to the mid-20th century. **Anne Roston** wrote the original piece on Helsinki, and **Sylvie Nickels** wrote on the Great Lakes region, Lapland, and the traditions of the Laplanders, the Sami people. The West Coast chapter was written by **Robert Spark**.

Like all Insight Guides, this book owes much to the superb quality of its photographs, which aim not just to illustrate the text but also to convey the essence of everyday life as it is lived in Finland. In this edition, we were spoilt for choice, with contributions from a large number of photographers. Many of the images were taken by **Lyle Lawson**, an American who lives in England and is an inverterate world traveller.

Other major contributors of new pictures added to the book were **Robert Fried**, **Jim Holmes**, **Michael Jenner** and **Layne Kennedy**. Picture research was undertaken by **Hilary Genin** and **Britta Jaschinski**.

This edition was proofread by **Bryony Coleman**, and the Index was written by **Isobel McLean**.

Map Legend

—••—	International Boundary
-----	Province Boundary
⊖	Border Crossing
—•—	National Park/Reserve
-----	Ferry Route
●	Metro
✈ ✈	Airport: International/Regional
🚌	Bus Station
■	Parking
❶	Tourist Information
✉	Post Office
☖ † ⴕ	Church/Ruins
†	Monastery
☾	Mosque
✡	Synagogue
⛫ ⛊	Castle/Ruins
∴	Archaeological Site
∩	Cave
𝟏	Statue/Monument
★	Place of Interest

The main places of interest in the Places section are coordinated by number with a full-colour map (e.g. ❶), and a symbol at the top of every right-hand page tells you where to find the map.

CONTENTS

Maps

Introduction

History

Features

Calm reflection in
Finnish Lakeland

Insight on ...

Information panels

Travel Tips

◆ **Full Travel Tips index
is on page 299**

Places

A PLACE IN EUROPE

The Finns are among Europe's least understood but most dynamic people, revelling in their new status within Europe

From the moment your plane lands at Helsinki Airport you are confronted with a characteristic of modern Finland, as the scramble for mobile phones begins. It is no exaggeration to say that this device, pioneered and developed by Finns and owned by well over half of them – an unequalled national per capita ratio – is at the heart of Finnish life at the start of the new millennium.

But the prevalent addiction to the phone and its attendant technology is just one aspect of life that, superficially at least, makes nonsense of the conventional wisdom about Finns. Reserved and reticent? You'd never guess it from the constant telephone prattle. The population's proficiency in languages other than its own obscure and difficult tongue also means that Finns, especially the younger ones, are ever happier to converse in English too. The stereotype of the hesitant, sullen Finn was always questionable, but now Finns are really starting to open up.

Since the 1980s Finland's capital Helsinki has swollen, draining the enormous, sparsely populated rural areas, maturing into a distinctive and vibrant metropolis with its own identity. Its restaurants have multiplied and improved; startling new buildings, such as the weird and wonderful Museum of Contemporary Art and the gleaming National Opera, have transformed the city's silhouette.

Celebrating its 450th birthday and the status of European City of Culture in 2000, Helsinki and its residents have found their place in the European scheme of things. Technological innovations, from the ubiquitous phones to state-of-the-art medical equipment and progressive Internet services, have begun to catch up on, and even overtake, Finland's still substantial pulp and paper industry in terms of economic prestige and significance. After a long struggle, there is confidence in the air.

Yet still, the local character is shaped by climatic extremes, of long nightless summer days and bitter winter nights, and its moods swing accordingly. From the rocky archipelago of the southwestern coast to the majestic sweep of the lakeland labyrinth stretching to the border with Russia and the sweeping fells of Lapland that traverse the Arctic Circle in the north, Finland's natural environment is one of Europe's wildest. And modern Finns, mobile phones and all, still claim a special affinity with this landscape, retiring to their lakeside cabins and saunas in the magical summer, gliding on skis through the snow-smothered woods in winter. The urban scene may have been the stage for the most visible recent changes, but the vast serenity of Finland's endless lakes and forests remains uniquely timeless. ❑

PRECEDING PAGES: Sami life as captured by the Sami artist Alariesto; shopfront for eager anglers; boathouses of the Aland Islands; at the heart of Finland's forests. **LEFT:** traditional dress at the Helsinki Midsummer Festival.

Decisive Dates

EARLY HISTORY: 8000 BC–AD 400

8000 BC Tribes from eastern Europe (ancestors of present-day Sami) settle the Finnish Arctic coast. They hunt bear and reindeer.

1800–1600 BC The Central European "Boat Axe" culture arrives from the east. Trade with Sweden begins from Bronze Age settlements along the Finnish west coast.

C. AD 100 The historian Tacitus describes the Fenni in his *Germania*, probably referring to the Sami.

C. AD 400 The "Baltic Finns" or Suomalaiset, cross the Baltic and settle in Finland, gradually absorbing the Sami population. Sweden's influence over its "eastern province" begins, although the migrants embark upon an isolated existence, living in clans and cut off from mainstream European developments.

SWEDISH RULE: 1155–1807

1155 Impatient with the danger posed by pagan Finnish clans raiding the Christians of southern Sweden, King Erik of Sweden launches a crusade into Finland; further Swedish invasions take place in 1239 and 1293, subjugating large areas of the country.

1323 The Treaty of Pähkinäsaari establishes the official border between Sweden and Russia, between today's St Petersburg northwest through the lake region to the Gulf of Bothnia.

1362 Finland becomes a province of Sweden.

1523 Gustav Vasa (1523–60) ascends the Swedish throne. The Reformation passes through Finland without any bloodshed. The Lutheran faith is introduced from Germany by Mikael Agricola (1510–57), a bishop of Turku, whose translation of the Bible forms the basis of the Finnish literary language.

1595 The 25-year war with Russia is concluded by the Treaty of Täyssinä; the eastern border now extends as far as the Arctic coast, allowing Finns to live in the far north.

1617 The Peace of Stolbovo. Russia cedes Ingermanland and part of Karelia to the kingdom of Sweden-Finland.

1640 Finland's first university is established in Turku.

1696 One third of the Finnish population dies of famine after a disastrous harvest. Sweden offers no assistance.

1714–21 The "Great Wrath". Russia attacks Sweden and occupies Finland. Under the Treaty of Uusikaupunki in 1721, the Tsar returns much of Finland but keeps Eastern Karelia.

1741 The "Lesser Wrath". Following Sweden's declaration of war Russia occupies Finland again until the Treaty of Turku in 1743. The Russians cede a section of Finland back to Sweden, but move their border westwards.

1773 Finnish attempts to gain independence fail. A peasant uprising results in several reforms.

THE RUSSIAN YEARS: 1807–1917

1807 Tsar Alexander I attacks and occupies Finland in an attempt to force Sweden to join Napoleon's economic blockade. The Treaty of Hamina, signed in September, legally cedes all of the country to Russia.

1809 The Tsar guarantees Finland beneficial terms at the Porvoo Diet. Finland becomes an autonomous Russian Grand Duchy.

1812 Because of Turku's proximity to Sweden, Tsar Alexander shifts Finland's capital to Helsinki.

1863 Differences of opinion between the Swedish-speaking ruling class and the Finnish nationalists are resolved, giving Finnish speakers equal status.

1899 Tsar Nicholas II draws up the "February Manifesto" as part of the Russification process. Jean Sibelius composes *Finlandia* but is forced to publish it as "Opus 26, No 7". Russian suppression lasts until 1905, fuelling Finnish resistance.

1905 Russia is defeated by Japan and the general strike in Moscow spreads to Finland. Finland regains a measure of autonomy.

1906 Finnish women become the first women in Europe to be given the vote

1908–14 Tsar Nicholas II reinstates the Russification programme and removes the new parliament's powers; any laws passed in Finland still have to be ratified by the Tsar.

1915 Finnish volunteers join the Tsar's army.

EARLY INDEPENDENCE: 1917–1939

1917 The October Revolution in Russia. Finland declares its independence from the new Soviet Union. The Finnish senate elects PE Svinhufvud as its first president. The new state is officially recognised by Germany, France and the rest of Scandinavia.

1918 A radical wing of the Social Democratic Party tries to introduce a Russian-style revolution, plunging Finland into Civil War. The "White Guard", right-wing government troops with German military support under the leadership of General Mannerheim, finally defeat the "Red Guard".

1918–19 Friedrich Karl, Prince of Hessen, is offered the Finnish throne but declines the invitation. On 17 July 1919 the Republic of Finland comes into being, under its first president, KJ Ståhlberg (1919–25).

1922 The Aland Islands are ceded to Finland and granted autonomy.

FINLAND AT WAR: 1939–1947

1939–40 Soviet territorial demands spark off the "Winter War" between Finland and the Soviet Union. Finland successfully defends itself at first, but soon Stalin is victorious. Under the 1940 Treaty of Moscow Finland is forced to surrender 11 per cent of its territory to the Soviet Union.

1941 Finland clings to its neutrality, but in fear of Soviet invasion is drawn closer to Germany. Hitler begins his Russian campaign. The "Continuation War" breaks out between Finland and the Soviet Union. Britain, allied with Russia, declares war on Finland.

1943 The Germans are defeated at Stalingrad.

1944 A peace treaty is signed between Finland and the Soviet Union. Finland is forced to give up the Petsamo region, and the border is restored to its 1940 position. War reparations are severe, and Finland is also compelled to drive the remaining Germans from its territory. The retreating German army destroys many towns in Lapland.

1947 The final peace treaty is signed in Paris on 10 February, reiterating the conditions of the armistice.

PRECEDING PAGES: the Battle of Poltava ends Swedish domination. **LEFT:** King Gustav Vasa of Sweden.
RIGHT: athlete Paavo Nurmi, the original Flying Finn.

FINLAND IN EUROPE: 1948–2000

1948 The Treaty of Friendship, Cooperation and Mutual Assistance (FCMA) is signed, laying the foundations for neighbourly relations with the Soviet Union.

1952 Finland joins in the formation of the Nordic Council. Helsinki hosts the Olympic Summer Games.

1955 Finland is admitted to the United Nations.

1972 The Strategic Arms Limitation Talks (SALT) are held in Helsinki.

1975 The Helsinki Accords are signed at the Conference on Security and Cooperation in Europe (CSCE).

1982 President Kekkonen (1956–81) steps down for health reasons. The Social Democrat Mauno Koivisto is elected as his successor.

1990 Finnish government declares several sections of the Paris Treaty of 1947 no longer applicable.

1991 The FCMA is replaced by a treaty emphasising good neighbourliness and cooperation.

1994 Social Democrat Martti Ahtissari is elected president by direct mandate.

1995 Finland joins the European Union.

1997 US President Bill Clinton meets his Russian counterpart, Boris Yeltsin, at the Helsinki Summit.

1999 Finland enters the first stage of its transition to the euro as the national currency, scheduled for completion in 2002. Finland also serves as President of the EU, hosting two Head of State summits.

2000 Helsinki celebrates its 450th anniversary and is one of nine European Cities of Culture. ❑

E igitur clementissime pater per iesum xpm filium tuum dominum nostrum supplices rogamus ac petimus vti accepta habeas ⁊ benedicas ✠ Hec dona ✠ Hec munera ✠ Hec sancta sacrificia illibata · In primis que tibi offerimus pro ecclesia tua sancta catholica quam pacificare · custodire · adunare et regere digneris toto orbe terrarum vna cum famulo tuo papa nostro · N · et antistite nostro · N · et rege nostro · et omnibus orthodoxis · atque catholice et apostolice fidei cultoribus ·

Memento domine famulorum famularumque tuarum · N · Memoria viuorum et omnium circumstantium quorum tibi fides cognita est ⁊ nota deuotio pro quib

THE FINNS ARRIVE

*The life of the early Finns is one of the most mysterious of all European cultures,
but by the 12th century Sweden had dominated its eastern neighbour*

Race study was an infant science in 1844 when M.A. Castren pronounced: "I have decided to prove to the people of Finland that we are not a... nation isolated from the world and world history, but that we are related to at least one-seventh of the people of the globe." Castren had persuaded himself that language equalled race and had concluded that the Finns were kith and kin with every single tribe which had originated in the Altai mountains of Siberia and Outer Mongolia.

A race apart

That the Finnish tongue is a branch of the Finno-Ugric language tree is undeniable and, to those who maintain, like Castren, that language kinship equals racial relationships, the matter ends there. "The Finns speak a Mongoloid tongue. Ipso facto they are a Mongoloid people." To a scientist-patriot such as Castren, his Siberian-Outer Mongolian theory had the added attraction of establishing a relationship between his own people and a large part of the global population.

Castren's and similar fanciful conjectures came about because of the exceptional isolation of Finnish as a language. Hungarian was, and is, often mentioned as a language akin to Finnish, but the connection is remote. Finnish and Hungarian are about as similar to one another as English and Persian, and only Estonian is close enough to perceive some common linguistic base with Finnish.

Castren's followers, and millions who may never have heard his name, swallowed his theory. This led to the long-held belief that the Finns were a race apart from the mainstream of Europe, their language firmly classifying them as being of Asiatic extraction. No other evidence was ever adduced and even their own scholars and nationalists did not attempt to dispute the issue.

LEFT: a page from Finland's first Bible, now on display at Turku Castle.
RIGHT: M.A. Castren, creator of race theories.

Theory rejected

This rather neat little slot in the huge and ever complex question of the origins of peoples and nations is still accepted by the world at large. The Finns themselves, however, at least those that think and those that research, have for some time totally rejected the theory. As one

leading scholar in the field of philology has written: "No valid reasons for this classification have yet been produced."

Research carried out in this century, based on archaeology, points to a Baltic people moving gradually into Finland from around 1500 BC to about AD 400. There are no signs of a migration from further east. All cultural contacts point to Western Europe and Scandinavia, even from the earliest times.

The anthropological verdict now accepted by all but Castrenite primitives is that the Finns and their racial forebears are "purely European". Tallness, blondness, long-headedness: Finns have these characteristics in common with Swedes and Norwegians (although they are slightly taller on average) and with Germans and Danes (who are slightly shorter, although there is a variant type known as the East Baltic).

Nevertheless, the migrants from the Baltic who took up residence in the land of lakes and forests to the north were destined to live an age-long existence isolated from the mainstream of Europe. A virile and questing people driven to sea and sea-borne exploits by an inhospitable climate and country would

> ### DIFFERENT FAITHS
>
> While Western Finns adopted Catholicism from Sweden, the Karelians followed the Orthodox faith, influenced by Russia across the eastern border.

appear to be a tailor-made fate for early Finland. But the Finns made no such moves. The longships left from the lands just over the Gulf of Bothnia or the other side of the Danish sounds and the trading, raiding and general sea roving of the Vikings seem to have lacked any Finnish participation. Instead, the Finns were hunters and gatherers, surviving largely on the abundance of fish in the country's lakes.

Secret past

Cut off in their sub-Arctic homeland from these early days, little light has been shed on the life and times of the early Finns. No single chronicler emerges from the forest mists to give later generations a glimpse of primeval life. There may well have been an oral tradition of poetry, song and story, a collection of folk memories passed down from generation to generation. The *Kalevala*, Finland's national epic, points in this direction, but the *Kalevala* was compiled and published in the 18th and 19th centuries and cannot itself therefore claim immemorial antiquity.

When Finland finally emerged into the history books through the flickering candles of Roman Catholic crusading, around the year 1157, we find the Finns living in clans. They had apparently never developed statehood; the clans were descendants of common ancestors, often warring with one another and submitting to priests who led them in the worship of nature and natural forces.

Taming pagan warriors

Just as Finnish scholars had established a theory of race and language, a parallel movement in academic circles was growing up on the subject of the arrival of Christianity. According to prevailing wisdom, the Finns were raiding the Christian people of southern Sweden and had become a nuisance and a danger. Furthermore, they were pagans. In 1157, King Erik of Sweden lost patience and set off on a "crusade" to Finland. Taming the Finns was a vital key to trading routes to the east, particularly Russia. Sweden was to control Finland for almost the next 700 years.

Once subdued, the Finns were submitted to baptism by an English-born bishop, Henry of Uppsala. Swedish secular dominance and, in tandem with it, Roman Catholicism, were thereby introduced into Finland.

Yet once again this theory, like the language theory, has all but gone out of the window. Rome has no record of these events and church documents make no reference to Erik or Henry. And again, the archaeologists have come to the aid of Finnish integrity with an assertion that the Finns practised primitive Christianity years before 1157. The Swedes brought Romanism to Finland, but not a new faith. ❏

LEFT: an illustration from the epic poem, *Kalevala*, which details ancient folk stories.

RIGHT: Orthodox religion came to Finland from Russia.

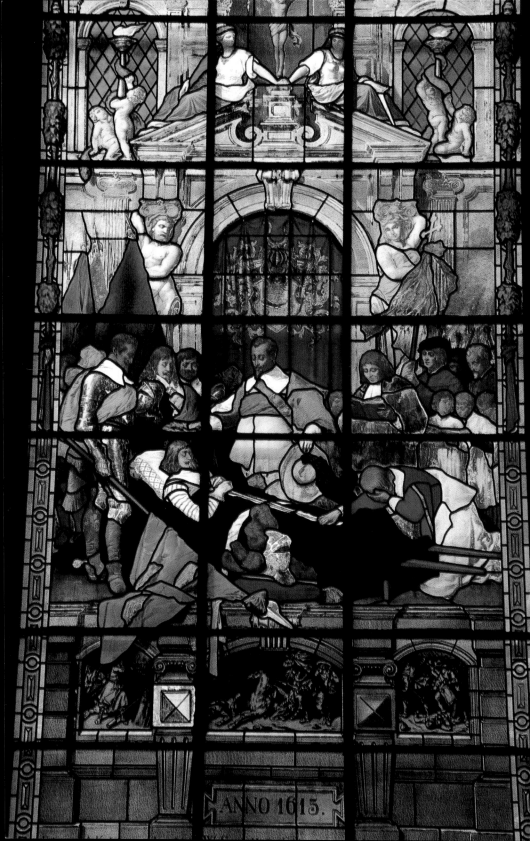

ANNO 1615.

BIRTH OF A NATION

Finland's relationship with Sweden was peaceful in the early days, but by the 16th century Russia wanted control of its western neighbour

The Finns were part and parcel of Sweden for seven centuries (*circa* 1200–1800), but there was never a Swedish "conquest" of Finland. Instead, a race had developed between Sweden and Russia – in those days known as Novgorod – to fill the power vacuum in the land of the Finns. Sweden won the race – and did so without resorting to conquest or dynastic union or treaty. Remarkably, the future relationship between Sweden and Finland was free for the most part of the stresses and strains that normally accompany such take-overs, and completely free of the vicissitudes of war.

A happy union

Although there is no official documentation, it is quite likely that Swedes had hunted, traded and settled in Finnish lands for centuries. On both sides of the Gulf of Bothnia the land had sparse resources and gave little cause for friction. In effect, Sweden and Finland merged as constituent parts of a larger whole. No distinctions in law or property were made, and the history of these two people under one crown has been described as "a seamless garment".

Finns took part in the election of the king, although they were not involved in the choice of candidates. In areas of mixed population language was the only real difference. Castles functioned as administrative centres, not as garrisons to subdue the people. The influences of the one people on the other were neutral largely because the cultures were identical. In one respect only did Sweden bring a dominating influence, and that was in the sphere of religion.

Spreading the faith

Various monastic orders began a slow but steady penetration of Finland during the 14th and 15th centuries. Dominicans, Franciscans and the Order of St Bridget took their place alongside the clergy and greatly strengthened the power and influence of the Roman Catholic Church. This activity gave impetus to church building and church adornment. Life became more settled in the relatively densely populated areas of Western Finland. Further east, it was more mobile, less settled, and depended on

LEFT: stained-glass window in Turku Cathedral shows Gustav II Adolf of Sweden.
RIGHT: Bishop Henrik in Hollola Church.

DANISH AMBITION

At the end of the 14th century there was an attempt to unite Denmark, Norway, Sweden and, by implication, Finland as a result of the ill-starred Kalmar Union of 1397. All the devices which had not been employed between Sweden and Finland were invoked in this fated union, the dream of the Danish Queen, Margrethe I.

In 1509 Finland, which had little say in the matter, became violently involved when the Danes burnt and sacked Turku (Abo), the "capital" of the country. It was just one incident in more than 100 years of conflict over the treaty, which was finally broken in 1523 in a rebellion by Gustav Vasa who became King of Sweden.

hunting across the sub-Arctic tundra, a region rich in animals and game birds, but not suitable for cultivation.

The most important centres from which the new influences spread were Turku (Åbo in Swedish, *see page 203*), with a bishop's seat and cathedral, and Vyborg (now Viipuri). Both towns had close links with Tallinn (Estonia), Danzig (now Gdansk, in Poland) and Lübeck (Germany) as well as with Stockholm. In these Finnish towns artisans and professions flourished alongside the clergy and an urban culture came into being, in contrast to the ruder ways of life further east.

Stirrings of nationhood

Sweden was now powerful and independent. The Middle Ages were over; the Reformation challenged Rome. Here was a cocktail of influences, almost modern in their impact. Sweden and Finland were both slipping away from the old moorings. Slowly, the relationship was changing. The first stirrings of nationhood date from this time, although they were small and they originally arose from the translation of religious text into the vernacular.

Many more Swedes and Finns fell under the influence of Martin Luther in Wittenberg. The Reformation also attracted Gustav Vasa,

"You are instructing your charges in a manner that is both nasty and lazy," wrote the Bishop of Turku, Mikael Agricola, to his clergy in 1548.

Agricola (1510–57) sent out this admonition with a translation of the New Testament in Finnish, a work he had undertaken to make sure, as he put it, "that not a single preacher or teacher could cover up his laziness by claiming that he did not know Latin or Swedish." Agricola created the first Finnish alphabet and Finnish writings, on a religious theme. The whole Bible was published in 1642, and in doing so, it created the first official document of the Finnish language in print, thus formalising the language.

because the Swedish crown needed more revenue and the church could provide it. In fact, the Reformation was so irresistible that Sweden was the first state in western Christendom to break with Rome.

The split took place in May 1527. All over Sweden and Finland the church suddenly lost property, authority, ceremonies and rites. Holy water, customary baptism and extreme unction were banned, so were colourful processions and the worship of relics. But transforming Finns from a Catholic to a Protestant people was not painless. The early Lutheran pastors were a motley rabble – "violaters of the laws of man and God." Yet Finns took a leading part in the transformation and Pietari Särkilahti, Mikael Agricola and Paavali Juusten aided their Swedish brethren in severing links with Rome.

Peasant soldiers

During the three centuries before 1809, when Finland finally broke with Sweden, the Swedish crown was at war for more than 80 years. Involvement in the Thirty Years' War and wars with both Poland and Russia raised taxes and took Finnish men away from the land – the burden of providing levies always fell

CALL TO ARMS

Military service was compulsory except for the cavalry, in which volunteers enlisted eagerly in order to escape the harder life of an infantryman.

The Dutch influence

In Turku, Helsinki, Porvoo and Viipuri, as well as in the other Baltic trading cities, many of the leading merchants, who controlled much of the foreign trade, were of German or Dutch descent. "The general area of our economic history during the 17th century and part of the 18th centuries bears a marked Dutch stamp," remarks V. Voionmaa, a prominent Finnish historian. The Dutch were well established, and foreign goods and ways of doing business gained ground in

heavily on the farmers. Finns were a vital part of the Swedish army, comprising a third of the foot soldiers and cavalry. In the wars with Russia, Finland bore the brunt of the suffering. City development became sluggish and, in any case, Finnish cities frequently went up in smoke. Turku (Abo) suffered 15 major fires between 1524 and 1624; the worst reduced the city to ashes. Pori and Viipuri also suffered a similar fate several times, though fires were not the only dangers that beset the cities.

LEFT: Mikael Agricola's 16th-century Bible translated into Finnish (Turku Cathedral).
ABOVE: building Häme Castle.

Finland. Foreign as well as Finnish capital fuelled industry and trade.

Sweden no longer dominated the land and conflicts with the Russians kept recurring. The wars were destructive to Finland and read like a litany: 1554–7; a 25-year war (interrupted by truces) which started in 1570; two wars in the 17th century (as well as a devastating famine from 1696–7) and the great Northern War from 1700–21; war again 20 years later; and yet again from 1788–90. In the mid-18th century Sweden regained partial confidence and began to improve Finnish defences with the construction of fortresses such as Suomenlinna (*see page 177*), but when Peter the Great founded St

Petersburg, just across the border with eastern Finland, Russian power was again in full force.

Carrot and stick

The Swedish crown demonstrated an inability to hold Finland against Russian assault. It lost Finland on two occasions (1721 and 1743). In 1808, Great Britain became a Swedish ally. The Russians now saw a dire threat to St Petersburg and to Russian naval access to the Baltic. Yet again Russia and Sweden fought. This time Russia held on to Finland and offered the country generous terms as part of a strategy of "carrot and stick" – offering Finns a large say in

constitutional monarch in the newly acquired territory. It was an experiment in kingship, a new departure for an absolute ruler. The experiment was an unqualified success for 60 years.

The Grand Duchy was declared before the end of the 1808-9 war with Sweden at the Diet of Porvoo. As a Grand Duchy, Finland benefited from Russia's precedent of allowing the countries annexed into its empire to retain their legislative and other social systems. The Baltic states, and later Poland, were granted the same rights. The enlightened policies of Alexander I, which included the granting of a degree of freedom for Finnish peasants, could be seen as a

the running of their land, but retaining Russian overall rule. The Swedish centuries had finally come to an end.

A nation is born

Sweden formally ceded Finland to Russia by the Treaty of Hamina on 17 September 1807. Along with Finland went the Åland Islands, between Sweden and Finland, which had long been an administrative part of the Finnish half of the kingdom. Finland became a separate state whose head, the Tsar-Grand Duke, was an absolute ruler; Tsar of all the Russias. Yet in Finland he agreed to rule in partnership with the Finnish Diet. This made the Tsar a

step towards wider, progressive changes planned in other parts of the empire.

For most ordinary Finns, very little changed. No pressure was put on the people to switch from the Lutheran Church to the Orthodox, and Swedish continued to be the language of government. Yet the setting up of a Finnish Diet, as well as an administrative Senate-led body allowed the gradual rise in influence of the Finnish language and, slowly but surely, the general spread of the idea of Finnish nationalism and independence. ❑

ABOVE: the house of Johan Ludvig Runeberg (1804–77), Finland's patriotic poet (*see page 95*).

A Winter Journey

At the end of the 18th century, Joseph Acerbi embarked on what was then the only practical way of crossing from Sweden to Finland in winter, by sledge across the frozen Gulf of Bothnia. The distance was 70 km (43 miles) but, using the Aland Islands as stepping stones, that left 50 km (30 miles) "which you travel on the ice without touching on land".

Acerbi was advised that his party of three, plus two servants, would have to double their number of horses and hire no fewer than eight sledges for the crossing. He suspected that he was being swindled by the Swedish peasants but, as things turned out, it was a sensible precaution.

Acerbi published the details of the difficult and at times terrifying journey in his work *Travels Through Sweden, Finland and Lapland to the North Cape. 1802*, as follows:

"I expected to travel 43 miles without sight of land over a vast and uniform plain, and that every successive mile would be in exact unison and monotonous correspondence with those I had already travelled; but my astonishment was greatly increased in proportion as we advanced from our starting-post. At length we met with masses of ice heaped one upon the other, and some of them seeming as if they were suspended in the air, while others were raised in the form of pyramids. On the whole they exhibited a picture of the wildest and most savage confusion... It was an immense chaos of icy ruins, presented to view under every possible form, and embellished by superb stalactites of a blue-green colour.

"Amidst this chaos, it was not without difficulty and trouble that our horses and sledges were able to find and pursue their way. It was necessary to make frequent windings, and sometimes to return in a contrary direction, following that of a frozen wave, in order to avoid a collection of icy mountains that lay before us.

"The inconvenience and the danger of our journey were still farther encreased (*sic*) by the following circumstance. Our horses were made wild and furious, both by the sight and the smell of our great pelices, manufactured of the skins of Russian wolves or bears. When any of the sledges was overturned, the horses belonging to it, or to that next to

---

RIGHT: Count Per Brahe, Turku governor at the time of Acerbi's journey.

it, frighted at the sight of what they supposed to be a wolf or bear rolling on the ice, would set off at full gallop, to the terror of both passengers and driver. The peasant, apprehensive of losing his horse in the midst of this desert, kept firm hold of the bridle, and suffered the horse to drag his body through masses of ice, of which some sharp points threatened to cut him in pieces. The animal... continually opposed to his flight, would stop; then we were enabled to get again into our sledges, but not till the driver had blindfolded the animal's eyes: but one time, one of the wildest and most spirited of all the horses in our train, having taken fright, completely made his escape...

"During the whole of this journey we did not meet with, on the ice, so much as one man, beast, bird, or any living creature. Those vast solitudes present a desert abandoned as it were by nature. The dead silence that reigns is interrupted only by the whistling of the winds against the prominent points of ice, and sometimes by the loud crackings occasioned by their being irresistibly torn from this frozen expanse; pieces thus forcibly broken off are frequently blown to a considerable distance.

"Through the rents produced by these ruptures, you may see below the watery abyss; and it is sometimes necessary to lay planks across them, by way of bridges, for the sledges to pass over." ❏

LIVING WITH RUSSIA

Finland's relationship with Russia was at first peaceful but, with Russia's own

political struggles, the union dissolved into revolt and war

Annexation by Russia defied all gloomy prophecies, at least at the outset. Tsar Alexander I seemed open to suggestions from the Finnish camp, and a group of leading Finns suggested that Finland should hold elections. Alexander agreed and the first Finnish Diet met at Porvoo in 1809. The Tsar had styled himself "the Emperor and Autocrat of all the Russias and the Grand Duke of Finland." Invested with this new title, the proto-type of future constitutional monarchs, Tsar Alexander formally opened the Diet. In return, he promised to respect and maintain the laws, religion and constitution of Finland.

A diplomatic success

The constitution's main pillar was a unique device in the statecraft of those days. Finland was to be in personal union with the Tsar. This meant that the Finns dealt direct with their head of state, bypassing the Russian government. Ultimately it became the cause of much jealousy, but the arrangement lasted for 90 years and was the basis of the relationship between Russia and Finland. When Nicholas I succeeded Alexander in 1825 a strong bond of mutual trust had developed. The change of overlord had brought advantages: the fear of attack from the east had gone; Finns could con-duct their internal affairs but, if they felt cramped, opportunities existed in the armed forces and civil service of Russia. The Finnish army was disbanded, though its officers received generous pensions. Russian troops garrisoned Finland but never in large numbers. Taxation was raised for domestic needs only.

Behind all this liberality lay firm policy: to pacify Finland and woo it away from Sweden. To keep Sweden sweet, Alexander concluded an agreement, in 1812, in support of moves to unite Norway with Sweden. This was the new Swedish ambition.

PRECEDING PAGES: Tsar Alexander I leads the Finnish Diet at Porvoo in 1809. **LEFT:** Russia's Imperial throne in Finland. **RIGHT:** Tsar Nicholas II.

The new capital

The Grand Duchy needed a capital and it was a small rocky fishing port that was chosen. Helsinki became a city of major importance on the Baltic within two generations. A visitor in 1830 remarked that the Finns were "convert-ing a heap of rocks into a beautiful city." The

urban centre was conceived and planned on an imperial scale, with Neo-classical buildings designed by the German architect C.L. Engel. The university of Turku moved to Helsinki's great square in 1828. The year before, Turku had suffered yet another disastrous fire, after which its eclipse was inevitable.

The university became a tug of war between languages. There was no discrimination against Finns as a separate linguistic group within the Russian Empire, and the idea of introducing Russian as a subject in schools was canvassed by a few bureaucrats, but not much was done. Finns wishing to serve the Tsar outside Finland had to learn Russian, but to serve the Grand

Duke of Finland the requirement, up until 1870, was to speak and write Swedish.

Peasant power

The all-important vernacular being promoted by nationalist Henrik Porthan already resided in the countryside, on the farms and in the forests. But the farmers and peasants of the country were slow to awaken to the power they possessed. In part, the peasants distrusted notions of independence. The rural poor, workers, smallholders and the landless were on the periphery of political life and thought. In contrast to the élite, they were indifferent to ideas of liberty and national independence, which were not hot topics among the masses. There was even some class-based hostility to such notions. When autonomy was in jeopardy under a changed Russian attitude at the end of the 19th century, some pamphleteers got to work to raise national consciousness. Grumpy peasants tossed back at them remarks such as "Now the gentry are in a sweat" and "These new laws don't concern us peasants, they're only taking the power off the gentry."

Yet, all the time, opportunities in higher education were increasing among such people. Into secondary education, university and the

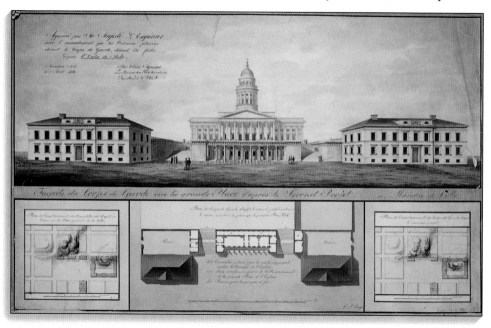

THE FATHER OF FINNISH HISTORY

Bold ideas of Finnish independence had been nurtured by educated Finns ever since the days when Sweden had started to lose its grip. Henrik Porthan (1739–1804), known as the "father of Finnish history," awakened intellectual leaders. "We must pray," he said "that Russia will succeed in situating its capital in Constantinople… But now that its capital city (St Petersburg) is located so near, I am afraid that Finland will … fall under the power of Russia."

Nevertheless, the Finnish people, he advocated, should use this as an opportunity, and not be despondent. They must think of themselves above all as Finns. History, language and folklore (according to Porthan) all pointed to a Finland that was ultimately free. But Russia – barbarous, Byzantine, eastern Russia – and not western, democratic Sweden, was the stepping stone to this end.

Porthan was ahead of his time, but his long-term, pragmatic philosophy took hold and became the prevailing wisdom of his own and succeeding generations of Finnish nationalists. Their patience was finally rewarded when, within living memory, the goal of nationhood was achieved. His disciples realised very quickly that if the Finnish language would be able to replace Swedish, the battle for independence, at least in the hearts and minds of Finns themselves, was three-quarters won.

new polytechnics they brought their language, which was vernacular Finnish. Russian was still not an issue, but Swedish was, and Swedish was gradually being supplanted. The peasants were also growing richer. The demand for timber increased and the price rose. Freehold peasant farmers with timber land grew rich. Their wives could now afford tables, sideboards and chairs in place of rustic benches and chests. Life for some was becoming genteel and not rough-hewn. Since 1864 peasants had been able to buy land on the open market. Now their sons were taking advantage of higher education, more Finnish language fodder.

Ruthless governor

Tsar Alexander III, who freed the Russian serfs, knew his Grand Duchy. His son, the ill-starred Nicholas II (1894–1917) did not. The conception of a docile and contented satellite country acting as a buffer on Russia's northwest flank, the cornerstone of policy for 90 years, was cast aside. A new Governor, General Bobrikov, fresh from a ruthless administration in the Baltics, was installed in Helsinki.

Finland lost its autonomy. Laws, soldiering and taxation, those pivotal issues which previous grand dukes had treated so delicately, were henceforth to be Russian concerns. "While leaving in operation the existing regulations for legislation on matters of local interest which bear only on the needs of Finland, we have considered it necessary to reserve to ourselves the final determination of matters of legislation which concern the whole Empire," ran a manifesto promoted by Bobrikov. It was too much for the Finns: 522,931 signatures on a petition were collected in just two weeks,

Abroad, another petition was launched in support of the Finns, signed by many eminent people. They addressed Tsar Nicholas: "Having read and being deeply moved by the petition of the 5th March of over half a million Finnish men and women in which they made a solemn appeal to your Majesty in support of the maintenance of their full Rights and

> **STUDENT SKIERS**
>
> Many of the signatures on the petitions to Tsar Alexander were collected by nationalistic students who skied from remote farm to distant cottage across the country.

Privileges first confirmed by… Alexander I in 1809… and subsequently re-affirmed in the most solemn manner by all his illustrious successors, we venture to express our hope that your Imperial Majesty will take into due consideration the prayer of the said Petition of your Majesty's Finnish subjects. It would be a matter of great regret if recent events in the Grand Duchy of Finland should retard the cause of amity among the nations of the civilised world which has in your Majesty so Illustrious an Advocate."

The "Illustrious Advocate" was unmoved. *The Times* of London thundered a declaration that "the Finnish Diet can, legally, only be modified or restricted with its own consent." This too fell on deaf Russian ears. They imposed strict censorship on the Finnish press. Conscription into the Russian army was the final straw.

The Finns revolt

Resistance started to stiffen and pamphleteers got to work. Half the conscripts ordered to report for military service in the spring of 1902 did not turn up. In 1904 the Governor General was assassinated by a patriotic student, Eugen Schauman, who then committed suicide by

---

LEFT: C. L. Engel's original drawing for the design of Senate Square in Helsinki.
ABOVE: statue of Alexander II at Helsinki Cathedral.

turning his gun on himself. Schauman became a national hero and is buried at Porvoo.

The Russian Revolution of 1905 and the Russo-Japanese war brought a respite. The Finns took the opportunity to put forward a bold measure. The franchise was by now outmoded. Industrial workers had no representation; women no vote. This was par for the times in Europe, although New Zealand had just granted women the vote. Finland proposed no less than a universal franchise and a unicameral parliament. The Tsar, doubt-less distracted by the stirrings of revolt in Russia – a chain of events that would eventually bring him down – agreed to the changes. The Finns got their modern parliament. The electoral role was increased tenfold. The Social Democrats won the subsequent election.

> ## NATIONAL IDENTITY
>
> "We are no longer Swedes, we will not become Russians, so let us be Finns," had been the cry for some decades by nationalists.

civil war which broke out between the "Whites" and the "Reds".

The cause, in short, was the overspilling of the Russian October Revolution into Finland, upon whose soil remained contingents of Russian soldiers who sided with the Soviets. Thus Finland had a Red Army in its very midst. Luckily the Soviet government did not officially participate in the civil war in Finland, but Russian aid played a significant part in the Red revolt. Finnish Red Guards were supplied with arms by the

Russians. Russian officers and NCOs provided leadership; in the case of the artillery, they provided the entire command.

The civil war's major contributory cause had been labour unrest. After the Bolsheviks had seized power in Russia, radical groups among Finnish socialists became determined to overcome their minority position in parliament with extra-parliamentary activity. A strike was the first step, accompanied by lawlessness on a considerable scale, including murder. Many parts of the country were affected. After a week the strike was called off, but events escalated, and a Central Revolutionary Council formed the Red Guards. They struck at the end of

Civil war

Now the country was united as never before in a determination to be free Finnish. The moment came during World War I, when the Russian army collapsed and Lenin seized power. Finland was allowed to go free, compliments of the Bolsheviks. Independence had come at last, but the event was to be marred by a bitter

January 1918, in the hope that Russian aid would be enough to secure a quick victory

Military genius

The legal government had no adequate forces at its disposal to meet this situation. It did, however, appoint a commander-in-chief to a non-existent army. General Carl Gustaf Emil Mannerheim was an inspired military leader on a par with Turkey's Kemal Ataturk and the British general Bernard "Monty" Montgomery.

Mannerheim had been persuaded by Premier Svinhufvud to organise a government force to uphold law and order. On 18 January, he went to Vaasa on the west coast of Finland, to plan for and organise a "White" army. Vaasa became the seat of government when war broke out. Four cabinet members escaped there from Helsinki hours before the Reds seized control of the capital on 28 January.

Mannerheim disarmed Russian garrisons in central and northern Finland, and then turned them into bases from which government forces waged war against the enemy in the south. Tampere, Helsinki and Viipuri were liberated by the spring. After a last stand on the Karelian Isthmus, the Reds capitulated on 15 May. On 16 May Mannerheim's "people's army" held a victory parade in Helsinki.

After a brief flirtation with the idea of a monarch, during which time both Svinhufvud and Mannerheim acted as regent, the Finns elected K. J. Ståhlberg, author of the Form of Government, as its first president.

Red defeat

The Reds, without full Russian support and up against the strategic ability of General Mannerheim, found their hopes short-lived.

LEFT: Eugen Schauman assassinates General Bobrikov in 1904.
ABOVE: White and Red troops at war in 1918.

An insecure start

In 1920 the conflicts between Finland and the Soviet Union were dealt with by the Treaty of Tartu, which recognised Finland as an independent republic and ceded to it the Arctic port of Petsamo. Some small adjustments were made to the border and Finland neutralised its islands close to Leningrad. However, the Soviets seemed unable to forgive the Finns for their bourgeois defeat of revolution; in turn, there arose an almost fanatical distrust of the Soviet Union in Finland. Fear of had been the upsurge of Red rebellion, which was ably put down but which caused a severe shock to the body politic. The second problem was emigration.

EQUAL RIGHTS

Finland was the first European country to give women the vote and an equal political voice when it became independent in 1906.

Land hunger

Once Russian overlordship had taken a nasty turn, the resulting insecurity had already started a trend towards emigration. But there were other causes, and land hunger was the foremost. "No land, no fatherland" was the cry. There was a landless proletariat of 200,000 in the 19th century, plus a host of peasants with

Russia, civil war, and the political polarisation that had caused it ran deep and affected the national psyche. Sandwiched between Communist Russia and neutral Sweden, and with a militaristic Germany to the south, independent Finland was born, one historian has noted: "not with a silver spoon, but with a dagger in its mouth". Finland survived because it learned the trick of "sword swallowing".

One matter that needed no adjustment in the constitution of independence was the Parliament Act of 1906, far ahead of its time in granting votes to both men and women. But social and economic disparities were not mitigated by legalities. Two symptoms were manifest. One meagre plots. These people looked to the New World for opportunities.

Before and after the civil war there had been near famine in the countryside. "Nature seems to cry out to our people 'Emigrate or die'," one university lecturer told his students in 1867. By the 1920s, 380,000 Finns had left for other lands, the majority to the USA. The Great Depression hit Finland in 1929, and by 1930 the figure for emigration had reached 400,000.

Divided politics

In the 1920s the two branches of the labour movement (the bulk of the "Reds") grew further apart. For public and election purposes, the outlawed Communist Party metamorphosed into the Socialist Workers' and Small Holders' Election Organisation, while the Social Democrats began to co-operate with the bourgeois parties, culminating in a Social Democrat government in 1926, led by their moderate leader, Väinö Tanner.

Anti-Communist feeling continued, nevertheless, and led to the Lapua movement which resorted to violent methods, such as capturing and driving suspected Communist leaders over the Soviet border. Even the respected former president

period of co-operation between the Agrarian Party and the Social Democrats, the aptly named "red-green" coalition.

IN SEARCH OF FOOD

"The heart pleaded no, but the stomach commanded yes," ran a line in the novel *Amerikkaan*, referring to Finland's emigration.

Cultural advances

Though the infant nation's priority had to be to survive and to strengthen its democracy, life was not all gloom. In the 1920s, sport, travel and the cinema all came into their own, with a profound effect on social habits. It was a time of strong cultural expression, particularly in architecture and design. Up until 1939, a degree of cultural and

Ståhlberg did not escape one attempt and was driven close to the border. In 1930, the Lapua movement inspired a great peasants' march to Helsinki, and led to armed rebellion in 1932.

The formidable duo of the Liberation period, Svinhufvud and Mannerheim returned and, after anti-Communist laws were passed, it was left to Svinhufvud to persuade the rebels to disband peacefully. Despite these strains, Finland grew closer to the Scandinavian countries, where democracy was advancing, with a long

---

LEFT: crowds riot in Turku in 1905 in support of Russian uprisings.
ABOVE: civil war bomb damage in Tampere, 1918.

commercial harmony had existed between Russians and Finns. Communism kept a low profile, while Fascists failed to gather significant support. By the time of the war, Finland's agriculture had developed and the forest industry took the lead, supporting progress in other industries; forest product exports to other European countries boosted national earnings. Optimism was rife, to the extent that, despite the growing threats in Europe (particularly from Germany) and Mannerheim's warnings, little was done to build up the country's armaments. When parliament eventually approved 3,000 million marks for military procurement in 1938, it was already too late. ❑

THE TWO WARS

The bravery and prowess of Finland's soldiers on their treacherous, ice-bound terrain became legendary during the Winter and Continuation wars

By the spring of 1938 Moscow was making demands on the Finnish Government to give guarantees that, in the event of hostile acts by Germany, Finland would accept Soviet military aid. The railway line between Leningrad and Murmansk was vital to Soviet security: hence Moscow's fear of German invasion through the Gulf of Finland.

Perilous times

The Finnish Government was reluctant to enter into discussions, fearing that to do so would be to compromise neutrality. The Munich Agreement of September 1938 prompted Finland to build up its defences and Mannerheim advised the government to carry out partial mobilisation. The Soviet Union again made representations to Finland, this time suggesting that the Finns lease the islands of the Gulf of Finland to them for 30 years. Soviet pleas to Britain and France for collective security had fallen on deaf ears and Leningrad was vulnerable from the sea.

Finland was still suspicious of Soviet ambitions. By April 1939, Hitler had managed to drive a wedge through Finland's policy of joint Nordic security. Estonia, Latvia and Denmark accepted a German plan of non-aggression, while Sweden, Norway and Finland refused.

After Sweden withdrew, and Germany and the Soviet Union had signed a non-aggression pact (which included a secret protocol on spheres of influence), Finland, placed within Moscow's sphere, was in a very dangerous position. After the German invasion of Poland, the Soviet Union began to press the small countries within its sphere to make pacts of "mutual assistance". Delegates from Helsinki travelled to Moscow for discussions. Mannerheim now pressed for full mobilisation of Finnish forces, and the Soviet Union moved swiftly on to a war footing.

PRECEDING PAGES: Finnish soldiers in the Winter War. **LEFT:** Field Marshal Mannerheim. **RIGHT:** Lotta-Svärld, leader of the Women's Group in World War II.

Winter warriors

The first Soviet demand was that troops be moved from the Karelian Isthmus. When Mannerheim refused, the Kremlin broke off diplomatic relations and launched an attack on Finland on 30 November 1939. What became known as the Winter War had begun.

Soviet forces had almost overwhelming superiority but they were untrained and ill-equipped to fight a war in severe winter conditions. Though short of heavy armaments, by contrast Finnish soldiers had already been training for just this sort of warfare. They were used to moving in dense forests through snow and ice, and the Finnish army's tactical mobility was on a high level. The Finns were also accustomed to the climate and dressed sensibly when winter set in and the temperature dropped several degrees below zero. Soldiers were issued with white "overalls" – now standard for winter warfare – to cover their uniforms so that they blended invisibly with the snow.

By copying the methods used by farmers and lumberjacks to haul logs from the forest, the Finnish army solved a second key problem: how to operate in the forests flanking the roads. They would open a trail in the woods using skis, avoiding gorges, cliffs and steep rises. When a few horses and sleighs had moved over this trail, a winter road would form along which a horse could pull up to a one-tonne load.

War preparations

Anticipating what might happen, the army had already perfected these techniques in its pre-war winter manoeuvres and, when war started in 1939, Finland had about half a million horses in the country. The army used around 20 per cent of them and, as half the reservists called up to fight were farmers or lumberjacks, there were plenty of skilled horsemen. During the summer of 1939, the Finns had also built dams in the small rivers on the Karelian Isthmus and elsewhere which raised the water level to form an obstruction against the enemy advance. When the Finnish army opened the gates in the Saimaa canal in March 1940, the Russians found operations in the flooded areas difficult.

Attempts to raise the water level were less successful during the coldest winter period; but

SURVIVING THE LANDSCAPE

One of the most difficult problems for winter warfare had already been solved by Finland in the 1930s: how to camp and make shelter in a winter wilderness. Finland had developed a tent for the use of half a platoon (20 men), which could be folded into a small and easily handled bundle. A portable boxstove was enough to keep the tent warm even if the temperature fell to −40°C. It was also relatively easy to prepare coffee and other basic warm food on top of the stove. The Finns also had the valuable know-how to operate for several weeks in uninhabited regions without tents by building shelters out of snow and evergreens.

equally, as the ice covered the uneven features of the terrain, the enemy had less shelter and was not concealed from air reconnaissance. Later, the Finns opened lanes by blowing up the ice and developed special ice mines which detonated when the Soviets approached.

Surprise tactics

Finns and Russians fought the Winter War during the darkest period of the year. In the area of Viipuri, daylight lasted from 8am to 5pm. On the level of Kajaani the day was a couple of hours shorter while, at the turn of the year, Petsamo in the north enjoyed hardly any hours of daylight at all. Finnish soldiers made use of the darkness for the loading and unloading of trains, transports and supply traffic. This prevented the enemy (with its command of the air) from noticing and disturbing operations. The troops carried out all their tactical movements in the forests, which offered even better protection.

As the Soviet Army moved west, the Finns had insufficient forces and equipment for classic air, tank, artillery and similar operations, and their aim had to be to force the enemy to attack under the worst possible conditions. But

> ### BOTTLES VERSUS TANKS
>
> To compensate for the lack of anti-tank guns, the Finns used gasoline-filled bottles and TNT-charges and destroyed a large number of tanks in this way.

pulled them along on sledges, which they also used to evacuate the wounded, often along the specially prepared winter roads through the wilderness. At night, for longer distances, they ploughed a road over the ice to bring troops and equipment. In any attack, surprise was the essence. Strike force commanders and their troops, all on skis, moved stealthily forward to block the road so that the sappers had time to destroy the bridges and lay mines to catch the tanks before any counter-attack.

the Finns, bred on the land, knew the terrain. The Soviet divisions, in contrast, had no choice but to stick to the roads, advancing in a tight column, strung out over some 100 km (60 miles). On either side lay a strip around 110–220 km (70–140 miles) wide of uninhabited, forest-covered wilderness, with numerous lakes and marshes, where the Finnish troops had all the advantages of surprise and manoeuvrability.

For these attacks, the Finns either carried their ammunition, mines and explosives or

LEFT: Karelians are forced to evacuate their homeland during World War II.
ABOVE: Finnish soldiers with a captured Russian tank.

The Finns fought against great odds during this Winter War (and partly during the Continuation War that followed). Their number of anti-tank guns was so limited that the troops could use them only against an armoured attack on an open road, and gasoline bottles and TNT-charges were more likely to destroy an enemy tank. Despite that, the advantages were not always on the side of the invading army. The ill-informed and often ill-clad Soviet troops could not move from or manoeuvre outside the roads and they, too, often lacked supplies when insufficient air drops left them short of ammunition and food. Throughout the war's skirmishes and more formal encounters, the "ski troops" inflicted hard blows on this badly deployed Red Army. (It was partly this poor performance that persuaded Hitler later to launch an attack on Russia.)

Honourable peace

Though the resourcefulness of Marshal Mannerheim's white-clad troops had grasped every advantage of territory and climate to achieve several victories, Finland could not last long against an enemy of much greater power. The Finnish army was forced to surrender at Viipuri, and

Winter War was mitigated for the Finns by the maintenance of national sovereignty.

The Winter War lasted exactly 100 days. But the European powers were still fighting and the inevitable result for Finland was to be swept up in yet another conflict. On 22 June 1941, Operation Barbarossa went ahead. Hitler attacked the Soviet Union, achieving complete surprise. Russian commanders signalled to Stalin: "We are being fired on – what shall we do?" Stalin replied that they were talking nonsense, and anyway why weren't their

the Soviet Union set up and then abandoned a puppet government on the Karelian Isthmus. But the long front held out to the end. This guaranteed pre-conditions for an honourable peace and, in 1940, the two sides concluded an armistice. The Soviet Union's original aim – a base in Hanko, in the southwest, and the moving of the border further from Leningrad – were its only gains.

Neverthless Finland had to surrender around a tenth of its territory, with a proportionate shift of population and, in this respect, suffered a heavy defeat. On the other hand it was obvious that Stalin's real intention had been to annex the whole of Finland, and their defeat in the

messages coded? There had been some collusion between the German and Finnish military authorities and the Finns had had to allow the west of Finland to be used for transit traffic. Partial Finnish mobilisation was ordered, and 60,000 civilians moved from front-line areas.

Alongside Germany

On the day preceding Barbarossa, Hitler had announced that "Finnish and German troops stand side by side on the Arctic coast for the defence of Finnish soil." Marshal Mannerheim was convinced that his statement was intended as an announcement of a *fait accompli*. "This will lead to a Russian attack," he said, "though, on the other hand, I am convinced that in any case such an attack would have occurred." The Russian High Command retaliated against the Finns. Russian bombs fell on Finland even before any were dropped on German targets.

The Finnish army was larger, war-hardened and better equipped than at the start of the Winter War. Eleven divisions stood on the frontiers, another faced the Russian base at Hanko, and the Commander-in-Chief had a reserve of four divisions, which he controlled from his old headquarters at Mikkeli.

PREPARED FOR BATTLE

During the Winter War, some units had been short of potatoes. Veterans reported for duty this time carrying their kit as well as a sack or two of potatoes.

Mannerheim but now he informed the Finnish government that "under no circumstances will I lead an offensive against the great city on the Neva." He feared that the Russians, faced with an advance on Leningrad, might raise irresistible forces and inflict a heavy defeat on the Finnish army.

The campaign aimed to reconquer Ladoga-Karelia, followed by the Isthmus, and finally penetrate Karelia. All these objectives were achieved. Mannerheim had some German units placed at his disposal, but he kept them at arm's

Even so, Marshal Voroshilov, who was in charge of the Russian Northwest Army Group, had formidable numbers under his command: 13 rifle divisions, two armoured divisions, a division of frontier troops, and specialist detachments. The Hanko garrison was estimated to consist of 35,000 men, and there were many fortress units.

Many in Finland expected the army to make an advance towards Leningrad. The idea of capturing this city had at one time attracted

LEFT: World War II gas masks in Hanko Museum.
ABOVE: like many Finnish towns, Rovaniemi was largely re-built after World War II.

length. The Finns were co-belligerents, not allies of the Germans. When the Finns had regained all of their old frontiers, Mannerheim commented: "Here we could have stood as neutral neighbours instead of as bitter enemies."

Admiring Allies

Fortunately, Finland and Great Britain never came to the point of fighting each other, although it was a close-run thing. Mannerheim and Winston Churchill showed great statesmanship in an exchange of letters at a moment when the outcome of the war, including the survival of Britain – and, for that matter, Finland – was far from clear.

Winston Churchill wrote to Mannerheim on 29 November 1941: "I am deeply grieved at what I see coming, namely, that we shall be forced within a few days, out of loyalty to our ally Russia, to declare war upon Finland. If we do this, we shall make war also as opportunity serves. Surely your troops have advanced far enough for security during the war and could now halt and give leave? It is not necessary to make any public declaration, but simply leave off fighting and cease military operations for which the severe weather affords every reason, and make a de facto exit from the war.

"I wish I could convince Your Excellency that we are going to defeat the Nazis. I feel far more confident of that than in 1917 or 1918. It would be most painful to the many friends of your country in England if Finland found herself in the dock with the guilty and defeated Nazis. My recollections of our pleasant talks… about the last war lead me to send you this purely personal and private message for your consideration before it is too late."

Field Marshal Mannerheim replied to Prime Minister Churchill: "Yesterday I had the honour to receive through the American Minister in Helsinki your letter of 29 November 1941, and I thank you for your kindness in sending

me this private message. I am sure you will realise it is impossible for me to halt the military operations at present being carried out before the troops have reached the positions which in my opinion will provide us with necessary security.

"It would be deplorable if these measures, undertaken for the security of Finland, should bring my country into conflict with England, and it would deeply sadden me if England felt herself forced to declare war on Finland. It was very good of you to send me a… message in these critical days, and I appreciate it fully."

Payment in full

The 1941–44 war is known in Finland as the "Continuation War" because it was understood as an extension of the Winter War and as an attempt to compensate for losses suffered in that war. In the Continuation War Finland's number of dead was 65,000 and wounded 158,000. Homes had to be found for more than 423,000 Karelians. After 1945 the Soviets insisted on show trials in Finland of the politicians who had given the orders to fight. These men received prison sentences, but served less than a full term and, in some cases, returned to public life with no damage to their reputation.

Finland also had to pay reparations to the Soviet Union, mostly in the form of metal products. The Soviets insisted on calculating their value according to the exchange rates of 1938, thus Finland paid almost exactly twice the price stated in the agreement. The reparations to the Soviet Union were paid in full. This was a point of honour to the Finns.

The years of struggle and of suffering were over at long last, and a war-weary Finland set about the business of national reconstruction. More poignantly, the dead soldiers, who had been removed from the battlefields to their home parishes, were buried with full honours in cemeteries alongside memorials to their courage and sacrifice. Unassuming, dignified and patriotic, the spirit of these graveyards and memorials is a fitting tribute to the memory of a people who had persevered and conquered. There never was and there never will be anything remotely neutral about Finland when the trumpet of war is blown in earnest. ❏

LEFT: Vammala war cemetery commemorates Finland's World War II dead.

The Great General

Carl Gustaf Emil Mannerheim was born at his family's country house at Louhisaari on 4 June 1867. The Mannerheim estate was in Swedish Villnäs, in the Turku district. The family was Swedish-speaking and of Dutch origin.

Furthermore, this great son of Finland to whom the modern nation state probably owes its very existence, was a Russian officer for 28 years before he ever served Finland's cause. Yet Gustaf (he used his second Christian name) was not following any family tradition when he enlisted as a cavalry officer cadet in 1882. He was even expelled from the Cadet School, and considered becoming a sailor. Fortunately for Finland he was given a second chance and went to St Petersburg for cavalry training; in 1889 he was commissioned into the Tsarist army, passing out in the top six, out of a total of 100.

While waiting for a Guard's commission he was posted to Poland as a subaltern in the 15th Alexandriski Dragoons. The Poles were far more restive under Russian rule than the Finns and had nothing like the same freedoms as the Grand Duchy. But Mannerheim later recalled: "The better I got to know the Poles, the more I liked them and felt at home with them." Transferred to the Chevalier Guards, he returned to St Petersburg to train recruits, and in 1892 married Anastasia Arapov, a relation of Pushkin. They had two daughters, and a son who died at birth. The marriage lasted seven years, although they did not divorce until 1919.

Mannerheim served as a colonel in the Russo-Japanese War, journeyed for two years through China and Japan, and then came back to Poland to command a cavalry regiment in 1909. In World War I, he served in the Eastern European theatre, fighting against Germans and Austrians. By 1917 he was a Lieutenant-General.

The Russian Revolution cut short his career in the Emperor's Army, and when the Tsar was murdered Mannerheim considered himself released from his Oath of Allegiance. Russia was seething with revolutionary activity, and the boiling pot overflowed into Finland.

His country had seized the moment and declared itself independent. The Senate named Mannerheim Commander-in-Chief of the armed forces in Finland. Quickly, he had to raise and mobilise an army against the Red Guards and Russian troops. When the war was over and won, the Senate appointed Mannerheim Regent of Finland but he lost the Presidential election. During the inter-war years he worked for the Red Cross and for the Mannerheim League for Children.

His finest military hour came with the onset of the Winter War in 1940, when Finland fought against Soviet Russia for three-and-a-half months under ferocious winter conditions. It came through the war with its independence intact, due largely to the deployment of mobile "ski troops".

Mannerheim was briefly President of Finland after the war, but retired due to ill health in March 1946. His final years were spent quietly, mainly in Switzerland, where he died in 1951, aged 83. His wartime ADC, Colonel Bäckman, recalls Mannerheim as kind, frugal, disciplined and fond of riding. His home in Helsinki is now a museum, presided over by Bäckman, and holds trophies and mementoes from the five wars in which he fought. On the library wall is a painting of military personnel on skis and in white overalls. Urgency in the human figures contrasts with the peace of the Finnish forest. Curiously, the painting is dated 1890 – an omen? Or rather an idea, which delivered Finland in its hour of desperate need. ❑

RIGHT: Field Marshal Mannerheim's statue stands proud in Helsinki.

A SHIFT IN BALANCE

In breaking free from Russia and moving towards a higher profile in Europe,
Finland has endured economic hardship. But its efforts are beginning to bear fruit

In 1980, Finnish statesman Max Jacobson wrote that outsiders persist in viewing Finland according to the state of western relations with the Soviet Union: "In 1939–40, Finns were idolised for their resistance against the Red Army; in 1941–44, ostracised for continuing to fight the Russians; at the end of World War II, castigated for their failure to heed western advice to trust Moscow; in 1948, written off as lost for signing a treaty with the Soviet Union; and finally, until the disintegration of the USSR they were subjected to a kind of character assassination through use of the term 'Finlandisation' to denote supine submission to Soviet domination."

The fact that this term, hated by the Finns themselves, has been almost forgotten is a sign of how this country has changed since the beginning of the 1990s. Finland has discarded its dual identity in which it was seen on the one hand as an enlightened, peace-loving Nordic nation, clean and unspoiled and heroic and healthy, and on the other hand as dictated by its position – physical and political – in relation to Russia. By committing itself in the long term to active membership of the European Union, which it joined on 1 January 1995, and by participating in the euro single currency system, Finland has sent a series of unequivocal signals of its wish to move away from the Russian sphere of influence.

Baltic attitudes

Yet as recently as 1991, President Mauno Koivisto was referring to the crisis in the Baltic republics as "an internal Soviet affair", causing dismay to some western and Baltic leaders. Most betrayed of all, perhaps, were the Finns themselves, among whom pro-independence sentiment for the Baltics, especially Finland's ethnic cousin Estonia, ran high. One newspaper

PRECEDING PAGES: President Urho Kekkonen. meets Soviet leader Nikita Khrushchev in 1960. **LEFT:** Workers' Statue in Helsinki. **RIGHT:** hydrofoil to Estonia.

editorial remarked: "Public opinion is finding it difficult to accept the realism of this country's foreign policy leadership and its appeal to Finland's own national interest."

Defenders of the government line explained their belief that interference from the outside would only increase tensions. (A week after the

Koivisto statement, Russian Interior Ministry troops attacked the Lithuanian TV station and more than a dozen ended up dead.) Some also reasoned that other countries could take stronger stances because they did not share a border with the Russians, and that this border has always made things different for Finland.

As well, Finnish Communists played a big role in organising the labour force that powered early postwar industry. At one stage they held 50 out of 200 seats in the *Eduskunta* (Parliament or National Assembly). The Russians used them as a vessel through which to channel influence. This method was most effective when the Communists were most powerful.

Twice, the Russians were able to wield enough influence to lead the government to resign.

There was a flip side. Until 1947, Finland was observed by the Allied Control Commission, which included many Russian officers. (The Commission among other tasks observed war crimes trials; the longest sentence given was 10 years, served on ex-president Risto Ryti for his dealings with the Germans.) The officers' presence was repulsive and frightening to anti-Communist Finns. The fear that Finland would go the way of Czechoslovakia in 1948 so rattled even the brave Marshal Mannerheim (who was president briefly after the war) that he

"bourgeois" European values. After the 1991 parliamentary vote, Finland was ruled by a centre-right alliance that was the most politically conservative in the republic's history.

The move right kept step with the economic growth of Finland, a phenomenon of rapid change. Divested in 1917 of the lucrative 19th-century trade links it had enjoyed as a trading post of Imperial Russia, Finland had to start from scratch. Until World War II, Finland had a stagnant subsistence agricultural economy. Postwar industrialisation pulled it out of this quagmire, and Finland became, eventually, rich, even if many of the richest individual Finns

made personal provisions to flee the country, just in case.

The Communist left eventually lost its grip. The Social Democrats (SDP), now barely left of centre, eventually became the dominant political party in Finland and held that position until 1991. The SDP found itself in a so-called "red-blue" coalition with the leading rightist party, the conservative Kokoomus.

Moving right

The Social Democrats' move right was emblematic of the political picture as a whole. Since the war, the sympathies of the majority have moved steadily towards more traditional,

were often forced to live abroad in order to avoid the massive bills imposed on them by their government's taxation policies. This accomplishment was of crucial importance to Finns, and also somewhat calmed western worries that the country was too close to the USSR.

But long before the economic miracle happened, Finland had to carve out its political place in the postwar world, a world that rapidly began to militarise along east-west lines. Finland chose neutrality. Fathered by J.K. Paasikivi, at first prime minister (1944–46) and then president (1946–56) of the Finnish republic, and Urho Kekkonen, president of the republic from 1956–83, the doctrine of neutrality was one that shunned commitment in favour of "peace orientated policy". Non alignment remains the official government foreign policy line, and was confirmed as such in a security and defence report in March 1997. But Finnish newspapers no longer temper their criticisms of their eastern neighbour, as was the case under Kekkonen's code of "self-censorship". Finland also allows itself the option of participation in NATO crisis management operations. A major instance of Finland's new association with, though not full member-

INTERNATIONAL VOICE

In 1955 Finland was admitted into the United Nations; in 1994 it became a member of the NATO Partnership for Peace programme.

tense mistrust that ruled east-west relations during the Cold War caused a foreign policy challenge that would have been formidable even to a nation far older and more powerful.

Finland, which was not even three decades independent by the war's end, resolved that it wanted "out" of the conflict, and bargained for postwar agreements along this line. The Soviet Union pushed hard for certain concessions, and depleted Finland had little to bargain with. Compromises were inevitable.

ship of, NATO was the deployment of Finnish soldiers in Kosovan peace-keeping duties in the summer of 1999.

Neutrality has meant many different things in many different situations. In postwar Finland, the neutral Paasikivi-Kekkonen line seemed to reassure Finns that their country would not become a battleground for the Soviet Union and its considerable enemies. To gain such reassurance, Finland had to play a tough political game and walk a narrow line. The

---

LEFT: the Finnish Parliament (*Eduskunta*) in Helsinki.
ABOVE: Finnish Parliament, with one of the world's highest quota of women, in session.

Soviet lease

The most controversial compromise was in the 1944 peace treaty with Moscow. In it, the Finns agreed to lease the Porkkala Peninsula (near Helsinki) to the Soviets for 50 years for use as a military base (*see page 187*). The situation was defused in 1955 when the two parties agreed to the lease's cancellation. Porkkala's return seemed to signal good things to the west, as Finland joined the United Nations; in the 1950s, the country also joined the International Monetary Fund.

When Paasikivi began formulating his foreign policy line he stressed "correct and irreproachable neighbourly relations" with the

Soviet Union. The phrase may have sounded ingratiating to western ears but made sense to the majority of Finns, who needed to believe that the Soviet Union could be bent into the shape of benign neighbour.

In 1948, Finland and the Soviet Union signed the Treaty of Friendship, Co-operation, and Mutual Assistance (FCMA), which was originally to have expired in 2003. This complex agreement was not a military alliance *per se*. Drawn up in clear reference to the Germans' having used Finland to attack the Russians, it demanded mutual protection; both pledged to prevent outside forces from using

their territory to attack the other; and Finland promised to join no alliances hostile to the Soviet Union.

This last measure was perceived by the Finns to be in line with the neutral policy they had already decided on. Other western nations, however, beginning to labour under sharp Cold War polarities, felt that if Finland was not for them, it could easily be against them. In this way began the declamations that Finland was teetering on the edge of becoming part of the Eastern Bloc.

The NATO question

Every other nation liberated by the western Allies in World War II eventually became NATO members. It was only Finland, the one country with a border with the Soviet Union to emerge outside the Eastern Bloc after World War II, and Yugoslavia who did not become Allies of either east or west.

When Finland joined in the formation of the Nordic Council in 1952, the Soviet editorials became hysterical: "Surely this means Finland will be joining NATO?" The fact that the Summer Olympics were set to be held in Helsinki also in 1952 added fuel to the fire. The Soviets interpreted preparations for the event, such as the building of a south coast highway, as proof of more plans to include Finland in a general military threat – perhaps even war – against the USSR.

Whatever else is true of the immediate postwar period, the fact that Finland did not decide to enter into the western fold but chose to go it alone did not endear it to the non-Communist world. A lone wolf is always suspect; Finland even refused to join the Marshall Plan.

SUPPORT FOR THE UNITED NATIONS

In addition to economic success, another Finnish accomplishment has been its deep commitment to the United Nations since it joined in 1955. Marjatta Rasi, the UN ambassador during the 1990–91 Gulf Crisis (Finland was a 1990 non-permanent member of the Security Council) says Finland "joined the UN after the difficulties of the immediate postwar period were safely behind and the main lines of our policy of neutrality had been laid down."

Finland strongly supports UN peacekeeping functions, in which thousands (nearly 30,000 by 1990) of Finns have participated. It has also contributed a high number of UN military observers and specialists. Involvement began during the Suez Canal crisis in 1956. There has since been a strong Finnish presence in peacekeeping operations in Lebanon, Golan, Gaza and the Sinai. But the most outstanding efforts were made on behalf of Namibia. On a Finnish initiative, in 1970 the UN set up a Namibia Fund, and Finland also pursued the 1971 International Court of Justice ruling that South Africa's presence in Namibia was illegal. When Namibia gained independence in 1990, it was Martti Ahtisaari who directed the transition.

Finland contributes generously to refugee aid programmes; the total Nordic contribution equals 25 per cent of the UN High Committtee on Refugees fund.

Economic progress

Nonetheless, economic progress began in earnest. The Finnish-Soviet 1944 peace agreement had included demands for war reparations of over $600 million. Ironically, this demand for money helped build the new economy. Postwar Finland was low on cash but met payments by negotiating the payment of some of its debt in manufactured engineering products such as farming and forestry machinery, and ships.

These items became staple sources of export income in Finland's postwar years as a growth economy. Before that economy got off the ground, however, most Finns lived in poverty. To this day, older Finns enthusiastically buy chocolate when they travel abroad because of postwar memories of chocolate being impossible to obtain.

Finland had to stretch its meagre resources yet further to deal with one of the largest resettlements of a civilian population in the world. Nearly 400,000 dispossessed Karelians (and a handful of Skolt Sami) were given free land and donations of whatever the others could afford to give, which was little. Most Karelians, already poor in their homeland, arrived only with what they and their horses could carry.

In 1950, a barter trade agreement was signed between the Finns and the Soviets. It was in force until 1990, when the Soviets abruptly announced they would not sign the next five-year extension. The reason given was that continuing it would hinder Soviet pursuit of survival on a free market economy basis. The true Soviet aim was to sell its oil for hard cash. While in force, the barter agreement was worth a fortune. It provided Finland with a completely protected market for tonnes of consumer goods each year. The heavy equipment and cheap clothes and shoes sent over were traded for Soviet oil, enough to cover 90 per cent of Finnish needs.

The Finnish trade balance suffered for the treaty's cancellation by a disputed but significant amount as the USSR was Finland's fifth-largest trading partner. Soviet-orientated Finnish producers foundered or went bankrupt. The Finns had to pay cash for oil and wait for the Soviets to pay them a $2 million debt.

LEFT: floating logs down lakes and rivers to Finland's busy wood and paper factories.

RIGHT: Martti Ahtissari, president since 1994.

Continuing crisis

While Finland was quickly able to shine in the United Nations arena, crises at home went on. In 1961, the USSR sent Finland a note suggesting "military consultations" regarding the 1948 FCMA. That note was probably sent because of Soviet fear of escalating (west) German militarism in the Baltic. The harm the note caused to Finland derived from the term "military consultations". Both sides had maintained the Treaty of Friendship, Co-operation and Mutual Assistance was not a military alliance, but an emblem of co-operation between two neighbours who were not allied.

Nikita Khruschev and Urho Kekkonen conferred privately and the consultations were announced "deferred". What the Soviets had been worried about, though, was clear: that Finland was not equipped to stop the west from using it as an attack flank. The Kekkonen-Khruschev exchange was never made wholly public, but after the "Note Crisis", Finland began shoring up its military forces. Finland sought, and got, from the British a reinterpretation of the Paris Peace Treaty of 1947 allowing it to purchase missiles, forbidden by the original treaty.

The Soviets throughout the 1970s were to try to make life difficult for the Finns several more times. One Soviet ambassador decided to meddle in an internal wrangle of the Finnish Communist Party – President Kekkonen demanded his recall to the USSR. The fibre of Finnish society was now more firmly established and the left-wing elements were mere ragged ends.

A more prosperous Finland was more difficult to "strong-arm"; by now West Germany, Sweden and the United Kingdom were Finland's major trading partners, not the USSR. Trees had become its "green gold", and it looked as though the pulp and paper industry's economic success would mean no looking back.

High living

In the 1970s and 1980s, Finland enjoyed one of the highest gross national products in the world and pulled up its standard of living and social services to be in line with Sweden's. In 1989–90, a survey showed Finland to be the most expensive country in the world, outstripping Japan. Fantastically high agricultural subsidies, and industrial cartels which set artificially high prices, were the main culprits and brought difficult consequences.

A lot of Finns, though, made a lot of money, and spent it with abandon. But it wasn't so easy to cover up the fact that they'd been poor

DISCUSSION ARENA

In 1975, the Final Act of the Conference on Security and Co-operation in Europe (CSCE) was concluded in Helsinki. It was a public relations victory, an event that could help Finland be seen as a place of diplomacy and neutrality.* Helsinki established itself as a "Vienna of the north", full of diplomats and police barricades. The CSCE resumed in Helsinki in 1992. Presidents Bush and Gorbachev met here in 1990 as the US sought to clear the way for action against Iraq in the Gulf War, and in 1997 presidents Yeltsin and Clinton held a Helsinki summit. The capital also held talks between US and Russian leaders on the deployment of peacekeeping forces in Kosovo in 1999.

cousins for so long. It is hard to believe when one explores Helsinki's well-stocked, stylish shops today, but even as late as the early 1980s one could look in shoe-shop windows and gasp at the ugly, out-of-fashion footwear on display; these were the designs that had been dumped on the Soviets for the past 30 years. One could buy Gucci shoes, but at costs that made Parisian boutique prices look like flea-market deals. There was little to choose from between the two extremes. By the end of the 1980s, the gap was closing, but prices were still wildly high, especially on imports. It was not until EU membership in the latter half of the 1990s that prices levelled and began to bear some resemblance to those in other western European countries. Helsinki, as it enters the new millennium, comes well down the rankings for the world's most expensive cities – rankings which it once topped.

Economic agony

Starting in the late 1980s, Finland went into economic recession. At the same time, the challenges of the "new" Europe were growing. When the rest of Europe was drawing together like a large mutual aid society, Finland seemed to repel the trend. The official word was that it had no interest in joining the European

European state since the 1930s. Between 1991 and 1993, the economy lost 14 per cent of its gross domestic product and unemployment soared from 3 per cent to just under 20 per cent. Pragmatists saw the need to shift from a commodity-based economy looking towards Russia to a manufacturing and service economy looking towards the west. Nokia, the country's leading electronics company, showed the way as its sales of mobile phones doubled its profits, and by the end of the 1990s the company had established itself as the world leader in its field. The changed circumstances also convinced many people that it would be worth seeking shelter

Community, but was firmly committed to continue as a European Free Trade Association member that endorsed a strong European Economic Space. Under such circumstances, however, the Finnish economy was less likely to improve quickly.

Those attitudes changed rapidly in the 1990s. The collapse of the former Soviet Union, which had accounted for a fifth of Finland's trade, combined with the world slide into recession to produce the worst slump suffered by any

LEFT: the Outokumpu Corporation's copper smelting plant in Harjavalta.
RIGHT: Nokia mobile phones infiltrate Finnish life.

within the European Union, and 57 per cent of the country's 4 million voters opted in a consultative referendum in October 1994 to become part of the EU from January 1995.

Reluctant members

Objections to EU membership were still vociferous. Many still argued that joining the European Union wouldn't change things for the better since the EU's agricultural policy was not one of its glories. However, in the first year of membership, food prices fell by 8 per cent, and the feeling of being part of a massive trading group created a sense of security that promised well for the future. The five-party "rainbow coalition" that came to power in 1995 promised little except austerity, but the new mood of realism enabled them to peg pay rises to 1.7 per cent and 2 per cent over two years, helping to keep inflation very low at around 1.5 per cent.

Deeply rooted agrarian loyalties were also hard to shake in Finland, even if full-time farmers were a dying breed. Finally, Finns had an instinctive wish to keep foreigners from buying a slice of their wealth-producing forests. For individuals, the

---

GO-BETWEEN COUNTRY

"It may take a generation before commercial order returns to Russia, but for sure it will do so," said one industrialist. "And when it does Finland will still be the natural gateway for western trade and investment."

---

only was Sweden one of Finland's most important trade partners, it was also a beacon of political and socio-economic policy for Finland.

Ten years previously, the country couldn't have contemplated a move such as joining the EU without first seeking permission from Russia, but now Finns began to enjoy the heady freedom of making their own decisions. They realised, though, that eventually Russia was bound to regain its economic strength and that they could

idea of foreigners buying forest brought fears of loss of privacy, something sacred to the national character. The forest industrialists had more pragmatic fears: namely, that introduction of foreign buyers would mean the break-up of the cartel-style domestic price-fixing mechanisms which helped shield the industry from real competition. Prices in this and other industries were thus artificially high, and in some sectors competition was virtually impossible.

The objection to EU membership had always been the risk of compromising Finnish neutrality, although neutral countries like Ireland had flourished in the EU and neutral Sweden was keen to join (which it did, also in 1995). Not

offer to the rest of Europe their own invaluable experience of negotiating with the Russians. There was some immediate benefit, too: because of poor facilities at Russian ports, western exporters began shipping bulk goods to Finnish harbours and transporting them on by road to Russia.

Pruning back the Welfare State

Until the recession that hit Finland in the early 1990s, the welfare state was one of the great sacrosanct untouchables of Finnish life. Using the model provided by its neighbour Sweden, Finland launched a programme to extend its state welfare facilities in the years following

World War II. Before the war these facilities had been relatively modest, with the first measure affecting the whole (still largely rural) population taking the form of a Pensions Act in 1937. A Child Allowance Act followed in 1948, giving state recognition to the need for child protection, and the Pensions Act was brought up to date in the late 1950s, along with the introduction of the private pensions option.

The 1960s and 1970s also saw the establishment of laws that made provision for sickness insurance and health care – and the whole time state spending on welfare measures mushroomed.

crisis which had to be solved with the backing of state funds. Pressure mounted on the availability of funds for welfare state provision, and the agreements between business, government and then influential trade unions no longer seemed written in stone. Charges for health care increased and taxation on pensions was introduced, at the same time as workers were encouraged by tax breaks to contribute to private pension schemes to supplement their less generous state pensions.

Finland's social structure has withstood considerable pressure from the increased poverty and unemployment that followed the recession.

For decades, Finns were prepared to endure massive income tax rates in return for generous and comprehensive welfare benefits. Unemployment was in any case insignificant in European terms, and poverty, which had been deep at the end of the war, was all but eradicated. Then came the economic turmoil of the early 1990s: suddenly, unemployment was soaring into double figures and reaching unprecedented postwar peaks of about 20 per cent, and Finnish banks found themselves in a

LEFT: Helsinki was named one of the European Cities of Culture for the year 2000.
RIGHT: female ministers of the Finnish parliament.

There is probably a bigger gap than ever before between the haves and the have-nots. For all that, the welfare state has held firm and still provides a sound, basic safety net. Finns have been prepared to see it trimmed and pruned, but they would still balk at the idea of removing it completely.

Electing a new future

The voters were certainly kept busy. In the country's first direct presidential election in 1994, Martti Ahtisaari, the veteran United Nations diplomat, topped the poll. And in 1995 the centre-right coalition government was ousted by a five-party "rainbow coalition" consisting of Social Democrats, Conservatives, Left Alliances (including former Communists), the Greens and the Swedish People's Party. Under Paavo Lipponen – known as "Moses" because of his towering figure and sonorous voice – the new government set about rebuilding the economy. The tough economic measures, partly in the unpopular form of public spending cuts, taken at the beginning of the 1990s began to bear fruit. Unemployment, though slowly falling, remained high at approaching 15 per cent, but inflation was kept at the low rate of under two per cent required for Finland to qualify for the first stage of the

European Monetary Union. The phenomenal success of Nokia fed a wider high-technology industry, and government policy guaranteed major investments to preserve growth in this field. The changeover from the Finnish markka to the euro as the national currency got under way on 1 January 1999, with the complete adoption scheduled for two years later. Meanwhile, President Ahtisaari travelled almost incessantly to improve trade links.

Scandal and success

Modern Finland is quite a different country from the one that started the 1990s in a daze of uncertainty about its future. Its brushes with corrup-

tion – or rather the exposure of its extent in public and commercial life – have brought it closer, paradoxically, to a "real world" from which it had always felt protected by the cocoon of its neutrality. The share scandal surrounding the resignation of the Minister of Transport and Communications, Matti Aura, in 1999 proved that accountability had become a valid word in the Finnish political vocabulary. Aura left his post when the president of the Sonera telecoms company, Pekka Vellamo, was dismissed for alleged share-holding irregularities at the time of the state-owned company's first share issue. In the unrelated but equally political sphere of the Olympic organisation, the Finnish IOC member Pirjo Häggman resigned from her committee position when she was implicated in investigations into the Salt Lake City Games bid.

The European dimension

At the same time, Finland has evolved into a more outward-looking and cosmopolitan country. It was often said that Finland, even under the shadow of Soviet influence, was one of the most Americanised countries in Europe: the continued proliferation of hamburger restaurants and the popularity of huge, fuel-guzzling American cars does little to contradict that superficial impression. But Finns, especially the younger urbanised generations, have chosen Europe as their centre of political reference.

Finland had its chance to prove this in the second half of 1999 when it served as EU President country, hosting over 70 special European meetings, including two major summits. Helsinki's European City of Culture role, shared with eight other European cities in 2000, and the celebration in the same year of the capital's 450th anniversary gave the whole country a confident platform upon which to enter the new millennium.

Helsinki has developed to such a point that it is now a city where many languages – English, Russian, German, Swedish, French and Italian, among others – are heard daily and on a routine basis (*see page 103*), yet where the local language remains as strong as ever. It is the capital of a country that is newly certain of its place in the world and which is learning to relish that self-confidence. ❑

LEFT: a ship unloads its cargo at Helsinki's busy harbour, an economic success story for Finland.

Ladies First

Finnish women seem to many to have some of the strongest advantages of their gender in Europe. They certainly claim a pioneering pedigree in equal rights, since in 1906 their country was the third in the world, after Australia and New Zealand – and therefore the first country in Europe – to enshrine in its law eligibility to vote and all other full political rights for women. It has been progressive in most areas of gender equality too, making it possible for Finnish women to join the clergy of the country's biggest church, the Evangelical Lutheran, in 1988, and passing an amendment to its Equality Act in 1995 committing national and local government committees to take a 40 per cent quota of women.

The country also very nearly voted in its first female President of the Republic in 1995, when Elisabeth Rehn, the candidate of the minority Swedish Speakers' Party, was only just pipped to the post by the eventual winner, Martti Ahtisaari. Rehn had already served as Minister of Defence, and went on to earn respect as a Member of the European Parliament and as an outspoken representative of the UN Human Rights Commission in the former Yugoslavia.

Finnish woman-power has spread through all levels of government too, with Eva-Riitta Siitanen, Helsinki's mayor at the end of the 1990s, a conspicuous example. Sirkka Hämäläinen was the first woman governor of the Bank of Finland in the early 1990s, and Tarja Halonen, a presidential front-runner in the 2000 elections, gathered plaudits as Minister for Foreign Affairs, a post she was appointed to in 1995. Riitta Uosukainen, whose eyebrow-raising memoirs included intimate details of her sex life, was still speaker of the Parliament as the new millennium approached. Indeed, women enjoy remarkable influence in government compared to other nations. The male-female ratio of parliament members in 1999 was 126 to 74, one of the highest for women in the world, and eight of the 17 Council of State or government ministers were women.

Although on the surface these figures appear enlightened, and although women lawyers, editors-in-chief, doctors and other professionals abound throughout Finland, a glance through the annual reports of the country's largest companies confirms that Finnish women have yet to make a significant breakthrough into the higher echelons of business. Sari Baldauf, the Nokia Telecommunications President, born in 1955, is a rare exception to this board-room gender rule.

"According to the official and theoretical version of things, we are very equal with men," says Anu Ek, a 42-year-old Finnish magazine editor. "But in private business, we still earn only about 80 per cent of what men are getting paid. Promotion is by no means automatic for women: men are usually first in line. And this is the case even though Finnish women are very highly educated.

More than 50 per cent of university students, for example, are female."

But legislative support for women at work is very strong and very effective. The Finnish woman who does not work full-time has become a rarity and time off to raise a family is not a hindrance. Since 1996, all children up to the age of seven are guaranteed a day-care place. Parents – father or mother – are entitled to child-care leave until their child turns three during which time their jobs are secured and an allowance is granted. Standard parental leave after the birth of a child, usually taken by the mother, of 158 days, is subsidised by an allowance equivalent to two-thirds of the parent's normal income. ❑

RIGHT: Tarja Halonen, the Finnish Foreign Minister, is just one of many high-profile women in Finland.

THE FINNISH CHARACTER

Blond, reserved, rustic – some of these stereotypes remain true, but Finns are moving with the times, embracing a more international approach to modern living

Are Finns manic-depressive by nature? What else can one become when the climate changes so abruptly from freezing winter (with almost total darkness 24 hours a day) to really hot summer months with no darkness at all?

Change is so deep-rooted in the Finnish soul that the nation accepts almost any new innovation with little resistance, be it the new currency, the euro, or technological features in mobile phones. "The only constant is change," Finns will tell anyone who asks, but despite this, traditions are never completely forgotten.

Change is most visible in nature – no new day is similar to yesterday. After the springtime thaw, everything grows rapidly until its time arrives for a slow death before winter. Only for a few weeks around the winter solstice, the nature stops, deep frozen, for a pause – but then Finns prepare for the busy Christmas time and their New Year's resolutions. The big wheel keeps on turning, another year means new opportunities for change, and daylight hours start getting longer again.

Pacifist nation

Finns have reached the end of the 20th century with both style and class. After Martti Ahtisaari, Finland's president, helped to broker a peace deal in the Balkan region, Finland is hosting the six-month EU presidency.

What a difference to the way the century began. A hundred years earlier, this small nation struggled to defend its language against the Russian Czarist regime. Being dominated by both Swedes and Russians, today Finns resent both nations, and small details such as success in sports or international trade are scrutinised carefully. Finnish Nokia mobile phones, for example, sell more than their Swedish competitors, and, in ice-hockey, Finns often defeat both Swedish and Russian teams. These things

PRECEDING PAGES: Tampere's funfair; reindeer races in Lapland. **LEFT:** typical Karelian dress. **RIGHT:** international designers now grace the ski slopes.

matter to Finns. Yet, although they may not forget, they are willing to forgive: across the eastern border, Finnish trucks carry emergency assistance to the struggling Russians now living in great poverty – only a decade after the traumatic period when Moscow dictated many internal issues within Finland.

By nature, Finns are peacemakers. At war, Finns always lose – there are few national war heroes of any note – but at peace, Finns certainly seem to be winning.

Ghosts from the past

To what extent can a land be judged by its ancient heroes? In the case of many countries, only an enemy would wish to invoke the memory of certain inglorious characters. With Finland, however, the idea is quite appealing. The main characters in the Finnish epic the *Kalevala* are patriotic, and the heroes are noble warriors (*see page 95*). Yet these strong men are troubled hair-tearers in private, and have great difficulty in waxing poetic when they set out to woo and win the girl. The women, in contrast, are strongheaded, matriarchal, and very family-orientated.

The land itself is full of nature and wood-spirits. No one in the *Kalevala* would deny that the woods have sanctity, and that the lakes and rivers are their little piece of heaven on earth. When one of the female heroes wants to escape her fate, for example, she simply turns into a nimble, stream-swimming fish.

> ### LIVING WITH SPACE
>
> Finns are greatly moulded by their numbers. Europe's fifth largest country in size has a population of just over five million, which is also largely homogeneous.

who's never happier than when he's showing off his possessions and singing his own praises.

Yet some stereotypes are universally recognised as true. "We are forest people," said Jarl Kohler, managing director of the Finnish Forest Industries Federation. "The forests are our security and our livelihood." And the security isn't just theoretical or a romantic notion of rural idylls: more than 400,000 Finns own a plot of forest and everyone has the right of access to the land *(see pages 128–9).*

One can only take the analogy so far, of course, but it's far better to start with a nation's self-made heroes, with at least some roots in reality, than the stereotypical characters others have created for them.

There are so many paradoxes in the Finnish character that it would be hard to convince the sceptical foreigner that there isn't more than a dash of schizophrenia in the national psyche. For every ranting drunk, there's a raving teetotaller. For every patriotic Finn who is as attached to Finland as to his own soul, there's one who leaves as soon as he can afford the fare, never to return. For every shrinking violet, there's an arrogant, cigar-smoking bombast

Nordic links

The "typical Finn" is the result of a genetic combination that is 75 per cent identical to that of Swedes or other Scandinavians, but 25 per cent derived from tribes that wandered to Finland from east of the Ural Mountains, though some experts now dispute this *(see page 21).* This more Oriental strain accounts for certain physical traits that set Finns apart from their Nordic neighbours – finely pronounced cheekbones and quite small eyes, which are slatey-grey or blue.

Karelians (Finns from the very east of the country) are stockier and also have more sallow complexions than other Finns. They are slightly smaller in stature than people from the west coast, whose ancestors merged with the gargantuan Vikings. Until the end of World War II, the Karelians' diet was extremely poor and they had one of the highest incidences of heart disease in the west, which may in part account for their slightly less healthy looks.

The rest of the Finns are taller, usually fair-haired (though, overall, Finns are the "darkest" of the Nords) and, much like any other nationality, vary greatly in most other ways.

Some of the most famous Finns are sportsmen and women, taking advantage of their generally strong and healthy physiques. As a

norm. And the infamous reserve applies as much to other Nords as it does to Finns.

City versus country

The ideas of those who would totally subjugate Finnish culture are no more appealing than those of the super-patriot who would have nothing change. Finns are on a pendulum swinging out towards the rest of the world, but they are far better equipped than they think they are to meet the challenges with equanimity.

For a traditionally rural country, Finland is becoming more urbanised. Some 80 per cent of Finns live on 2 per cent of the land. Domestic

nation, Finns are great lovers of the outdoors and of sport, and some young Finns seem to live for little else but their athletic activities (*see page 111*).

The Finnish personality is harder to pin down but, if you go to Finland with preconceived stereotypes at the ready, you will no doubt be able to satisfy any or all of them. You can't help but notice the drunks, for instance, but if that is what you are expecting to see, you will no doubt see disproportionately more than is the

LEFT: out of the sauna and into the ice pool is a healthy winter tradition.
ABOVE: in summer, al fresco dining is fashionable.

A RESERVED NATION

It is characteristic of Finns to speak quietly, even in stage whispers, when a couple are conversing in a public place. If you converse loudly, you will draw stares. (Perhaps many who drink heavily do so in order to gain licence to shout.) Finns put great value on privacy. The summer cabin (*kesämökki*) also tells you something of Finnish privacy. These are usually set back from the lakeshore among the trees, and as far from other dwellings as possible. The idea of time spent here is to revel in your own plot. However, young women are becoming more demonstrative – in Helsinki they greet each other with hugs, kisses and big smiles.

emigration is accelerating – Finns are moving from small towns to Greater Helsinki, Tampere, Turku and Oulu. The much publicised *"etätyö"* (distance working via the Internet) has attracted quite a few, but most people still try to escape to cities. This is often a result of unemployment and decreasing services as post offices, shops and bus services close in villages.

But rural life has its attractions. People tend to live in large houses surrounded by gardens. Farmers are fewer but get enough subsidies to continue a comfortable lifestyle. Farm holidays are common, although some wonder whether rural Finland is turning into a tourist reserve.

Gypsy Roots

One of the oldest groups in Finland who are not ethnic Finns are the Romany gypsies, whose womenfolk are instantly recognisable by their elaborate embroidered lace blouses and voluminous skirts. Although today most speak only Finnish, few have intermarried, so their dark good looks stand out against fairer Finns.

Although most gypsies are no longer nomadic and live instead in houses and flats, some families still tend to wander, especially in autumn, from one harvest festival to another. Little horse-trading is done these days, however, and the gypsies' appearance at these fairs is little more than a vestige of nostalgia.

Society and culture

Although Finns fought a bloody class war in 1918, modern Finland is less class conscious than it has ever been. Distinction between town and country is more relevant as the "rainbow government" *(see page 61)* includes both left- and right-wing parties, and the "rural" Keskusta party is outside the government.

But the traditional welfare society is losing its grip. The rich are getting richer, the poor remain poor. Unemployment was cut from over 20 per cent to around 10 per cent during the second half of the 1990s, but poverty still haunts certain suburbs in Helsinki and entire regions in the northern half of Finland.

Popular culture has grown, along with commercial media (there are now four national TV channels, two financed commercially, and many local TV stations) embracing young and old. Even the Swedish-speaking minority is persuaded to consume the mainstream culture, especially in big towns. Many younger Finns, shedding their parents' unease, have gone on to study, work and travel abroad, as well as welcoming all things foreign to Finland. While some older Finns still have not abandoned the dreary, grey outfits that used to dominate the clothing racks, their grandchildren sport fluorescent clothing and embrace fads from Britain and the US with near-fanatical fervour.

Things seem to be turning upside down. While Finns traditionally were very observant towards the law, an increasing number of the populace accepts the new liberal society, although strict traffic rules (compulsory safety belts for back seats, for example) are generally accepted. The grey sector of the economy is estimated at around 20 per cent of the GDP, as one of the highest tax rates in the world tempts Finns towards tax evasion.

The home is still highly venerated and Finns spend a considerable amount of time and money on their properties. As a contrast to many southern countries where people dress well and live poorly, Finns live like royalty but dress crudely. One female minister recently raised eyebrows in an international meeting by wearing a violet jeans jacket. Despite their move towards international lifestyles, sartorial style remains low on the Finnish agenda. ❏

LEFT: Finns are brought up with a deep appreciation of their countryside.

Finnish Youth

Be it rollerskating or bungy jumping (one Finnish company claims to have the tallest bungy-jumping crane in the world), young Finns keenly jump on each new band-wagon and let loose until the next craze comes along. Even Finland itself creates new trends, which transfer to the youth of other nations. Mobile phones and pagers are more common here than anywhere else in the world (Nokia is Finland's largest company); every minute a beep announces a new message in buses, public libraries or restaurants. Young kids get given mobile phones from worried parents – a sort of an electronic nanny which announces meal times. Many parents pay hundreds of pounds each month for their children's phone bills – a heavy price for mere gossiping.

The Internet is another daily tool among Finnish youth. Domestic chatting channels, such as Kiss Chat or City Chat, attract thousands of teenagers daily, to gossip or to talk dirty. Internet is available at most schools and public libraries for free, and home usage is increasing fast. IRC attracts an equally large amount of Finnish "nerds".

Subcultures are strong, from religious networks within the Lutheran or other churches to Devil worshippers who occasionally feature in national headlines through their attacks on graveyards. Indeed, Finland is no longer a land of innocents – if it ever was: almost any phenomenon can be found, from punk hairdos to drunken teenage girls.

Finns watch a Scandinavian version of MTV, but equally enthusiastically a Canadian-created youth programme by the name Jyrki ("George"). Jyrki has a studio in the Lasipalatsi media centre in Helsinki, and the daily live programme attracts large crowds who want to spot their favourite rock stars in the flesh. In 1999, one of Jyrki's hosts, Joonas Hytönen, started his own talk show at the tender age of 24, which has not only been immensely popular, but the most credible Finnish version of the popular American audience-led chat shows, something the older generation never managed to create in Finland.

More commercial attractions are available: vast multiplex-style cinemas have arrived in Helsinki, Tampere and elsewhere – Finnish film production has been booming since 1998. Local radio stations

have mushroomed, including Kiss FM and the French-owned NRJ, and popular music keeps getting heavier.

Young rock bands may be homegrown, but success has to be sought internationally. Hybrid Children, a heavy rock band that has been playing since 1991, sells well in Japan, but in Finland, although it attracts an audience of 13 to 25-year-olds, sells only a few thousand records domestically. "It's not a way to get rich – we earn about the same as being on the dole," says one band member. However, numerous summer festivals mean both bands and fans can party and dance almost every warm weekend away.

Innovation is the password among young Finns who hardly remember the near-socialist era of the 1980s. Ari Tiainen ("Arska") is one of the key figures. At the age of 20, he founded his own record company Levy-yhtiö (literally "Record Company") and now publishes records by Tehosekoitin and Apulanta, his own band, some of the most popular Finnish rock bands.

Drugs, alcohol and teenage sex are on the increase and Finnish parents find it increasingly difficult to understand their children. Perhaps the recession in the early 1990s was to blame: parents were unemployed and the youth culture boomed, with unpredictable results. Some argue that it's merely part of the new liberal Finland. ❏

RIGHT: Summer festivals are the most likely events to see Finnish youth getting together.

ART, ARCHITECTURE AND DESIGN

*Finland's struggle for national identity has led to an artistic heritage
that swings between ancient rural traditions and sparkling Modernism*

When Diaghilev, founder of the Russian Ballet, divided the Finnish painters of the 1890s into two camps – "those with a nationalistic outlook and those who follow the west" – he described a tension which has been present in Finnish art ever since.

Association with the art world of western Europe and the artistic expression of Finnish nationalism have been persistently seen as opposing forces. Taken to extremes, artists either belonged to Europe or to Finland. Paradoxically, those who have achieved world renown were able, by creating something essentially Finnish and therefore unique, to leap over national boundaries. Today, Finnish design and architecture are among Finland's best-known products, partly because they combine a universal modernism and a Finnish quality.

Because Finland is still relatively young as an independent country, much of the art produced during the past 100 years has been concerned with creating a national cultural identity. Until the 1880s, the nascent Finnish cultural scene was influenced by the country's political masters – first Sweden, then Czarist Russia. The few practising Finnish artists who were able to make a living from their work either trained or lived in Stockholm or St Petersburg.

Searching for identity

The seeds of a specifically Finnish culture were sown when organised art training began in Turku in 1830. In 1845, Finland held its first art exhibition. The Finnish Art Society was founded in 1846. But it wasn't until the 1880s and 1890s that a truly Finnish artistic idiom began to emerge and Finnish artists were at last afforded some recognition at home and, by the end of the 19th century, internationally.

European artistic influences were strong as painters such as Albert Edelfelt (1854–1905) utilised the style of French naturalism. Yet,

PRECEDING PAGES: Karelian women, painted by Albert Edelfelt in 1887. **LEFT:** Rovaniemi Art Museum.
RIGHT: Akseli Gallén-Kallela, Finland's "national" artist.

while his style was initially imported from abroad, the subject of Edelfelt's paintings became increasingly Finnish in character.

In the 1880s, a motley group of painters took up the struggle for cultural identity, which paralleled the growth of Finnish nationalism and the desire for independence. Among those

artists were Akseli Gallén-Kallela (1865–1931), Pekka Halonen (1865–1933), Eero Järnefelt (1862–1937), Juho Rissanen (1873–1950) and Helena Schjerfbeck (1862–1946). They looked to the Finnish landscape and to ordinary Finns for subjects which were quintessentially Finnish. Within that framework, artistic styles varied from powerful realism to mythology, and sentimental bourgeois or fey naturalism.

National Romanticism

While some painters, like Hugo Simberg (1873–1917), followed idiosyncratic, transcendental and Europe-based symbolist paths, a body of artists came to represent what was to be called Finnish National Romanticism. Their focus on Finnishness – a subject dear to the heart of every Finn – meant that these artists enjoyed, and continue to enjoy, considerable popular appeal in Finland. Several artists chose deliberately to move among people whose mother-tongue was Finnish (at that time many urban intellectuals spoke Swedish) and whose traditional folk culture and rural living had, the artists believed, remained largely uncorrupted by either Swedish or Russian influences. They maintained that the Finnish peasant was the true Finn, and that a rural landscape was the only credible Finnish landscape – the country's cities had been planned and designed under the sway of foreign rulers.

Nationalist hangover

In a general sense, the legacy of National Romanticism is large, and has often been something of an incubus which restricted later artists who wished to look at urban Finland, to follow European movements, or to pursue abstract styles. Finnish popular taste in art continues to be dominated by both a nationalistic and a naturalistic preference. This conservatism has frustrated many an artist who wished to forge ahead in new directions.

KARELIAN INFLUENCE

Still in hot pursuit of the essence of Finnishness, several painters began to go on forays to Karelia. Gallén-Kallela, often acclaimed as one of the most original talents in Nordic art, went to Karelia in 1890 and started the "Karelia" movement which sent 19th-century artists and writers to the area in droves, and continued the earlier travels of the author Elias Lönnrot *(see page 95)*. Aino, *The Defence of the Sampo (Sammon puolustus)* and *Joukahainen's Revenge (Joukahaisen kosto)* show his use of a stylised, allegorical idiom. A seminal figure in Finnish culture, Gallen-Kallela's enormous contribution laid the foundations for contemporary Finnish design.

Groups like the October Group, whose motto was "in defence of Modernism, against isolationist nationalism", pushed hard against what is sometimes forbiddingly described as the "Golden Age" of Finnish art. Sculptor Sakari Tohka (1911–58) was a founding member of the October Group. Overthrowing the classicism of his Finnish forebears, he cast his sculptures in cement.

The October Group was not alone. Townscapes and urban Finland were the chosen subjects of another artistic backlash group, the "Torch Bearers", which consisted of Väinö Kunnas (1896–1929), Sulho Sipilä (1895–1949) and Ragnar Ekelund (1892–1960).

Today, contemporary art in Finland is well supported by state and private grants, and the work on show in the permanent and temporary exhibitions at Kiasma, the new Museum of Contemporary Art in Helsinki, would hardly be recognised as art by the National Romantics. "There are more opportunities to be experimental in Finland because of the support for the arts," says Minna Heikinaho. Her three-screen video installation *"Mun koti on katu ja se onnäytelmä"* ("My home is the street and it's a performance") was one of Kiasma's early shows, and her work epitomises the bolder attitude of Finnish artists born in the early 1960s.

Square and the Cathedral, the architectural leaders of National Romanticism – the partnership of Herman Gesellius (1874–1916), Armas Lindgren (1874–1929) and Eliel Saarinen (1873–1950) – used peasant timber and granite architecture as their sources.

Another leading exponent of the movement was Lars Sonck (1870–1956). Decidedly Gothic in outline, and uneasy on the eye because of the clash of smooth timber or symmetrical roof tiles with rough-hewn granite, National Romantic buildings like Helsinki's National Museum (designed 1901) and Tampere's Cathedral (designed 1899) have a gawky

"Artists are finding different contexts for what they do, making links between theatre, space and performance."

National architecture

The pattern of Finnish fine art – swinging from nationalism to modernism – is mimicked in other art forms: crafts, architecture and design. Turning their backs on the Neo-classical designs of their predecessor C.L. Engel (1778–1840), whose buildings include Helsinki's Senate

LEFT: the Modernist Kiasma, Museum of Contemporary Art in Helsinki.
ABOVE: Alvar Aalto Museum in Jyväskylä.

ugliness. The partnership trio of architects did, however, begin to draw on more soothing, elongated Art Nouveau influences too. The plans for Helsinki Railway Station, originally designed by all three, were amended by Saarinen. The building as it now stands is far more Art Nouveau than National Romantic.

After independence in 1917, the driving need for a national identity diminished in the face of the need to rebuild the country. Beyond the capital, there are abundant instances of original and well-considered municipal architecture: the public library in Tampere, for instance, completed in 1986 is named *"Metso"*, Finnish for capercaillie, the forest bird whose shape its plan resembles. The forest reference is deliberate, but the attractive combination of copper and granite, both indigenous Finnish raw materials, transcends the gimmick. The library's design, like many public Finnish buildings, was the result of an architectural competition and was the work of the husband-and-wife team of Reima and Rauli Pietilä.

Struggling with Modernism

Finland, a relatively new nation whose cities were also deeply scarred in World War II, has bravely embraced Modernism and tried to make a virtue of it. Not all its efforts have been successful, however. The Merihaka estate of apartment blocks near Helsinki's Hakaniemi Square is bleak and heartless, while individual buildings in the Sörnäinen district make one wonder quite how Finland earned its reputation for fine architecture.

Neither is there a universal consensus about the virtues of various showpieces which shot up in central Helsinki at the end of the 1990s. Kiasma, the extraordinary Museum of Contemporary Art designed by American Stephen Holl and opened in 1998 *(see page 173)*, sprawls in metallic asymmetrical splendour behind the statue of the national hero Field

ALVAR AALTO

One designer who became a household name in Finnish architecture was Alvar Aalto (1898-1976), who managed to fuse something Finnish with Modernism and revolutionised 20th-century architecture in the process. Aalto was the prime mover in Finland in the struggle to get the principles of modern architecture, and Modernism as a whole, accepted there. Once that was achieved, he then turned his attention to the rest of the world, via his two Finnish pavilions at the Paris exhibition of 1937 and the New York world fair of 1939. This was primarily to prove that Finland could contribute internationally to the world of architecture and design.

Aalto practised "organic" architecture, designing buildings to suit their environment as well as their purpose. Some of his buildings (the Enso Gutzeit building in Helsinki) appear to be of the archetypal, scorned "concrete block" variety – but, aesthetics aside, they are respected because they were the first to employ nakedly modern materials. Far more highly-regarded is Aalto's Finlandia Hall, the capital's concert and congress complex which gained in stature when it served as the main venue for the CSCE summit in 1975. Its crisp white profile seems to complement the contours of the park overlooking Töölö Bay, and it's hard to imagine the Helsinki profile without it.

Marshal Mannerheim, and it was this bold contrast that was condemned by older Finns, who also lamented the fact that a national architect was not chosen for the job. In fact it provides an ingenious counterpoint to the stolid, humourless Parliament House situated across the road.

The adjacent glass cube of the Sanoma-WSOY media group head office is regarded as cold and transparent by some, while the stately new Finnish National Opera House (Karhunen-Hyvämäki-Parkkinen, 1993), another landmark near Töölö Bay, is condemned by some as a characterless block *(see page 170)*.

It's an environment that has given rise to the creative spirit of the spiky inventions of internal and industrial designer Stefan Lindfors (born 1962) on the one hand, and the gentle paper jewellery of Janna Syvänoja (born 1960) on the other. Finland's giant names in plastics (Neste), ceramics (Arabia), textiles (Finlayson, Marimekko), jewellery (Kalevala Koru, Lapponia) and glass (Iittala, Nuutajärvi) industries periodically introduce pieces by new designers as well as those with established reputations such as that of Yrjö Kukkapuro, whose contemporary furniture is now in New York's Museum of Modern Art.

Superb designs

There is boldness in the field of design too. Whatever the object – a tap, a telephone, a bowl, a chair – if its lines are smooth, if it employs modern materials like chrome or plastic with confidence or reinvents glass or wood, and if it fits its purpose perfectly, it is likely to be Finnish. Encouraged, like architecture, by the financial and prestigious carrot of open competitions, everyday items are ceaselessly redesigned.

LEFT: Marimekko textiles on sale in Helsinki.
ABOVE: the Pentik factory, producers of fine glassware and ceramics.

A legacy of Alvar Aalto is the Artek design and furniture company set up with his wife Aino, critic Nils-Gustav Hahl, and arts patron Maire Gullichsen in the 1930s and which still has a showroom in central Helsinki. The company's designers, working with bold colours and geometric shapes, have created products which are as identifiably Finnish as the handicrafts – woodcarving, rag-rug weaving and tapestry-making – which pertain to traditional culture. The distinctive and popular Fiskar scissors (Fiskars being a small village in southern Finland and a once thriving foundry) is one more example of how Finnish design has invaded international consciousness.

A talent for invention

Just to the west of Helsinki, in the neighbouring city of Espoo close to the Helsinki University of Technology, is the Innopoli Building, housing the Foundation for Finnish Inventions. Started in 1971 with backing from the Finnish Ministry of Trade and Industry, the Foundation epitomises Finland's encouragement of the inventive spirit. But this is not a case of inventiveness for its own sake. The Foundation states its function as serving "as a link between inventors, innovators, consumers, businesses and industry in Finland or other parts of the world". The Foundation's activities are also a sign of

how Finns have recognised the need to diversify their industry. The staples of pulp and paper and related metals and engineering remain strong, but there has been a need to look in new directions.

Finland's most conspicuous and commercially successful inventions are those being placed on to the market with dizzying regularity by Nokia. The company, often mistakenly believed to be of Japanese origin, takes its name from the small and uneventful town in central Finland where it was founded. It has stayed ahead of the field in mobile phone technology by virtue of the slim and stylish designs of its basic cellphone models, but also because it has

recognised the need to continuously refresh its product selection with innovative gadgetry. Its development of videophone technology is known to be at an advanced stage (prototype designs were made public as early as 1998), while the Nokia Communicator – a combination of miniature laptop PC and compact telephone – was almost instantly upstaged in 1999 by the Nokia 7110, which performs as a mobile shopping centre, banker and information provider, as well as a mere telephone.

Nokia has given Finnish information technology a powerful boost: evidence of this is provided by the work, for example, of Risto Linturi, one of whose missions as head researcher with the Helsinki Telephone Corporation was to supervise the Helsinki Arena 2000 project, placing every aspect of Helsinki daily life and services on to its own Internet "mini-web". Elsewhere, California-based Finn Linus Torvalds was the inspiration behind the Linuxcomputer operating system, a set-up which had Bill Gates and his mighty Microsoft glancing over their shoulders with concern in the late 1990s.

A better margarine

But Finnish innovation is not confined to communications technology. It spreads to Benecol, for instance, a margarine which not only contains no cholesterol but which has been proved to decrease blood cholesterol levels by as much as 14 per cent, an effect of the ingredient stanol ester, a birch pulp extract. The only problem for the manufacturing company, Raisio, is how to bring the price of this product, a headline-grabber in the fanatically health-conscious USA, down to a level close to that of other margarines. Birch is also the source of the sweetener xylitol, pioneered in Finland in the late 1970s, used to flavour chewing gum and confectionery, and clinically proved to prevent tooth decay.

Finns have exploited their maritime heritage to good effect as well: shipbuilding innovations include the Azipod propulsion unit, a module that can be adopted by different vessels. The Azipod was developed and installed in vessels made at the Kvaerner-Masa ship-builders, whose yards in Helsinki and Turku have turned out the most advanced icebreakers and the biggest passenger ships in the world. ❏

LEFT: Finnish linens incorporate ancient traditions of textiles production.

Glass and Wood

In view of the prominence of its modern glass design, it is surprising that Finland's glass-making industry dates back only to the late 17th century, when the first glass factory, at Uusikaupunki on the west coast, enjoyed a brief life. Just the same, it is not only one of oldest industries in Finland but the first design industry to make attempts at breaking away from copies of standard European prototype designs, although this only happened in the 1920s. A turning point was a competition staged by the Riihimäki glass company (named after the southern Finnish town of the same name, today the home of the Finnish Glass Museum) for the design of cocktail glasses. Individual glass designers began to make names for themselves, not least Aino Aalto, who was upstaged by her designer/architect husband Alvar in 1936 when he contributed the celebrated Savoy vase to the Milan Triennale (see page 80).

Gunnel Nyman became well known in the following decade for his designs for Iittala, Riihimäki and Nuutajärvi, setting standards which were then equalled and surpassed by designers such as Tapio Wirkkala (thanks to him the frosty surface of the Finlandia vodka bottle), Kaj Franck and Timo Sarpaneva. Eero Aarnio and Yrjö Kukkapuro were other design innovators of the period.

Their traditions of style and a distinctively Finnish grace have been maintained more recently by the likes of Brita Flander, Vesa Varrela and the 1998 winner of the Kaj Franck Design Prize, Heikki Orvola, all of them making sure that Finnish glass is still some of the most beautiful in the world. Items of Iittala and Nuutajärvi's frequently updated glassware ranges include some of Finland's most popular and desirable gift items and souvenirs and a prime export industry. Pentik is another popular glass company.

Finland has also been exceptionally good at taking its natural resources and utilising them for design purposes. Finland's forests have always been (and "touch wood", always will be) the country's most plentiful and ubiquitous natural resource, and Finns know as well as any race on earth their potential as a raw and essentially functional material.

The traditions of woodcraft were crucial to every

aspect of Finnish agrarian life right into the early 20th century, providing shelter, tools and even clothing. Old wooden quarters of the earliest urban milieus were vulnerable to, and were frequently ravaged by, fire but the old parts of Porvoo, 50 km (30 miles) to the east of Helsinki (see page 196) and Rauma on the west coast, preserved since the 17th century (see page 237) contain charming remnants of wooden house-building skills.

These basic timber patterns used in rural buildings around the country are today preserved in the structure of the log cabins and saunas that pepper the shorelines of Finland's thousands of lakes and which remain the summer retreats for

much of the population (see page 250).

On a more intimate scale, the use of wood has been adapted with characteristic Finnish innovation to everyday functions. Paving the way for modern wooden furniture design was Alvar Aalto, who pioneered the "bentwood" technique in the 1930s, skilfully moulding birch wood into laminated fluid curls and curves.

The wooden ornaments, everyday utensils and bowls, and jewellery on sale at the Aarikka gift shops are still testament to the continued Finnish versatility and sensitivity when it comes to their most precious and plentiful raw material. ❏

● For information on the best places to buy glass and wooden Finnish souvenirs, see page 313.

RIGHT: glassblowing in action at the Iittala factory near Helsinki.

MUSIC AND FILM

Finland's musical heritage has long been associated with Sibelius, but modern classical musicians, rock bands and film directors are keeping the country's arts alive

When people think of Finnish music, they still think of Jean Sibelius. The great Finnish composer, after all, sprang from a little-known country to become one of the most famous composers of all time – and Finland's most famous export. But there is much more to modern Finnish music than simply Sibelius, and audiences everywhere now recognise this. A startling number of Finnish musicians and orchestras have won both domestic and international acclaim.

Classical music

The Association of Finnish Composers today numbers over 100 members. All have had works performed professionally, and many possess distinguished discographies. Playing their works in Finland are 13 professional orchestras, 18 semi-professional or chamber orchestras and numerous ensembles. Helsinki is home to two symphony orchestras: the Finnish Radio Symphony and the Helsinki Philharmonic.

For a country of only 5 million people, this is nothing short of remarkable, but the seemingly disproportionate number of musicians is not coincidental. Finland takes its music seriously and has proved it through a generous policy of funding for musicians and musical institutes. Close to 130 such institutes, with a student body of 50,000, offer free primary instruction and talented graduates can audition for one of the seven free conservatories or the celebrated Sibelius Academy in Helsinki.

Professional opportunities for musicians are also wide. As well as holding regular concert seasons, Finland sponsors a number of annual music festivals *(see page 92)* attracting both native and foreign artists. Two recording companies concentrate on Finnish musicians.

Finnish instrumentalists have also been winning global attention. Cellists, of whom Finland has an especially strong tradition, have

done particularly well. Arto Noras, second prize winner at the 1966 Tchaikovsky Competition, and Erkki Rautio are renowned *virtuosi*. Now garnering laurels are Anssi Karttunen and Martti Roussi, both born in 1960. Cellists aren't the only ones. As a classical guitarist, Timo Korhonen (born 1965) is less known, but he looks set to fill the shoes of André Segovia. Pianist Ralf Gothoni commands a confirmed place in Europe and further afield, as does pianist and composer Olli Mustonen (born 1967) – "Finland's Mozart" – who performed his own concerto with the Radio Symphony Orchestra at the age of 12. Esa-Pekka Salonen is the most notable achiever, a principal conductor with an international reputation second only to Sibelius.

After Sibelius and Salonen, however, it is Finland's singers who have gained the most fame. Foreign audiences adore Finnish basses: Matti Lehtinen in the 1950s, Martti Talvela before his premature death in 1989, and now

---

PRECEDING PAGES: the Sibelius Monument in Helsinki.
LEFT: conductor Esa-Pekka Salonen.
RIGHT: Aino Ackte, Finnish soprano opera singer.

Matti Salminen and Jaakko Ryhänen. Baritones Jorma Hynninen, Tom Krause, Walton Grönroos and tenor Peter Lindroos grace houses like the New York Met, London's Covent Garden and Berlin's Deutsche Opera. Nor have sopranos missed out; Ritva Auvinen, Anita Välkki, Taru Valjakka and Karita Mattila have attained stardom, and Soile Isokoski, winner of the Elly Ameling contest, is joining their ranks.

Although its sopranos have sought fame overseas, the Finnish National Opera, now happily settled in its new showpiece National Opera House in Helsinki, doesn't seem to suffer too much. It made, for example, operatic history in 1983 as the first foreign company to be invited to perform at New York's Met.

Vocal works have always been the backbone of the Finnish musical tradition, which may, perhaps, explain why about three new Finnish operas are published every year. Among recent ones to have been performed in leading houses outside Finland are Aulis Sallinen's *Ratsumies* (*The Horseman*), *Punainen Viiva* (*The Red Line*), and *Kullervo*, and Joonas Kokkonen's *Viimeiset Kiusaukset* (*The Last Temptations*).

These operas offer additional proof that Finnish composition, too, lives on beyond Sibelius. Joonas Kokkonen might be called the

WANDERING MAESTROS

Talented Finns are often lured abroad, thereby spreading the musical word. Finnish conductors are particularly in demand. Every Nordic capital has had a symphony orchestra with a Finn as principal conductor. The country has many world-class maestros, including Paavo Berglund, Okko Kamu and Salonen. Prolonging the fine tradition are the likes of Sakari Oramo, who became conductor-in-chief of the City of Birmingham Symphony Orchestra in 1998. The well-loved Leif Segerstam has been extremely active and prolific; both as a conductor in Finland and around the world, and as composer of about 20 symphonies, as well as many songs and concertos.

country's pre-eminent living composer but excellence is also to be found in the works of Erik Bergman and Einojuhani Rautavaara, two other acclaimed senior composers. Among younger composers, Magnus Lindberg (born 1958) and Kaija Saariaho (born 1952) are of special note. Lindberg's KRAFT (1985) won the Nordic Council's music award and the Koussevitzky disc award. *Le Monde de la Musique* has called him "one of the best composers in the world of his age." His most recent orchestral work, *Fresco*, made its world première with the LA Philharmonic, conducted by Esa-Pekka Salonen. Saariaho, an electro-acoustic innovator, has also received much acclaim.

Popular music

One of the refreshing aspects of Finnish art generally is its lack of élitism. Still, the lines are as well drawn between classical and rock music here as in most places. Finnish rock thrives but on its own terms. The best-known Finnish band was probably Hanoi Rocks, now disbanded and remembered for their kitsch image as much as for their music. Neither has Finland had an answer to the phenomenal global appeal of neighbour Sweden's

OPERA FESTIVAL

Even the most recalcitrant sopranos come home for the annual Savonlinna Opera Festival. Held in a 500-year-old castle, it is one of the most delightful summer opera festivals in the world.

heels in especially deep). But their style is still sufficiently Finnish to restrict them largely to an exclusively Finnish audience.

The language, of course, is what sets many Finnish bands apart. If you don't understand Finnish, you have no hope of grasping the essence of Juice Leskinen's dismal whine, for instance. Yet the pop and rock music scene is proudly eclectic, embracing the techno experiments of Jimi Tenor as well as the sophisticated, harmonic folk-pop of Värttinä, a group

glossily produced pop, such as that of ABBA, Roxette or The Cardigans.

Certainly, there is nothing inferior about Finnish rock music. The best-loved bands, such as the veteran Eppu Normaali outfit, the bluesy J.J. Karjalainen and his various line-ups, and the raucous Don Huonot, can all play as well as any rock group in Europe, and are affected by the same fashions (especially punk and heavy metal bands, which seem to have dug their

LEFT: Finnish composer Magnus Lindberg.
ABOVE: Seppo Kimanen (left), cellist and cultural director of Kuhno Chamber Music Festival; and Ralf Gothoni (right), pianist.

of girl singers who have adapted the traditional motifs of ancient styles to a modern, radio-friendly swing, and whose albums have risen to the top of the World Music charts

One other aspect of the Finnish music scene which is a true regional phenomenon is the passion for the tango. It may sound unlikely, but Argentine melodrama converts convincingly to the melancholy of the Finnish crooner. The Tango Festival at Seinäjoki is Finland's best-attended summer gathering: the dancing continues through the night, in the streets, in the bars and restaurants, and a Tango King and Queen are elected. Seinäjoki is also the host for the annual Provinssirock festival (see page 93).

Generally, the further north you travel, the louder the music gets – and, some say, the more interesting. Windy and cold Oulu in northern Finland has the most intense core of rock fans, as well as the only male choir in the world that doesn't even try to sing: *Huutajat* (literally "the Shouters"). Dozens of long-haired men in black suits and gum ties shout their hearts out in perfect order – Arctic hysteria at its best.

Finns on film

It is the Kaurismäki brothers, Aki and Mika, who are largely to thank for wrenching the Finnish cinema industry from stagnation and

to worldwide attention with their rough-edged individuality and prolific output. Contemporary Finnish cinema received little exposure until the advent of the brothers. Refracting a range of influences, from the French *nouvelle vague* to American rock 'n' roll, through a Finnish sensibility, the brothers have created a body of work that has been seen in 65 countries, won prizes at international festivals and brought Aki the accolade of being the youngest director ever to receive a retrospective at the Museum of Modern Art in New York

Born in Helsinki in 1957, Aki toiled as a postman and film critic before working as a scriptwriter, assistant and actor on his elder brother's 1980 film *Valehtelija* (*The Liar*). The following year, the two men formed a production company. They also own a distribution company, a cinema in downtown Helsinki and were among the founders of the Midnight Sun Festival held each June in Sodankylä, Lapland.

Aki, the better known of the siblings, worked with Mika on the 1983 rock documentary *Saimaa-Ilmiä* (*The Saimaa Gesture*) before striking out with a freewheeling adaptation of *Crime and Punishment* (1983). A lugubrious figure of laconic manner and dismissive attitudes to his work, Aki has a self-proclaimed reputation as "the biggest drinker in the world". His films revel in the deadpan humour of morose outsiders desperate to escape the confines of a gloom-ridden country. Frequently shot in monochrome, eschewing dialogue whenever possible and rarely running to more than 80 minutes, his films range from *Calamari Union* (1985), an unscripted comedy in which the 17 characters are all called Frank, to *Hamlet Liikemaailmassa* (*Hamlet Goes Business*) (1987), a modern-day version of Shakespeare set in a rubber duck factory, and *Ariel* (1988), which begins with a suicide and offers tribute to the Finnish tango. Aki then moved his settings away from his native land with the Ealing-style comedy *I Hired a Contract Killer* (1990), filmed in London, and more recently *Hold On to Your Scarf* and *Drifting Clouds*.

Mika, two years older, studied film in Munich and has worked in a variety of genres from the road movie *Helsinki Napoli* (1987) to the comedy *Cha Cha Cha* (1988) and *Amazon* (1990), set in the Amazonian jungle.

Flying the Finnish flag in quite a different way is the Hollywood action specialist, Renny Harlin, the director of special-effects blockbusters like *Cliffhanger* and *Deep Blue Sea*. Closer to home is *Helsinki is Made at Night* (1999) by Ilkka Järvi-Laituri with Hollywood star Bill Pullman in the lead. Finns seem to have rediscovered their own environment as a setting for film. In 1999, Finnish films attracted half the cinema audiences, entertained by old-hand Raimo Niemi's *Poika ja Ilves* (*Tommy and the Wildcat*), Aleksi Mäkelä's *Häjyt* and Markku Pölönen's *Kuningasjätkä* (*King of the Lumberjacks*), all of them set in Finland. ❏

LEFT: the film maker Aki Kaurismäki at work on one of his many films.

Jean Sibelius

It cannot be easy for a man to find himself a figurehead in his country's search for an identity, yet it was this label rather than the simple genius of his music that many Finns tied on to their most famous composer, Jean Sibelius (1865–1957), during the years before Finnish independence. His tone poem *Finlandia* in particular became an emblem of everything Finnish, and this aura of reverence must have sometimes irked the composer.

Yet Sibelius did embody many things Finnish; even his ancestry took in areas of Finland as far apart as the coastal town of Loviisa, near the Russian border, the Swedish influence of Turku, the northwest Gulf of Bothnia and, nearer at hand, Häme province where he was born. The family already had a daughter but Jean was the first son of Hämeenlinna doctor, Christian Gustaf Sibelius, and his wife Maria. Later, another son, Christian, followed.

Though his father's family in Loviisa was wealthy, Dr Sibelius was better known for his medical care than as a financial manager and when, three years later, he died looking after his patients in the typhus epidemic that raged during Finland's last great famine, Maria had little choice but to file for bankruptcy. The family remained in Hämeenlinna. All three children showed musical talent, displaying their concert skills on family visits to Loviisa. The birthplace has a photograph from that period which shows the young Jean (violin), Linda (piano), and Christian (cello) during a recital.

Although it is simplistic to think of Sibelius as being solely influenced by the Finnish landscape, he was undoubtedly part of the late 19th-century movement of artists, writers and intellectuals who turned for inspiration to Finland's land, people and past. Yet, after the first performance of his early *Kullervo* symphony, based on Finnish folklore at the height of the National Romantic movement *(see page 77)*, Sibelius withdrew the work and it was not played again until after his death.

The great Sibelius scholar Erik Tawaststjerna insists that Sibelius moved in the mainstream of European music and was influenced by Beethoven, as well as by Bruckner and Tchaikovsky. His relationship to Wagner's music could be described as love-hate.

RIGHT: bust of Jean Sibelius on display in the Sibelius Museum.

Certainly Sibelius travelled to Bayreuth and Munich in the 1890s and planned an opera, something he did not achieve though some of its proposed music went into *The Swan of Tuonela*. He wrote his First Symphony just before the turn of the 20th century and followed it with the popular Second in 1902, around which time he started to plan the Violin Concerto, now regarded by many as his greatest work. Its first performance in 1904, arranged hurriedly because Sibelius had financial problems, was not a success and it was revised.

Not long after, the family moved to Ainola *(see page 224)*, close to the retreat of his friend the artist Pekka Halonen. The site for Ainola (named

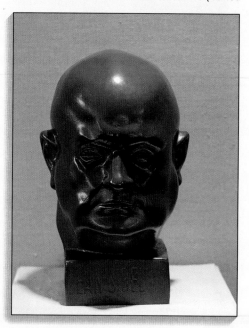

after his wife Aino) was located by the painter Eero Järnefelt, Aino's brother. Another friend, architect Lars Sonck, designed the house, and Sibelius wrote some 150 works there, including the remaining symphonies. Sibelius lived for 53 years at Ainola until his death in 1957, and the small artistic colony spent much time in one another's houses. To compose, Sibelius needed silence: his children went away to friends and the servants crept around on tiptoe.

In his final years, Sibelius left no music. Until his death, there were constant rumours of one more symphony; but, though many believe Sibelius continued to compose, nothing can have satisfied him. The Seventh Symphony was his last. ❏

FINLAND'S SUMMER FESTIVALS

In common with other Nordic countries, Finland has a long tradition of festivals which make the most of summer nights in music, song and dance

The soprano Aino Acte founded Savonlinna in 1912, and it remains the most dramatic setting for any music festival the world over. After this came Jyväskylä, opened in 1955 by the composer Seppo Nummi. The tradition for music festivals continues today, many in rural areas and many which now draw international audiences. One of the most remote is the Kuhmo Chamber Music Festival close to the Russian border, founded in 1970 by cellist Seppo Kimanen. It now draws 150 international musicians to more than 60 concerts.

Other arts festivals include: Tampere (theatre); Kuopio (dance); Pori (jazz); Imatra (big bands); Lieksa (brass bands) and Sodankylä (film).

FOLK FESTIVALS

One source of traditional festivals was the old-time fire brigades, who got together to play music and dance at annual festivals. Some festivals have their roots in a more sinister past: in 1643, the Ruovesi Witch Trials condemned Antti Lieronen "as a witch most obvious and potent" and burned her at the stake. Today's "trials" include drama and concerts but no one is burned.

In 1968 Finland Festivals was formed, to monitor festivals, propose new ideas and guarantee high artistic level. New festivals are born every year.

◁ ONE WORLD
Finland's festivals are not just local events – international artistes bring their own shows and costumes.

▷ CASTLE SETTING
In all, Savonlinna has seen the world premières of no less than five operas by Finnish composers in a country where the composing and playing of classical music flourishes as never before.

△ SUMMER MADNESS
Finland's all too brief summer is certainly cause to celebrate when it arrives – the Helsinki Midsummer Festival attracts hordes of revellers.

△ SAILING FRENZY
It's not surprising that a country with so much water at its disposal holds regular rowing and boating regattas in the Lakeland region.

▷ FOLK TRADITIONS
Throughout the nine days of Kaustinen Folk Music groups of musicians from many countries hand on old traditions and develop new styles of folk music.

ROCK, JAZZ AND BLUES FESTIVALS

◁ FISH FESTIVAL
It is not only arts and music that get the festival treatment; food is also celebrated, such as at this Herring Festival on Helsinki's harbour.

▽ LEARNING THE STEPS
The Kuopio Dance Festival (*Kuopio tanssii ja soi*) is one of the finest events concentrating on dance from around the world.

Finland has a broad rock scene, highlighted by a number of summer rock festivals.

Provinssirock, held in Seinäjoki in early June, traditionally marks the opening of the rock festival season. A four-hour train ride north of Helsinki, Seinäjoki turns into a rock heaven for one weekend. As well as the best of the Finns, Provinssirock attracts big names from abroad, such as REM and David Byrne. As elsewhere, there are beer tents selling brew. (Drugs are low-profile in Finland and you are unlikely to see any.)

The other important summer rock festival is Ruisrock at Turku. The oldest rock festival in Finland, Ruisrock faded for a few years but has now revived and hosts some of the biggest names. Recent guests have included Bob Dylan and Billy Idol.

Even President Mauno Koivisto favours the artists featured in the huge Pori Jazz Festival. Another festival with a family atmosphere is Puisto Blues in Järvenpää, north of Helsinki, at the beginning of June.

THE WRITER'S DILEMMA

Finnish literature emerged in the 19th century as an embodiment of the national character. Today, Finnish writers continue to use writing to understand their world

Eino Leino, poet, novelist and playwright, said of Finnish literature in 1910: "Literature is the country's interpreter. Literature is the nation's mirror. Without literature the nation is like a blind man, like a deaf mute."

The story of the past two centuries of Finnish literature is the story of a country struggling to find its voice and its identity. Mimicking Finland's political development, there have been peaks and troughs, high expectations and disappointments. Writers have expressed the fortunes of their country by veering from romanticism to cynicism and realism. The written portrait of the Finn has covered the spectrum from noble hero to drunken buffoon.

A blank canvas

The high expectations came first, partly fuelled by the blank canvas on which the first writers of the 19th century worked. Until that time, Finland's literary tradition had been primarily an oral one. Because there was no written precedent, writers had a free hand to invent the Finn on paper, and many made him a hero.

Johan Ludvig Runeberg (1804–77), Finland's national poet, offered just such a romantic vision of his countrymen. In his three collections of Swedish-language poems, *Dikter I–III* (*Poems*), and in his patriotic ballad series, *Fänrik Ståhl Sägner I–II* (*The Tales of Ensign Ståhl*), he created loyal, gracious and noble Finns. They were readily embraced.

In the 1820s, Elias Lönnrot (1802–84) began a project which was to generate yet more national pride. Lönnrot travelled through Finland recording folk poetry. The resultwas the *Kalevala* of 1835 (now commonly called the *"Old Kalevala"*). A new, longer version was published in 1849.

The *Kalevala* is easily misunderstood as merely "Finland's epic poem", not paying due attention to its literary value. Technically

LEFT: Elias Lönnrot, creator of the Finland's national epic poem, the *Kalevala*.
RIGHT: Gallén-Kallela's illustrations of the *Kalevala*.

speaking, the *Kalevala* is based on metrical foot, "quadrisyllabic trochee" which makes it rhythmical and easy to recite. There are four pairs of syllables on each line, and two or more lines have a synonomous meaning. Alliteration is also typical, which makes translations impossible – they merely follow the narration. The

poem itself is an heroic epic on the scale of *The Odyssey* or *The Iliad*. But it is also a rag-bag of narratives and light interludes, existing to preserve old customs and songs. The narrative is interrupted by poetic "charms", some of which belong to the realms of Shakespearian comedy. Lönnrot's Finn is a participator in the creation of the world. The characters are classical figures with a Finnish twist. The context – sea, farm, forest – is entirely Finnish.

The *Kalevala* managed to include in its poetry a national fiction-cum-history which stretched back to the beginning of time, and which did not include the humiliating details of real life – never-ending domination by foreign rulers. In Lönnrot's mythical Finland, power lay with the good and the just. Lönnrot compiled the work in the mid-19th century, yet it reads like a piece of literature as old as the classics or, at the very least, as old as the Norse sagas. And, because it is drawn from a dateless oral tradition, it is impossible to question its veracity while under its spell.

At the same time as Lönnrot was compiling the *Kalevala*, other Finnish-language writers such as Aleksis Kivi (1834–72) were celebrating rural life, casting the ordinary people in the role of heroes: true Finns led virtuous lives among the forests, harmonious with nature.

Twentieth-century works

By the early 20th century, real events began to cast doubts on this unimpeachable national character. Political achievements – especially that of independence – were quickly soured by subsequent developments and crises. It became the job of writers to make sense of events like the Civil War, or the effects of industrialisation, that lay heavy on the nation's conscience. Mainstream Finnish writing concerned itself with events in the world at large.

Notable exceptions include Mika Waltari (1908–79), an escapist writer. His main work, *The Egyptian*, has been translated into more than 25 languages. F. E. Sillanpää, too, wrote about the mystical rural life and won the Nobel Prize for literature in 1939 – his books include *Meek Heritage* and *The Maid Silja*.

During this time, Swedish-language writers drifted away from the main pulse of Finnish writing, becoming more isolated. Some, like the poet Edith Södergran (1892–1923), nonetheless enjoyed considerable popularity. Christer Kihlman, author of *Den Blå Modern* (*The Blue Mother*) and *Dyre Prins* (*Sweet Prince*), and Tove Jansson's Moomintroll books, show just how idiosyncratic Swedish-Finnish writing has become.

The years after the war expurgated many people's consciences. The fate of refugees from Karelia was one literary theme. Väinö Linna's successful and controversial novel *Tuntematon sotilas* (*The Unknown Soldier*) turned wartime events into a psychological story among a group of Finns from various parts of the country, each reflecting a regional character with a typical dialect.

By the 1960s, the literary trends were those of the rest of Europe – protest poetry, working-class novels, middle-class angst and, because of rural depopulation, a scrutiny of rural life.

Contemporary voices

Today, Finnish heroes no longer have to act as vessels for the nation's pride. They are as troubled and beset by worries as the heroes of other literatures. Modern writers like Leena Krohn and Pentti Saarikoski reflect Finnish humanity. Veijo Meri is seen as a reformer of Finnish prose with his *Manilla Rope*.

As modern Finnish writers become more international, the *Kalevala* may still be reflected in popular Finnish literature. The best-selling authors, Kalle Päätalo, Laila Hietamies, Arno Paasilinna and Veikko Huovinen place their stories in the same regions where the *Kalevala* was collected. Päätalo's nostalgic rural landscape and Hietamies' lost Karelia both evoke the eternal yearning for youth. Paasilinna and Huovinen both work in a Karelian-style setting and use onomatopoeic words – the backbone of both the *Kalevala* and modern Finnish short stories. Both work on the far side of the Finnish culture where reality and imagination meet, as in the *Kalevala*. ❑

LEFT: Viejo Meri, one of Finland's most respected modern writers.

The Moomins

At first sight Tove Jansson's Moomin books seem like storybooks to buy children as gifts. But the mystical fairytale world of mighty nature and ever-changing seasons inspire even die-hard realists.

Tove Jansson was born in 1914, to an artistic family – both brothers are artists and writers. A tiny Swedish-speaking woman, meek to the point of humility, Jansson has lived much of her life with her female friend on a small island off the southern coast of Finland. Here Jansson created another world like C.S.Lewis and J.R.R. Tolkien. But, where Tolkien was a perfectionist and a scientist, Jansson is a humanist, an artist and a storyteller. Nature is the main element, and nature is always respected.

Moomin books appeal to both children and adults, because their basic philosophy is about acceptance, quest for space and solitude. Some titles, in fact, are too advanced for children, but raise many questions in adults.

The books are all led by the Moomin family characters. The Bohemian Moominmamma takes care of everything, while the Moominpappa is a philosopher, who writes his memoirs and becomes active only when it's time to explore the unknown. The Moomin house is always open to adopted children and strange creatures that seem to appear from the valley. Love and tolerance reign; difference is always accepted. There are no wars, no alcohol is consumed and nothing threatens the idyll except the natural phenomena.

Each character is a sensitively illustrated personality, so every reader will identify oneself with at least one of them. Children fear the monstrous Groke who only appears in winter. He is cold as winter and no one wants to be near him. But even he has human qualities – lonely poor Groke suffers greatly while missing contact with just about anyone. Little My is an adventurous girl, who, along with Moomintroll, is perhaps Tove Jansson's own alter ego. Snufkin is a world traveller who prefers wandering alone. Snitt is a coward; the Fillyjonk is a neurotic pedant. Hemulen is an absent-minded botanist and Snork an engineer who does little else than design a light aeroplane. The Snork Maiden, Snork's sister, is extremely feminine. The strange, worm-like electric creatures Hatifnatters

represent foreigners, with whom communication is possible if not easy. All these characters lend themselves to fine psychological drama.

The Moomin life pauses for hibernation when the winter comes, and is reborn at the thaw when Snufkin returns from his world travels, except when the magical winter is brought to life in *Moominland Midwinter*. The four seasons are dominant – from springtime optimism to autumn isolation.

These unpretentious little books have conquered the world, having been translated into over 30 languages. In Finland, there is the Moomin World in Naantali, the Moomin Museum in Tampere and yet another theme park being planned – of all places –

in Hawaii. The Japanese love the Moomin figures, and a TV cartoon series was produced in co-operation with a Japanese company. Finnair has had Moomin figures painted on aeroplanes flying to Japan, and Finnair's flight attendants sell enormous quantities of Moomin paraphernalia to travellers. Several stamps have been issued on Moomin characters, but the commercialised Moomins are not entirely faithful to the originals.

Jansson's world really exists near the village of Pellinki, south of Porvoo. Around this cape, one will find islands, caves and the sea, but the lighthouse that became the Moomin house is no longer there. But the Moomin world is alive anywhere that love and tolerance are understood. ❑

RIGHT: the Moomin Valley Museum in Tampere is perennially popular with children and adults.

FINNS WHO SPEAK SWEDISH

Finland is officially bilingual, using both Finnish and Swedish, a tradition that goes back centuries between these two neighbouring countries

Why do so many Finns speak Swedish is a question that is often asked by visitors. The main reason is that for 600 years, Finland was a part of Sweden. In that time it is not so surprising that Swedish became the language for administration, and many Finns adopted the language to survive in the society. Some of their great-grandchildren still use Swedish, the language having been passed down the generations. But the answer isn't quite as simple as that – politics and education have also played their part.

Early settlers
The earliest inhabitants on the Aland Islands and many other coastal communities were Scandinavian settlers, adventurers and fishermen, who brought their language with them. Many who still live on these islands speak a unique Swedish dialect which may be hard to understand, even by Swedish tourists.

As Finland was a lucrative territory, many Swedes also emigrated, mostly to Nyland ("New Land") and Osterbotten (as opposed to Västerbotten, eastern and western "Bothnia", respectively). Some came as industrialists and founded factories and saw mills. Many of these ancient communities remain, including the cardboard factory in Verla, now a UNESCO World Heritage site.

The military also played a major role in the Swedish "take-over". In many cases, successful soldiers in the Royal Swedish Army were granted privileges in Finland, such as territory and tax-free status, which brought with them a Swedish upper class to many previously remote regions of Finland.

As Swedish soon became the lingua franca in large towns such as Turku, Helsinki and Vyborg, many German, Jewish or Russian burghers living in these areas adopted Swedish, and this usage remains today.

LEFT: bilingual road signs are a common sight: this sign puts the Swedish language first.
RIGHT: a typical Swedish area near Turku.

A bilingual nation
This is something visitors to Finland find difficult to understand. Swedish-speaking Finns, or Finland-Swedes as they are described by the government, are not immigrants, nor are they Swedes. They may not even have any family connections with Sweden.

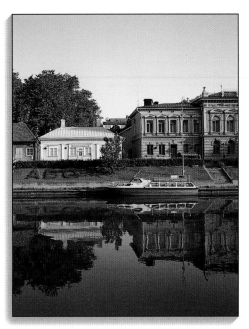

When Finland is described as a "bilingual" nation, it means that the two languages are given an official status, very much the same as English and French in Canada – one may assume the right to use either Swedish or Finnish at offices or even in shops in "bilingual" towns. However, this is not always successful – in some cases Finns have to resort to English in order to understand each other.

Swedish as a language is many things in Finland. At one hand, it is a living language (including numerous dialects), used by 300,000 people. It is also a "compulsory" language taught to practically every Finnish child at school. It is an "official" language, which the president uses to address the nation. It is also a "semi-official" language in the sense that the law provides certain minimum services in Swedish, say, regular TV and radio programmes on national channels.

Linguistic roots

Swedish-speakers are a throwback to the 600 years when Finland was the eastern part of the Kingdom of Sweden. Then, and even during the time when Finland was a Grand Duchy of Russia, from 1808 to independence in 1917, Swedish was the official language, the language of the civil service, of the law, of higher education, at the University of Turku (Abo in Swedish), and of the monied classes.

Fed by students from Turku University, Finnish cultural life was dominated by Swedish-speakers too. It was not until 1828 that the university established a Finnish language lectureship, and not until 1850 that a professorship of Finnish was introduced.

Because the Swedish language held sway in this way, it was the principal language of the nascent Finnish mid-19th-century cultural and political life. Early political activists like the Fennomen, who supported the Finnish language and campaigned for its recognition as an

official language, often faced the paradox that they were Swedish-speakers whose love of their country was paramount. A number of 19th-century cultural ambassadors, painters and writers, who searched determinedly for an artistic expression of Finnish nationalism, were also Swedish-speakers.

It was not surprising, therefore, that when Finland gained its independence, the 1919 Constitution decreed that Finland should have two official national languages: Finnish and Swedish. At that time, Swedish-speakers accounted for 12 per cent of the Finnish population. Today, the figure has shrunk to around 6 per cent.

Swedish-speakers are very much spread out around the country. About half of them live in purely Swedish regions in Nyland, around Turku, on Aland and on the west coast. Regional centres, such as Ekenäs (Tammisaari in Finnish), Borgå (Porvoo) and Jakobstad (Pietarsaari) have their indigenous Swedish culture, and larger towns such as Abo (Turku), Vasa (Vaasa) or the capital Helsinki (which Swedish-speakers call Helsingfors) house about half of the Swedish-speakers.

DIFFERENT WORDS

Swedish spoken in Finland is not identical to that of Sweden; many local dialect words which have their roots in Finnish are included in Finland's Swedish.

Accusations that Finland-Swedes were more wealthy or disproportionately powerful have rumbled on over the decades.

Highs and lows

Sadly, the population of Finland-Swedes is decreasing. Figures may be misleading, however. In 1960, there were 21 Swedish-language newspapers (182 Finnish); in 1988, the figure was 14 (with 374 Finnish publications). Finland-Swedes have a choice of papers from either Sweden or Finland. Daily papers from

With encouragement from individuals like Czar Alexander II, who made it official in 1863, Finnish gradually became the dominant language and the language of power. But political disputes over the two languages and their relative prominence have flared up from time to time, especially in the 1920s and 1930s when it became a central political issue. Common comparisons with the Republic of Ireland are not far-fetched – the difference is that, in fact, English has been more dominant than Swedish.

LEFT: the League of Nations meets to decide the fate of the Aland Islands' status in 1921.
ABOVE: Alanders enjoying traditional Swedish dancing.

large publishers in Stockholm are always available in Finland's Swedish-speaking centres, and Sweden's culture, politics and daily gossip is popular among Finland-Swedes.

In fact, Finland has been dubbed a model for minority policy. The government spends much more money per capita on Swedish radio and TV programmes, and the largest Swedish daily in Finland, *Hufvudstadsbladet*, manages a circulation of 60,000, which means one paper for each five Swedish-speakers. Some observers note that, as a comparison, Wales has no daily newspaper in the Welsh language – a language that is spoken by more than 15 per cent of its population.

As Finland and Sweden entered the European Union in 1995, Swedish became an official language once again, which boosted its significance all over Europe. Finnish-speaking Finns, therefore, readily understand the usefulness of Swedish in both domestic and European communication.

The growing number of "mixed marriages" between Finnish- and Swedish-speakers also doubles the number of bilingual Finns – many families choose to use both languages at home, and Swedish schools are becoming popular once again, even among purely Finnish-speaking families.

A unique situation

The case of the Aland Islands, which lie off the southwest of Finland almost halfway to Sweden, is unique. Though this is Finnish territory, the roles are reversed. When Finland became independent in 1917, the Alanders' background and culture were (and are) more clearly Swedish and they voted overwhelmingly in a referendum to become part of Sweden. After much wrangling, the matter went to the infant League of Nations in the early 1920s and, in the way of international bodies, it complicated what could then have been a relatively simple settlement by deciding that the Aland Islands remain Finnish but that the

islanders' use of the Swedish language would be safeguarded.

The official language, therefore, is Swedish, and Swedish culture is preserved by law. However, the 25,000 residents consider themselves to be autonomous, with their own flag and postage stamps. The Alanders have their own parliament and government to run their internal affairs out of a proportion of the Finnish budget. They also send a member to the main Parliament in Helsinki (*see page 229*).

The argument goes that as part of Sweden, Alanders would be "normal" citizens. As part of Finland, they may retain their "special" status. Aland became even more of a special case on 1 July 1999, when tax-free sales became banned within inter-EU travel. Aland is "outside" the Union, however, thus all ferries between Finland and Sweden stop briefly at the Långnäs pier, where popular tax-free sales continue unabated.

Political representation

The main political party representing mainland Finland-Swedes, the Swedish People's Party (SFP), was founded in 1906. Other political parties claim to be multilingual or bilingual, but the SFP's power base has been constant in recent years. It won 5.3 per cent of votes in the 1987 parliamentary elections (13 seats) and 5.1 per cent (11 seats) in 1999.

Frequent coalition governments have resulted in some Cabinet prominence for SFP Members of Parliament. Jan-Erik Enestam held a number of ministerial posts, including Minister of Defence in 1999. The SFP's Elisabeth Rehn was the first female Minister of Defence in the early 1990s, and was a candidate for Finland's president (*see page 63*).

Talk to Finland-Swedes about the problems of being a linguistic minority and they will often tell you of the difficulties of not being able to express themselves fully in both languages. The plus side is that many, used to switching between two languages, become able linguists, taking on board German, English, French, Danish and Norwegian with ease.

And, despite coming from such diverse backgrounds, they benefit from three cultures: Sweden, Finnish Finland and Swedish Finland. ❏

LEFT: Swedish People's Party (SFP) leader Ole Norrback addresses a rally.

Immigrants

In the heat of the summer of 1999, Romany refugees from Slovakia caught Finns off-guard. Within two weeks over 1,000 had arrived. The government acted immediately, with a new visa compulsion for Slovakian nationals, and the flow soon reversed. The Slovakian "gypsies" became the first news item during the traditionally quiet midsummer weeks.

Finland is no promised land that can take any number of foreigners. It seems that few can arrive without anyone taking notice. The numbers of arrivals are constantly increasing, however.

These days Helsinki is fully international, with over 5 per cent of the population speaking a foreign language (other than Swedish). It doesn't compare with Stockholm where more than 15 per cent are foreigners but the figure is growing. The densely inhabited Kallio suburb in Helsinki is a playground for hard-working immigrants. Bangladeshis run pizza restaurants, Thai women keep massage parlours and ethnic food shops abound.

Finland became a sort of a cul-de-sac when the Soviet Union restricted travel, especially from Russia to Finland. Therefore, the biggest influx of foreigners occurred soon after the Soviet downfall – Russians and Estonians now constitute the largest foreign groups in Finland (35,000) and one per cent of all Estonians live in Finland.

Among Asians, the Chinese are the largest ethnic group, working in restaurants or studying. More than 3,000 Vietnamese also live in Finland, most of them originally as refugees. The arrival of the Vietnamese, in fact, was a media event. Many of them were hand-picked at Asian refugee camps by Finnish government officials. At the same time Finland gave developmental aid to the Vietnamese government. This was, and still is to some extent, the official refugee policy – a few hundred "quota" refugees who were given full financial support. The other nationals that arrived with refugee status came mainly from Chile, or the Kurdish regions in Turkey or Iran.

When the Somalis came, however, the situation changed. Already some 6,000 Somalis live in Finland, a minority well visible in central Helsinki. Rumours abounded about the enormous amounts of tax-payers' money being spent just to clothe them. Gang wars against Somalis occurred, especially during the harsh recession years in the early 1990s when Finland's unemployment figures hovered above 20 per cent. The small town of Joensuu became notorious for a "skinhead" gang who terrorised foreigners. Things have now cooled down, although unemployment among Somalis remains high.

Restaurants are typical employers for many Chinese and Indians in Finland, and Turkish kebab shops are ubiquitous in even smaller towns. Most employers demand full knowledge of Finnish, and most foreigners have low-paid jobs that Finns refuse to accept.

Loneliness or isolation is one of the biggest problems among foreigners. Some refugees will be located in tiny towns where contacts with locals are practically non-existent. Finns seldom "small talk" with strangers, let alone foreigners. One Australian co-habited six winter months in a student apartment with a shy Finnish man. After several months' silence, he one day broke the silence: "It is your turn to buy toilet paper".

Many immigrants choose Finland over warmer countries: some fall in love with a Finn, Finland has useful social benefit schemes, a very high standard of living and, perhaps most importantly, an increasing amount of fellow foreigners – some 90,000 citizens now carry a foreign passport. ❏

RIGHT: Somalian refugees seeking Finnish citizenship at Helsinki airport.

THE SAMI AND THEIR LAND

The Sami of north Finland have a distinct culture that, rather than being destroyed by modern life, is increasingly valued by Finns and by tourists

For the Sami (Lapps), who on the whole prefer to mind their own business and hope other people will mind theirs, the second half of the 20th century has brought mixed blessings, putting pressure on a fragile ecology already under threat. Against that, the many changes have also triggered a much greater awareness of their own identity.

Early development

Most specialists agree the Sami descend from a people who, following the retreating edge of the continental ice, reached Finland and East Karelia in the latter millennia BC. Their contacts with an indigenous proto-Sami people gave birth to the earliest Sami culture. Later came the Finns, also speaking a Finno-Ugric tongue, and thus sharing a common linguistic heritage originating in the Ural mountains.

The cornerstone of early Sami society was the *siida*, a community of several families and the territories in which they co-operatively hunted, trapped and fished. Place names in southern and central Finland suggest that Sami communities thrived until the Middle Ages. But as the Finnish settlers moved in, so the Sami – those who were not assimilated – moved on, ever northwards. In Finland today they are concentrated in northern Lapland around Utsjoki, Karasjoki, Inari and Enontekiö (*see page 285*). Based on language criteria there are an estimated 6,500 Sami people in Finland, considerably fewer than in Sweden and Norway.

Land of the midnight sun

The Sami home in Lapland (Lappi) is Finland's northernmost province and covers nearly a third of the country's total area, most of it north of the Arctic Circle. Away from the few towns and scattered communities its extraordinary beauty is still predominantly primeval wilderness. Extensive swamps and forests of conifer and

birch rise in the far north to bareheaded fells, the highest topping 1,300 metres (4,270 ft); all this is laced by swift rivers and streams and punctuated by lakes and pools.

You may think of it as the land of the midnight sun which, depending on latitude (and cloud cover), is visible for up to 70 summer

days. In winter there is an almost equivalent sunless period, tempered at times by the flickering veils of the Northern Lights or, around midday, by the lingering dawn effects from the invisible sun or the inescapable, all-pervading whiteness of the snow. Spring is a swift green renaissance in the wake of the big thaw. And autumn flares in colours so spectacular the Finns have a special term for it: *ruska*.

You may also think of it as the land of the Lapps. They, however, prefer their own name for themselves: Sami (pronounced Sah-mi) a preference which is now respected. Today the Sami's territory extends across northern Scandinavia and into the northwest corner of Russia.

PRECEDING PAGES: Sami's midday meal during a reindeer drive. **LEFT:** Skolte Sami woman in Nellim Church. **RIGHT:** a modern Sami girl.

Society and spirit

Inevitably the Sami's fragile, less structured society was threatened by rivalry with the Finnish newcomers over natural resources, by growing contact with Finnish social organisation and, not least, the effects of Finland's innumerable wars. The nomadism associated with the Sami people of Norway and Sweden has never been so widely practised among the predominantly Forest Sami of Finland's Lapland and, gradually, an economy based on hunting and fishing evolved into one dominated by reindeer husbandry as the wild herds once vigorously hunted were semi-domesticated. Early on, many Sami adopted the more settled life of the Finns, keeping a few cattle and tilling scraps of soil to grow oats and potato, the only viable crops in these latitudes. In reverse, many Finns have opted for the reindeer economy.

Integral to early Sami culture were the shamanist beliefs rooted in the power of nature which so profoundly affected their lives. Everything it was believed, living or inanimate, had a soul and the spiritual world was as real as the material one. The wise man (*noaide*) was skilled in interpreting one world to the other achieving a state of ecstasy with his magic drum and entering the spirit world.

WORDS AND MUSIC

The religious missions that came to Lapland to convert the Sami not only brought the influence of God, they also brought education. However, the Sami already had a rich oral tradition that ensured a wealth of tales and legends as well as centuries of acquired wisdom were passed from one generation to the next. There was also their simple brand of pictorial art. Also very special to Sami culture – and surviving still – is the *yoik*, a kind of yodelling chant, each a unique improvised tribute to an event, a landscape, an emotion or a person.

Sami culture has always lacked early written sources, and the first books in Sami were exclusively of a religious nature. Later, with education, came grammar books and dictionaries and, finally, though not until well into the 20th century, the beginnings of a Sami literature.

Ironically, education has brought not only advances but also its own threat to Sami culture as youngsters increasingly abandon traditional occupations to enter almost every branch of trade and the professions. On the other hand, Finland's Sami today have their own publication, *Sápmelias*, founded in 1934, as well as theatre, and arts and crafts organisations. In the field of music, the *yoik* has begun to make strange alliances with modern music forms. And in 1991 for the first time a Finnish Sami writer, Nils-Aslak Valkeapää, was awarded the Nordic Council prize for literature.

Not surprisingly, as soon as the Sami began to penetrate these remote regions, religious missions made every effort to discourage such goings-on; yet, despite drum-burning and other deterrents, shamanism survived well into the 19th century. Its eventual submission was largely due to the teachings of Lars Levi Laestadius whose emotion-charged, fire-and-brimstone form of Christian worship must have struck a familiar chord among the Sami. The old gods gave way to the new and today many of the brightest events on the Lapland calendar are associated with church festivals – notably Lady Day and Easter: popular times for Sami weddings, lasso competitions, reindeer races, and get-togethers for scattered families.

Into the 20th century

No century has left a greater impact on Lapland than the 20th century. The rebuilding programme following the devastation of World War II marked the beginning of changes that have altered its face forever. Since 1945, Lapland's population has soared to 203,000 (predominantly Finns), though in an area of nearly 100,000 sq. km (38,600 sq. miles) this is hardly overcrowded: the population density is just 2.2 persons per square kilometre.

The administrative capital of Rovaniemi has been virtually rebuilt and expanded to take in a satellite sprawl of light industry. Communities have burgeoned from hamlets into modern mini-townships. A network of new or improved roads penetrates regions only accessible a few decades ago by foot or ski. Rivers, notably the Kemi, have been tamed for their hydro-electric power. Two large man-made lakes, Lokka and Porttipahta, have been created. And a trickle of visitors has grown into a steady stream, spawning a whole range of facilities.

Organisations dedicated to Sami interests go back to the turn of the 20th century but their efforts were uncoordinated until 1956, when the Nordic Sami Council was founded to "promote cooperation on Sami issues between Finland, Norway and Sweden." It was the first body to provide all Sami with a common platform from which to coordinate their aims and inform the world at large. A few years later a State Commission for Sami Affairs was established by the Finnish government and in 1973 Finland's Sami population acquired a parliamentary assembly, elected by them from among themselves. It has no legislative mandate, but it does provide a forum for promoting Sami concerns. Paramount are their rights to territory and its traditional usage in northern Lapland – age-old rights which have been gradually eroded (though never legally removed).

One may regret the adulteration of a culture under pressure, but people outside Finland are beginning to realise the enriching potential emerging from the Sami's ancient culture. ❏

LEFT: reindeer round-up at Vuotso, Lapland.
RIGHT: Sami man wearing the traditional national dress of the Lapps.

A VERSATILE BEAST

The docile reindeer has always represented much more to the Sami than a meal on four legs, its skin contributing to bedding and winter clothing, antlers and bones raw materials for tools and utensils. It has also provided a major means of transport, sledge-hauling across the winter snows, only recently ousted by the noisy, motorised skidoo. Even now, the annual cycle of the reindeer – rutting, herding, separating, slaughtering, calving, marking – moulds the north Lapland calendar. The winter round-ups are among Europe's most colourful events, resembling scenes from a Wild West film transposed to an Arctic setting.

FROM RALLY DRIVERS TO RUNNERS

A strong physique and a determined nature have combined to make Finns a force to be reckoned with in the world of national and international sports

Later on in his life, when asked about the relationship between Finnish independence and the performance of Finnish athletes in the early part of the 20th century, the great Finnish runner Paavo Nurmi commented: "The higher the standard of living in a country, the weaker the results often are in the events which call for work and effort. I would like to warn this new generation: do not let the comfortable life make you lazy! Do not let the new means of transport kill your instinct for physical exercise! Too many young people get used to loafing and driving in cars even for short distances. I believe that I must thank sports for the fact that I am an independent, self-supporting man."

Despite his warnings, Finns still perform remarkably well in sport and achieve international reputations. There is the football player for Holland's Ajax team, Jari Litmanen, Olympic cross-country skier Mika Myllylä, and Teemu Selänne, one of a number of top-notch hockey players, to name but a few. However, some old-timers hold with Nurmi's views and believe that, because of the complacency of the generations that succeeded him, Finland will never produce another athlete in Nurmi's class.

A sporting tradition

The Finnish sport tradition is unlikely to die out, though, because it is honoured and well established, engrained in every child from the moment he or she is put on skis at the age of two. In the centuries before motorisation, Finns often invented athletic ways to get across their great distances and traverse their vast forests and lakes. The best known was the church boat race, a rowing competition between villagers to see who would arrive at church first.

Sport was associated with religion at other times of the year, too. At Easter, there were competitions in tug-of-war and high and long

jumping, while Christmas was the time for shows of strength by weight-lifters and plough-pullers. Finland has, by virtue of its landscape, always produced a healthy crop of cross-country skiers. Even now, cross-country skiing is as much a form of transport as an enjoyable winter pastime.

Finnish schools today have rigorous sports programmes and, as Finnish officialdom likes to say, sport is the country's biggest youth movement. Whether or not this is strictly true, anyone visiting Finland will nonetheless be both amazed and impressed by the number of sports institutes scattered around even the remotest districts of the country, not to mention the skiers practising on roller skis throughout summer and windsurfers converted to ice surfers in the winter.

In fact, in postmodern Finland, sports has entered a deadly serious state. A recently opened snow tunnel in Vuokatti sports centre, not far from Kajaani, enables skiers to practise

---

LEFT: the great long-distance runner Paavo Nurmi lights the Olympic flame at the 1952 Helsinki Games. **RIGHT:** Eero Mäntyranta, gold-medallist in the 1960s.

in a realistic environment when ordinary people enjoy the few hot summer days.

Formula One racing

Take any group of rally drivers – men and women who drive their cars into a pulp through forest, desert and farm tracks – and among them you are likely to find a puzzlingly high number of Finns. The top Finnish rally stars, Tommi Mäkinen, Ari Vatanen and Hannu Mikkola, and top Formula One drivers, Mika Häkkinen and Mika Salo, may be known only to lovers of motor sports, but more non-Finns could probably name one of these sportsmen than could identify Finland's current prime minister. The British magazine *Motoring News* has called the Finnish rally drivers "devils from the backwoods". Rally enthusiasts, from fans to the competing drivers, have marvelled at the way the Finns seem to give their heart and soul to the sport.

No one has satisfactorily explained why Finns should excel in this particular field, but the answers perhaps apply to all successful Finnish athletes: the fact that Finns come from a quiet northerly country that feels a need to make its mark on the world must have something to do with it. Another reason is, of

FINLAND IN THE OLYMPICS

Outstanding performance in sport is a point of national pride which dates back at least to the Stockholm Olympics of 1912 (the last before World War I), when Finland was still part of Russia. During those games, the Finnish medal winners far outstripped the Russian winners, gaining 23 medals against the Russians' three, although officially Finland and Russia were competing under the same flag.

At the 1912 Games, the Finnish competitors made a point of leaving a 50-metre (150-ft) gap between themselves and the Russians in the Games' opening ceremonies. They also dared to raise a Finnish flag at the medal ceremonies, the first sign that the yearning for

Finnish independence was not to be taken lightly. The gesture was not in vain: the world took notice. Five years later, Finland was an independent republic.

But at the 1996 Olympics in Atlanta, the Finns were disappointed to win only a few medals: one bronze in athletics (Seppo Räty, javelin), and two silver medals, one in swimming (Jani Sievinen) and one in wrestling (Marko Asell). Nevertheless Finland applied for the 2006 Winter Olympics, submitting a well-financed and sponsored bid. Their proposal was to divide the games with Lillehammer (Norway), which hosted the winter games in 1994. However, Torino, Italy, finally won the bid.

course, the landscape: anyone who can orientate himself or herself in the Finnish wilderness already has a strong, built-in sense of navigation (which certainly comes in useful in the more circuitous rally routes) and must therefore have a distinct advantage over someone who comes from a more "civilised", well laid-out country.

Finally, one must look beyond the physical features of the country and examine the Finnish personality. There is one feature of the Finnish character which the Finns themselves call "*sisu*", a quality so central to their being as to make a dictionary definition nearly impossible.

Sprinters

As proof of their durability, Jalmari Kivenheimo was still exercising and running every day even after his 100th birthday. His more famous, but not quite as long-lived running mate, Hannes Kolehmainen, scored gold in the 1912 Olympics.

But the Finnish runner whose name has been famous for most of the 20th century was just under competition age in 1912: Paavo Nurmi (1897–1973). A multiple world record-breaker and medal-winner (with four gold medals), Nurmi first competed in the 1920 Olympics. Variously known as the Flying Finn, the

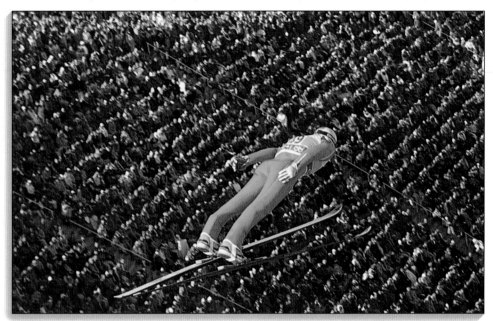

Roughly speaking, the word conjures up an enigmatically tough, independent personality. Hand in hand with the toughness is a determined staying power, even under the most adverse conditions.

Sisu has certainly played its role not only in sporting achievement but in Finland's most important pursuit: independence itself. From the republic's very early days – in fact, even before Finnish independence – sport and freedom were inseparably intertwined.

LEFT: champion racing driver, Mika Häkkinen, perhaps Finland's best-known modern sportsman.
ABOVE: ski-jumper Matti Nykänen in action.

Phantom Finn and the Phenomenal Finn, he is still remembered for his extraordinary running style, speed, and tough character. That champion of the Olympics movement Avery Brundage said of Nurmi: "No one seeing Nurmi's running style can ever forget him. His running rhythm was his endurance secret; it went beyond majestic movement, and the mathematical use of time."

John Virtanen, one of Nurmi's biographers, adds the observation that Nurmi seemed to disregard gravity as he ran. One reason for this was his incredibly long stride, which was measured during a one-mile race at 2.25 meters (7ft 4½ ins).

Nurmi had running in his blood from an early age. Although his father, a religious man, did not approve of running, believing it to be a frivolous pastime, Nurmi exerted his independence and spent every spare moment running with boys in his neighbourhood. He ran in competitions at school, and also alone in the woods. John Virtanen suggests that sports competition between Finnish-speaking Finns and Swedish-speaking Finns was particularly keen in Turku, Nurmi's home town in southwest

SKATING ON WATER

With its network of lakes frozen into ice for much of the winter, all Finnish children grow up as competent on a pair of ice skating blades as on their own feet.

support his family while he was still attending school. But, as he lifted heavy loads and worked under what were no doubt appalling conditions, Nurmi used to tell himself that all physical labour was good for his dream of being a champion runner.

Snow and ice

Not surprisingly, skiing is one of the top sports in Finland, and the sport most readily associated with this snow-covered nation. Along with its Scandinavian neighbours, Finland has produced cham-

and heavily Swedish-speaking Finland *(see page 203)*, which may have further fired his ambition.

If indeed some of Nurmi's determination was spurred by local ethnic competition, it is interesting to note that later, according to Virtanen, "no ambassador could have been more effective than Nurmi" in attracting positive international attention and even investment to the fledgling Finnish republic while it struggled to build a modern political and economic life for itself.

Nurmi's father died when Paavo was in his early teens, and from then on economic circumstances forced the boy to work to

pion cross-country and downhill skiers, who benefit from an extended winter season in which to perfect their sport.

But skiing is not the only winter sport in which the nation excels. Ice hockey is also one of the most important team sports in Finland. Almost all males participate at school, and the élite are filtered through and chosen for the best teams. Many Finns play in the North American NHL and many foreigners play in Finnish teams.

Ice hockey is also commercialised: one of the leading teams, Jokerit (the Jokers, referring to a deck of cards rather than humour) is run like a large company. Teams in Helsinki, Tampere and Turku are usually the best, and spectators can number up to 10,000 per game. Some Finnish teams participate in the newly established European Hockey League. The annual Ice Hockey World Championship Tournament in April and May (being held in St Petersburg in 2000) is one of the main spectator sporting events for Finns. The 1995 World Championship became a nationwide festival and in 1999 players wept openly after the final game was lost to the Czech Republic.

> ### UNUSUAL GAMES
>
> Less conventional Finnish sports include the annual Wife-carrying Championships at Sonkajärvi (Savo) and Rubber boot-throwing, also in Savo.

Track and field

Pesäpallo is a Finnish version of American baseball, first developed by Tahko Pihkala. The game soon became a "national" hobby, especially in rural Finland. The best teams now participate in the national Super Pesis League, which is well organised and has becomeincreasingly commercial.

Finns also consider athletics as one of the most interesting and "Finnish" of all sports. Despite Nurmi's legendary performances, long-distance running now only has one male runner, Samuli Vasala, to keep up Finnish hopes, but javelin-throwing is constantly well represented. Sporting fields are available to schoolchildren and individuals in every town and village. Local governments finance these institutions and usage of equipment is free. Local championships start from elementary school, and reach their peak in the national level at the annual Kaleva Games.

Although summer sports are not generally associated with Finland, the golf scene has boomed in the last decade. For such a large country 94 courses may not seem a great number nationwide, but the wealthy Greater Helsinki area has 12 greens alone serving the capital's golfers. Land is expensive, and practically every golf course is full throughout the summer months. Memberships are available only after several years' waiting period, and cost about 25,000 mk (£2,800/US$4,500) a year. But while the summer golf season is relatively short, the smart Rovaniemi enthusiastics will even play golf on ice in winter.

LEFT: All-weather, practice skiing tunnel.
RIGHT: pursuing their love of golf in Rovaniemi, Lapland, despite the snow.

Sport and scandals

The national news agency STT recently announced that one Finnish skiier had used illegal substances to improve his capabilities. In an ensuing law battle, the athlete was given the largest ever compensation pay-out in Finnish history. Other greedy sportsmen, however, have not been so lucky. In the national pesäpallo league of 1998–9, all teams decided on the game results beforehand. Prior to the games, most players had taken part in a national baseball lottery, and

consequently won hundreds of thousands of markkaa, as the unanticipated results were so unlikely. Practically all the pesäpallo community was caught, the court ruled the players guilty and the players lost their money and some even their right to play.

Yet sport continues to dominate even the top level of Finnish society: Finland's president Martti Ahtisaari plays golf; Prime Minister Paavo Lipponen played water polo in his youth; the Financial Minister rollerskates; former president Mauno Koivisto plays volleyball, and another former president, Urho Kekkonen, is an avid skiier. Who ever said Finns don't take the sports seriously? ❑

FOOD AND DRINK

Traditional Finnish cuisine makes fine use of its native ingredients, such as fish and game, washed down by strong coffee or locally brewed beer

Finland is a land of forests and lakes with abundant possibilities for fine dining. Take the trees – Finns have finally found edible substances in each variety: birch gives Xylitol, a sweetener very kind to teeth; spruce spring shoots are used to make sweet jam, a delicacy served with desserts; pine is a good source of tar, an aromatic substance, not oil but extracted from pine in traditional tar-burning pits. The light tar is a soothing aroma, used in Finnish sweets and ice-cream. Pine is also raw material for the Finnish-invented Benecol margarine-style spread that has been found to have cholesterol-lowering qualities.

Unusual varieties

Finnish food is as innovative as Xylitol or Benecol demonstrate – the years of agricultural conformity are over and the "rural" Keskusta party is kept outside the government. Be it ostrich farms, strawberry wineries or herb producers, Finnish food is becoming more varied by the day – more Finnish restaurants are opening up, and rarities such as bear meat or unusual fungi can be found more regularly on menus. Herbs are pleasant surprises, and often the least likely choices yield the best sensations – try the tiny vendace (*muikku*) with garlic and cream, an unpretentious fish that has more taste than all tropical varieties combined.

It's the taste that Finland is worth visiting for. The changing seasons, endless daylight in summer, deep forests, thousands of lakes, unpolluted environment, all help Finland to produce interesting culinary delights.

This is a country that also produces "non-vegetables" (varieties that are too small to be "accepted" by the European Union directives) but that is often the very point: the "new" potatoes (the first in the season), which are tiny but full of aroma. Small strawberries, blueberries or handpicked fungi from the forests all taste

PRECEDING PAGES: smoked fish is a Baltic delicacy.
LEFT: selling smoked fish at market.
RIGHT: preparing traditional Finnish pies.

better than their fertilised varieties produced in bulk in warmer countries.

Finnish food as we know it today has a short history. Traditionally Finnish food was made up of fat, and was always homemade. Restaurants were non-existent until enough demand justified imitations of exotic meals, say

"Hawaii Cutlet" which consisted of a piece of pork and a slice of tinned pineapple. Hamburgers, kebabs and pizzas satisfy most of the fast food requirements in modern Finland, but tourists should now have no trouble finding genuine Finnish delicacies.

Water-fed diet

Take fish, for example. Finland has lakes, rivers and the sea, brimming with local species, and many Norwegian varieties are imported. Fish has always been an important diet for Finns, and it is part of a long culinary tradition. Smoked fish must be the speciality, although it may also be grilled, glow-fired, steamed, or basted in the oven. Fried fish is, fortunately, rare in Finnish restaurants.

Salmon soup is another subtle delicacy: only a little bit of salt is added to the liquid, but the main taste comes from the fish. Each way of cooking salmon in Finland gives a distinctive experience, but *graavi lohi* (raw salmon marinated for a day in salt and herbs) is delicious served with potatoes. "*Graavi*" is the Finnish version of *sushi* – but instead of rice and seaweed, small potatoes and dill are used.

CRAYFISH SEASON

Rapujuhla (crayfish parties) are by invitation only, although all fine restaurants serve crayfish during July and August. Much of the red delicacy is imported, as each small creature costs about 20mk.

various roes and Baltic herring. In winter, turbot is the seasonal variety. But imported fish is always available, and it's up to the chef whether the food is fresh and well-cooked.

Hunting nation

Much of Finland's tasty elk meat disappears into private deep-freezes during the hunting season, but semi-domesticated reindeer is more common. The Lapland speciality is *poronkäristys* (reindeer casserole), served with mashed potatoes and

While Finnish salmon should not be missed, don't forget to try *siika* as well. This white fish has a more subtle taste, and is also best in the *graavi* variety, with potatoes and dill. *Silakka* (Baltic herring) and *muikku* (vendace) are small fish, very typical in Finnish restaurants, but lamprey is confusingly not fish at all. It is a vertebrate, and is only caught from the rivers of western Finland. Charcoal-grilled and eaten whole, it's another fine experience of Finnish *haute cuisine*.

Fish is very much a seasonal fare. The spring and summer are good for salmon and perch; crayfish dominates in July and August. Autumn is the season for lampreys, white fish, vendace,

cranberry (lingonberry). It's an excellent way to fill oneself up after a week-long trek in Lapland's wilderness but weight-watchers should be wary. Some westerners feel strange about eating meat from an animal that traditionally helps Santa Claus to deliver his gifts, but reindeer herding is an important livelihood for the Samis in Lapland (*see page 109*). The best part of reindeer is fillet steak, usually worth its price.

The best restaurants in Finland will also serve rare game birds during the season. Wild duck is most common. Its hunting season only runs from late summer to autumn, and it is worth trying when available.

Sausage (*makkara*) is also very popular in summer – best grilled with local mustard. Typically Finnish sausage has more flour than meat but quality varies. In Tampere, *mustamakkara* ("black sausage") contains spices, barley and blood in real gut. Blood may also be added to the Aland Island's *svartbröd* ("black bread"), a distinctively sweet brown bread.

Regional dishes

Regional differences are notable around Finland. The Karelian menu is completely different from, say, western fare. Salted fish, pies and pastries are typical in Karelia (avoid the pre-

a baked rye bread – although it is an acquired taste to some. The northwest coast is renowned for salmon soup and *leipäjuusto*, a bread-like cheese, often eaten with yellow cloudberries (a sour berry that grows on marshlands).

Potato is the staple food, available all year round, but one restaurant, Ursulan Viinitupa (Pohjoisesplanadi 21 in Helsinki), recently introduced barley to replace rice and pasta (which are common in Finland too). Barley is softer, bigger and, some believe, tastier than rice, but sadly quite rare in restaurants. Barley, oats, rye and rice are all used for porridges, which are typical breakfast items in Finnish

packed Karelian pies at supermarkets, which bear no resemblance to their originals). Rye dough is filled with barley or potato and then turned inwards to create the distinctive Karelian pie, baked in the oven and eaten with mashed four-minute eggs and some butter. Another laborious meal is Karelian meat stew (beef) which takes 12 hours to prepare.

The Lakeland provides plenty of fish, as one would expect, and *muikkukukko* is a typical Savo delicacy, consisting of vendace fish inside

LEFT: Helsinki harbour is a good place to find fresh fruit, vegetables and fish.
ABOVE: traditional salmon and Finnish beer.

WHERE TO FIND SPECIALITIES

Helsinki is the best place to look for fresh or smoked fish at supermarkets or markets for self-catering tourists, as small towns rarely serve culinary delights even for locals – there simply isn't enough demand. An exception is a smørgåsbord, or *seisova pöytä*, which can be outstandingly good or simply bad. Many theme restaurants, such as Karelian houses along the eastern border, serve an excellent variety of marinated and smoked fish, pickled herring or "*graavi*" salmon, salads and other vegetables. The larger hotels prepare invariably a great breakfast buffet, and there are also innovative Finnish versions of international buffets.

homes. The authentic Finnish recipes in this particular restaurant are bravely advertised as "homemade" which perhaps hides the elaborate preparation of the ingredients and complex cooking techniques. Some recipes take hours, even days to cook. Although traditional edible beets, such as swede or turnip are seldom considered as "gourmet food" in modern Finland, why not try one that has been on low heat for a day – fully softened swede requires no spices!

Finns, in fact, seldom use spices. Many raw ingredients have a naturally strong flavour that may simply be lured out by the right cooking technique, with no need for additions.

One special element in Finnish cuisine is the abundance of ingredients that are available free on the forested landscape, including a wide range of berries, fungi and herbs. No one owns these foods and Finnish law allows free access to the forests. However berry- and mushroom-picking is hard work and time-consuming and there is always a small price tag, unless you do it yourself. Blueberries are readily available in July, the native sour cranberries (lingonberries) by September. Numerous varieties of delicious edible mushrooms enter restaurant menus by the autumn, quantity depending on the heaviness of the rains.

SEASONAL FARE

Christmas food in Finland is very traditional, to the point of being mediocre – what was perhaps special and expensive 100 years ago and saved exclusively for Christmas festivities, is very much simple and inexpensive today, and certainly fattening: ham, salmon, casseroles, dried codfish and plenty of desserts including ginger biscuits and the popular star-shaped plum tart, *joulutorttu*. At Easter, Finns consume *mämmi* (a malt-based pudding), and *sima* (mead) and *tippaleipä* pastries on May Day. Finnish food varies seasonally, geographically and in quality – an endless source of fascination and pleasant surprises.

Bread

Ryebread is unique to Finland – Russians and Swedes produce similar but use different recipes and Finnish ryebread is usually less sweet than its counterparts. All are very different to the German variety. It is healthy bread, available as crispbread (rougher and again less sweet that the Swedish variety), soft and fresh or slightly stickier and harder (*jälki-uunileipä*). The latter variety keeps edible longer and is good with cheese and cold milk.

Finnish ryebread is made of sourdough with water, salt and flour added. The distinctive taste is a result of lactic fermentation during the proving process.

Alcohol

The Finnish *ravintola* may be a restaurant, bar or pub, and most often people go there to drink. Beer is ubiquitous, and one of the "big five" is most usually served: Koff, Lapin Kulta, Karhu, Olvi or Karjala. But there are many more: micro-breweries are popping up with more frequency, often located in historical buildings, across the country.

The same goes for wineries, which for the time being seem unique for Scandinavia;

> ### DESSERTS AND CAKES
>
> Typically, Finns partake of *kahvi* (coffee) and *pulla* (wheat buns) after their meals. Cakes are also abundant; cream cakes topped with strawberries are typical.

Where to eat

Whether it's culinary delights, fast food, coffee or a pint of lager, you will always find it: there is a restaurant or just a simple kiosk on practically every corner. The kiosk is another Finnish institution that sells chocolate and groceries when other shops are closed.

Helsinki is the best place to savour Finnish delicacies. A La Maison (Salomonkatu 19) has more than a few ways to prepare vegetables. Here, Finnish food is art – each plate is so beautifully arranged that

Finland gave up part of the restricting alcohol policy (a system similar to other Nordic countries) and allowed private wineries, which number at least 20 around Finland. Strawberries, blackcurrants and redcurrants, among others, are used to produce a distinctive red wine – not exactly Burgundy but it is a well-balanced berry drink with a 12 per cent strength! In the same way, local producers are now experimenting by adding other berries to stronger alcohol.

LEFT: cranberries are just one of the many berries that abound in Finland's forests.
ABOVE: Savoy Restaurant in Helsinki.

one can barely bring oneself to destroy the effect. Havis Amanda (Unioninkatu 23) specialises in fish and seafood. Kanavaranta (Kanavaranta 3) runs its own cooking school and offers four-course meals with a pre-selected accompanying wine, certainly a reliable choice for gourmet dining, competing perhaps only with Savoy (Eteläesplanadi 14), an expert on seasonal varieties.

Lappi (Annankatu 22) is a truly Lappish experience, with a rich menu of Arctic specialities, including reindeer. The other end is represented by Zetor (Kaivopiha), with a rural 1950s decor and plenty of typically Finnish meals on the menu. ❏

IN DEFENCE OF GREENNESS

Despite the familiar images of Finland's lakes and forests, the country is struggling like the rest of the world to find solutions to environmental problems

Finns have long looked to their country's natural environment for a sense of national identity. The national anthem celebrates the country's summer landscape; its blue and white flag is said to represent the white snow of winter and the blue lakes of summer; literature, fine art, design and architecture have all drawn on the environment for a Finnish idiom.

As the environmental campaigner Martti Arkko put it in 1990: "We depend on nature and the environment for everything. If we allow our forests and lakes to become polluted, our Finnishness will disappear too. The hearts of the Finnish people lie in the lakes and forests. They are our identity, our capital and riches."

The defence of Finland's lakes is high on the political agenda, looked on as a battle to preserve nationhood and to save the country's greatest assets and, as a race, Finns really care. Surveys in the late 1980s indicated that more than half of the population was willing to support civic action to protect the environment. Outstripping education, health and housing, the environment came second only to employment on the list of subjects of major public concern.

Enter the politicians

The environment became a political issue in the 1980s and has continued be into the 1990s. In 1987, the Green League won four parliamentary seats (4 per cent of the votes). In the 1991 general election, this figure rose to 10 seats (nearly 7 per cent of the votes), and in 1995 and again in 1999 they joined the five-party "rainbow coalition" government. In the 1999 EU Parliament election, they won two seats. A "green" Finland was on the agenda.

Public concern for the environment is nothing new in Finland. Like other Nordic countries, civic organisations have been committed to protection for years. The Finnish Nature Conservation Association, which became the

Finnish Environmental Protection Association (FEPA) was founded in 1938, taking as its brief the creation of nature reserves and the preservation of rare plants. Today, the FEPA has around 16 regional and 170 local branches. A sister organisation, *Natur och Miljö* (Nature and the Environment) exists for Swedish-speakers.

Alarming incidents

As long ago as the early days of national independence, the young republic introduced legal protection for the forests and threatened species, and the Forestry Act of 1886, which was intended to curb wasteful uses of the forests, predated the republic by 30 years. Later laws prohibited the devastation of forests and defended threatened forests areas. Yet, when the owners of the private Lake Koijärvi decided to drain it, people who protested were prosecuted for civil disobedience.

The Ministry of the Environment was set up in 1983, and the 1980s was the decade when the government surveyed, theorised, and made

---

PRECEDING PAGES: haystacks under an autumn sun.
LEFT: Pyhähäkki National Park.
RIGHT: Heidi Hautial, Finnish member of the EU.

policies and assessments. Their conclusions appeared in the 1987 National Report on Environmental Protection in Finland, a substantial overview of the state of the environment. It identified many problems and put forward suggestions for controls, concluding: "General environmental protection goals have been comparatively little considered in Finland, especially from a long-term perspective."

Finland's problems are the basic ones shared by industrial nations everywhere: air and water pollution, energy conservation, the despoilation of the natural landscape, endangered species and waste management. Finland has

Doom-laden though this may sound, it is well to remember that, by comparison with the really polluted areas of Europe, Finland is a model of purity. Where the country does suffer, perhaps more acutely than others, is from the atmospheric and water pollution of its near-neighbours. Russia is the principal offender, but Poland and what was the German Democratic Republic have also contributed to the pollution of the Baltic Sea.

Since the 1987 report, the government has acted on some of its suggestions. There has been more talk – conferences and summits on the state of the Baltic, on the Arctic and on

generated more solid municipal waste *per capita* than any other European country, but recycling schemes have increased recently.

The biggest issue concerns emissions and a long-term solution for suitable energy sources. Implementation of the Kyoto Protocol in 1997 is crucial, as Finland's carbon dioxide emissions are one of the largest *per capita* in the EU. Finland is determined to reach the 1990 level by year 2010. The main argument is about the fifth nuclear power plant, that industries want and environmentalists don't. Eurajoki, home of two of Finland's nuclear power stations, has been chosen as the location for nuclear waste, but the decision has faced legal hurdles.

acidification – and Finland has put its clean-air and clean-water industrial technology at the disposal of Russia and Eastern Europe.

Forest threats

Driving through Finland, you might feel there is little cause for concern about its endless green forests and lakes, but the Finns nevertheless brought a Wilderness Act into force in February 1991 to defend the areas which remain in their natural state. The Act designated as "wilderness" 12 areas in Lapland, each roadless and some 150,000 hectares (380,000 acres) in size. Protected zones now account for nearly one-third of Lapland's area. Forestry will be restricted here and limited to "natural forestry" only, where operations are adapted to the natural development of the forest. No extensive felling, no clearing, and natural regeneration are the prime components.

Finnish forestry accounts for 78 per cent of the total land area, some 230,000 sq. km (90,000 sq. miles). It is Finland's largest resource and major export, and forestry and mining provide a large proportion of the country's income. Yet forestry, timber processes, and mining can do the most environmental damage.

Planting, bog-draining for plantations, fertilising, and felling have all had severe conse-

After Finland joined the EU, the ill-fated Natura protection scheme soured relations between private landowners and the Ministry of Environment. Some landowners have been notorious for clear-felling their forests next to a national park, and the Natura programme sparked widespread protests and even more clear felling on private land. The initially popular minister Pekka Haavisto thus lost his seat in the *Eduskunta* (Parliament) in the 1999 election.

Finnish lakes are in a better shape than 20 years ago, but fertilising residues from farmland still pose a threat to the environment.

quences, changing natural habitats and the balance of Finland's water courses, and over-exploiting the soil. Responsible forest management, planned on a national scale, has been the government's solution but, as the state owns only 27 per cent of the forests, it has also had to offer incentives for private owners to subscribe to the national plan. In 1998 a forestry certificate system was initiated. Overall, forestry has undergone extensive reforms to conform to EU and global requirements.

LEFT: the image of summer that every Finn wants to preserve.
ABOVE: building a road from tyres in Toivakka.

HUMAN THREATS

The green sanctuaries that are Finland's forests are also Finland's recreational playgrounds. The right of common access permits free access to all the country's forests and allows such activities as the picking of berries and mushrooms, and fishing in the lakes, which are national summer pastimes. But greater use of the forests for recreation also brings more problems: the dispersion of litter and different forms of pollution, such as the noise and emissions of too many vehicles, not to mention the selfish drivers who thoughtlessly plough their cars at speed through uncharted territory.

While afforestation and exploitation of the forests have spoiled some habitats, the trees are threatened by air pollution or acidification ("acid rain"). Like other countries, Finland has legal limits designed to control industrial emissions. Policing of these emissions and the question of whether the limits are pitched at an acceptable level are the nub of the issue. Environmentalists push for tighter controls; industry argues for economically "realistic" targets.

Making improvements

"Green" policies have for some time been part of everyday Finnish life. Recycling schemes

and attempts to improve house insulation continue, and the government has repeated its commitment to public transport. If you want to cause a heated argument, try a casual mention of a subject such as the construction of a fifth nuclear power station – a proposal which has been resisted powerfully in the wake of the Chernobyl disaster. New worries, such as the damage salt on winter roads may do to the water courses, also rear up regularly. The Baltic Sea is an on-going concern, and global environmental catastrophes continue to preoccupy Finns, as they do people everywhere.

Small-scale Finnish projects, which could solve some of the western world's ecological problems, hit the headlines from time to time. The pioneering idea of building a road out of chopped-up rubber car tyres was intended to have a dual "green" purpose. Firstly, it gave a use for tyres, which are notoriously difficult to dispose of. Secondly, the experiment was an attempt to find a durable road surface able to resist the strains of the fierce winter ice, which calls for frequent road maintenance and endless resurfacing. Other experiments have involved research into biodegradable plastic – especially carrier bags – as a sideline of Finland's oil refineries.

In the world of design, too, specialists have been applying their minds to ecological considerations, with the maximum use of recycled and recyclable materials, the minimum use of energy during the manufacturing process, and the longest possible life for the product.

From a visitor's point of view, Finland may already represent a supremely unspoilt environment. The main selling line of the Finnish Tourist Board has been the country's landscape, supported by photographs of summer in Finland's green forests, its blue waters and its leafy towns. Human habitation appears in its proper context, a tiny sprinkling of buildings in a vast forested terrain.

This is a true picture of Finland, nevertheless. In a country which is the seventh largest in Europe, the 5 million-plus inhabitants are just a blip on the map, highly influential but outnumbered several thousand to one by trees. For this reason, if no other, it is in Finland's interest to protect its natural domain. ❑

RAISING REINDEER

In Lapland, there is a different cycle of difficulties and paradoxes. The cultural traditions and the livelihood of the Sami, or Lapps, both contribute to environmental damage and are threatened by it. Reindeer herds are a fundamental part of the Sami's lives. Chernobyl was a disaster and meant that hundreds had to be killed. Yet, in that same summer of 1985, the Sami reindeer herds exceeded quotas (introduced to prevent over-grazing and the destruction of young trees) by almost 100,000. Another contradictory factor is the predators – wolves, lynx, eagles, wolverine – protected by the government but seen by the Sami as a threat to their reindeer.

LEFT: the true Finnish home is in the forest.
RIGHT: Finland's lakes and forests.

A WILDERNESS EXPERIENCE

It may have been slower to adapt to tourism than its more popular neighbours, but

Finland's natural splendour is attracting an increasing number of visitors

Finland, often forgotten or sometimes ignored, is one of the best-kept secrets in Europe. It's a country with few world-renowned attractions: no fjords, no medieval Orthodox monasteries like its Nordic neighbours. Yet Finland has an indigenous culture with much regional variety, thousands of lakes, rivers and islands, and unlimited possibilities for activities.

Slowly, the world is taking notice. Finland, a member of the European Union and the euro currency area, offers unspoiled wilderness, quaint historical attractions, peace and quiet and free access to practically anywhere – all forests are potentially yours for trekking, berry- and mushroom-picking or short-term camping.

Finland has its share of great European legacy – about 70 medieval stone churches, several imposing castles and plenty of old and new art in museums. Its own traditions are preserved in numerous museums around the country – indeed, there may still be more museums than hotels in Finland!

Statistically, Finland is a very quiet place. In the most recent year for which statistics are available, 657 hotels in the whole of Finland attempted to house tourists – about the same amount as in the city of Prague, and fewer than in many other large cities. Occupancy rates were on average below 50 per cent; not even Greater Helsinki managed to get above 60 per cent. Many hotels are small: there are only 43,000 hotel rooms in the country, or an average of 65 rooms per hotel. In fact, not all tourists choose hotels. There are campsites, lakeside holiday villages, guesthouses, youth hostels, and some even camp privately in the wild. Supply increases when the summer comes, exactly following the demand.

Finns view tourism as an escape, choosing the elements over Mediterranean warmth. Until recently, the industry has not been taken seriously. Domestic tourism has been slow to pick up and, so far, mass tourism has remained elsewhere, but individuals are beginning to arrive in greater numbers.

Local attractions

The Finnish Tourist Board lists the Top Twenty tourist attractions, including five spas, three

amusement parks, two churches, one casino and one festival – only eight are conventional tourist attractions such as museums or theme parks. No wonder, tourists are confused. Therein lies the dilemma of the Finnish tourism industry – no one would travel all the way to Finland just to visit third-rate versions of Disneyland, and much of the existing hoopla is around locally popular entertainment.

World-class attractions in the Top Twenty are few – Kiasma, the Museum of Contemporary Art *(see page 173)*, Bomba House in Nurmes *(see page 275)* or the Ateneum Art Museum in Helsinki *(see page 156)* are worth a visit. Little-known wonders attract few visitors, which is

LEFT: braving the white waters of Finland's vast network of lakes.
RIGHT: light traffic is good news for cyclists.

partly explained by the lack of guidebooks. Indeed, Insight Guides Finland was the first modern guidebook in English when the first edition was published in 1992.

Finns really turned outward towards the end of the 1980s. Prior to this, there weren't even money exchange services available in Helsinki centre at weekends. With a language few can understand, Finns were, and still are, seldom understood. They still have a gauche, slightly perplexed attitude to tourists. Finns don't always smile at you when you'd expect them to, and do when you wouldn't. They remain silent when you want to hear an explanation, or they talk (in Finnish) when you'd rather enjoy the serenity. In many cases, tourists still experience the unconditional warmth when they are treated as guests, not as customers, especially in farms, only to experience the greediest con artist in a rip-off tourist trap the next moment.

If Finns are eccentrics, so are some of the attractions. The wife-carrying championships are an international media event, as was the first Kutemajärvi sex festival, exclusively for old and stout people. There are offbeat art exhibitions, weird festivals (the annual tango festival is the biggest in the country) and mad habits –

SPECIAL INTEREST HOLIDAYS

As Finland lacks mass tourism, most visitors have an individual approach to the country, with specific needs. It may seem that Jyväskylä is packed with architecture buffs pointing wide-angled lenses at buildings designed by Alvar Aalto; architecture fans may choose functionalism, Art Nouveau, modern or Neo-classical "tours". Music lovers may choose among hundreds of small or large festivals, or follow Sibelius' footsteps from Hotel Kämp in Helsinki to Ainola to North Karelia. Visitors interested in design can tour various glass factories and pottery studios. Santa Claus can be visited in Rovaniemi. People who want traditional saunas will discover the very roots of Finnishness.

saunas are too hot, and in winter, you're supposed to jump into a hole in the ice!

Savonlinna, the opera festival held in a medieval castle *(see page 92)* has been a success. In Retretti, a man-made cave became an eerie but hectic summer art exhibition *(see page 257)*. Modern architecture shaped the Forest Museum Lusto to become an interesting exhibition on anything wooden – now the region is one of the top destinations in Nordic countries.

Nature Calls

As Finnish nature is so varied and so accessible, the only limit is imagination. Activity holidays are increasing. Several bird-watching towers have been built near major lakes and bays – the Worldwide Fund for Nature has financed Liminganlahti near Oulu. Individual tourists have about 180,000 lakes to choose from for canoeing, swimming or skiing in winter when ice covers all lakes. Fishing is possible in lakes, rivers, rapids and seashore – a permit is required. Moving from one place to another is possible with skis, dog sleighs or snowmobiles in winter, by bicycle or trekking in summer.

Many tourists seek natural experiences in Finnish national parks. Finland's unique park network is mostly administered by the Forest and Park Service, which controls 29 national

National parks are just the tip of the iceberg. Local municipalities often finance recreational hiking routes for local needs. Many of these can be combined, and thus was born the Karelian Circle Trek, Finland's longest trekking route with approximately 1,000 km (620 miles) of marked trails.

The Karelian Circle Trek offers genuine wilderness routes, variety in four different national parks, and a possibility to combine walking with mountain biking or canoeing. Fishing gear is common, and some even carry a hunting gun. This a friendly wilderness, with no fear of dangerous wild animals, and locals

parks, 14 strict nature reserves and over 350 other protected areas. The organisation rents interesting accommodation in isolated wilderness cottages, often of relatively high quality. It's a network that works from the main information office Tikankontti in Helsinki to excellent park headquarters near the park entrances to assistant wilderness guides who can be reached by a handy mobile phone – and each rentable wilderness hut is now featured on the Internet.

LEFT: the snowmobile is a fast and fun way to get around in winter.
ABOVE: ice-breakers are a popular tourist attraction.

are also friendly. More than 6 million marks (£600,000/US$960,000) have been spent on this route. Sleeping is possible in bed-and-breakfast locations, free wilderness huts (or ones that have to be reserved in advance) or lean-to structures. Pitching a tent is legal (and free) almost everywhere along this route.

Organised tours

Small service companies are now popping up around Finland. One of the biggest is Experiences Unlimited, based in Helsinki, which mostly caters to Finnish customers. Owner Timo Heinaro calls himself an adventurer: "Finland lacks the Alps, but with innovation, we have been able to avoid the mass tourism and concentrate on small individual groups." Heinaro's company has grown rapidly – 20 per cent of his customers are foreigners. "We believe incoming incentive tourism will grow enormously in years to come. Most of all, Finland has genuine experiences available, good infrastructure, reliable facilities: safety and cleanliness are key words."

In Nurmes, the Metsänväki Group recently moved to the new Safari House (tel: 13-480 126) near the famous Bomba tourist centre. The company provides full-range adventure services, including winter outfits for 150

the shallow, lukewarm water, riding horses across dirt tracks, paddling in the lake, then savouring an enormous buffet with fresh farm produce, game, fish and wonderful cakes. The opportunity for individual freedom is an experience in itself – nothing is actually forbidden – as you have the forest tracks and lakes to enjoy all for yourself.

Naturally, the peace and quiet is not to everyone's taste. One wealthy German arrives regularly at a certain small lakeside cottage in the heart of Finland, enjoys the solitude for two weeks and then returns happily to his hectic business life in Germany.

people. Activities may include husky tours, or snowshoe treks to wilderness in winter. Here gateway services are available on the tourist path although real adventure takes place off-road – canoeing, rafting or trekking in summer.

Farm holidays

As the EU membership decreases chances among Finnish farmers to earn from agriculture alone, many families are now turning their estates into guesthouses. Bed-and-breakfast may be the official term, but most farms provide the visitors with a full range of options. It's an experience that will always be unforgettable – bathing in a lakeside sauna, with a dip in

Lakeland leisure

Increased tourism along Finland's lake system is bringing the lake steamers back into business. There are now regular passenger routes on several of the lake systems but the oldest and probably the most romantic are those across Saimaa's vast expanses *(see page 253)*. Steam first came to Saimaa, wheezing and belching its thick black smoke, in the 1830s. It revolutionised the timber business, until then reliant on sailing vessels – and, in turn, their dependence on the vagaries of the wind – enabling easier transport of Finland's "green gold" from forest to factory during the short summer months.

The heyday of passenger steamers was in the early years of the 20th century, when the well-to-do of St Petersburg arrived by the night train at Lappeenranta for a leisurely nine-hour steamer trip to Savonlinna, then a new and fashionable spa. In due course the steamers covered the four points of the Saimaa compass, picking up and dropping off the lakeland's scattered inhabitants, along with livestock and every imaginable form of cargo, at communities of all sizes or no size at all. One of the great sights of Savonlinna each morning and evening was the Saimaa fleet of wooden double-deckers. Several still survive.

unmistakable sleek shape and the long-nosed jet slips elegantly down from the sky.

And it's here that Santa Claus himself may be visited 365 days a year, around an ever-growing tourist village by the name of Napapiiri (Arctic Circle). It's a similar attraction to the Equator – one can officially experience the midnight sun to the north of the Arctic line, which is clearly marked across Napapiiri village. This is the biggest tourist trap in the entire country, but a nice reminder of the meek character of the whole country – a theme village built around a character who couldn't possibly be more sympathetic to his guests. ❏

Christmas visitors

The most recent newcomer to Finland's skies is Concorde, now a regular midsummer and midwinter visitor to the Arctic Circle with its full complement of passengers eager to "meet" Santa Claus on home territory (see page 138). It is still enough of a novelty to attract a large number of Rovaniemi's citizens. As arrival time approaches, a steady stream of traffic heads out to the airport. There is an appreciative murmur as a distant speck materialises into that

LEFT: enjoying a winter break in Espoo.
ABOVE: fishing in the rapids near Viitasaari.
RIGHT: dry slope bob sleighing.

TRAVELLING WITH POSTMEN

Finland is a large country. Distances are long but accessibility is easy with public transport. About 90 per cent of all Finland's public roads carry regular coach services, including the admirable yellow postbuses which reach deep into areas where few visitors penetrate. Though slower than their more commercial rivals, they provide closer contact with the Finnish ethos. The driver is also the ticket-collector, guide, mentor, friend to country ladies struggling back from market, and postman, delivering mail by a flick of the wrist into rows of roadside postboxes, sometimes far from any visible habitation.

LAPLAND: THE HOME OF SANTA CLAUS

Everyone "knows" that Santa Claus comes from Lapland, and today he is fast becoming the biggest tourist attraction in Finland

Since the beginning of the tourist boom in the 1950s that played on the legend of Santa Claus and Lapland, some 600,000 children in a total of 158 countries write to Finland's Santa every year. Sweden's Jultomten is the biggest competitor to the Finnish Santa, but more than 32,000 letters arrive daily in Lapland in the run up to Christmas, most often from the United Kingdom, Poland or Japan, all expressing their Christmas wishes for that year.

Santa Claus and the Arctic Circle bring 400,000 visitors annually, and there may be 30 nationalities represented any day. Santa "speaks" several European languages – including the essential phrases in Chinese and Japanese.

PROTECTING A LEGEND

Sinikka Salokorpi is a Santa Claus expert in Finland and has written the official Santa "thesis" for the Ministry of Trade and Industries. It is literally an official publication and includes photos of authentic Santa Claus garments. Although written with a tongue-in-cheek attitude, the booklet defines more than the dress code. It tells us, among other things, that although there is harmony with foreign Santas, the "real" Santa lives in Finland. "It's a commercial battleground – Santa is big business," says Salokorpi.

◁ **FACE TO FACE**
Young children from around the world delight in their visit to the "real" Santa Claus on specialist trips to Lapland.

▷ **RED-NOSED REINDEER**
Although Santa sometimes "uses" helicopters these days, he still uses several reindeer to get around, including Rudolph and friends.

△ HOME SWEET HOME

Santa officially "lives" in a small hut at the Korva-tunturi, a 483-metre (1,580-ft) hill at the Finnish-Russian border.

▽ SANTA TRAIN

To meet Santa, you must get off the Santa Claus Express train at Rovaniemi and proceed 10 km (6 miles) to Napapiirii.

△ SANTA TRAINEES

In reality, there are many working Santas. The Santa Claus Academy started in 1998, and graduates can be hired via the Santa Claus Office.

▷ CHRISTMAS DREAMS

Even letters addressed to "Santa, North Pole" or "Reindeer Street" still find their way to the Arctic Circle, Finland.

SANTA CLAUS THEME PARKS

The Arctic Circle was never an entity until German soldiers marked the spot during World War II, but still no one took much notice until Eleanor Roosevelt paid a visit in 1950; a simple shack was built for the occasion. Mrs Roosevelt became an unofficial sponsor for the growing Santa Claus village, which now includes shops, a Santa Claus Office and, of course, Santa's post office.

The recently founded Santa Park, in co-operation with British theme park experts, is the biggest Santa-related tourist trap in Finland. Just 2 km (1 mile) from the main Arctic Circle area, the "park" found an inge-nious location inside an artifical cave. You walk 200 metres (220 yards) inside Syväsenvaara hill and find the Magic Sleigh Ride and other attractions. A digitally produced photo with Santa is available in two minutes – a popular souvenir – but other companies want their share: Christmas para-phernalia and Finnish design is also for sale.

PLACES

A detailed guide to the entire country, with principal sites
clearly cross-referenced by number to the maps

Nobody has managed to count with any degree of certainty how many lakes and islands there are in Finland – almost enough, it seems, for every Finnish family to have an island or lake of its own, with plenty of space for visitors too. No wonder an ideal Finnish summer is based on a wooden cabin at the edge of lake or sea and a wooden smoke sauna house nearby. With some fishing, swimming, and a small boat tied up alongside, this is Finnish perfection.

There are seemingly endless expanses of untouched landscape, crossed by endless straight roads running between tall trees. Roads like these eat up the distances, though beware in case the sheer ease of navigating the long avenue stretching ahead encourages a tendency to doze off at the wheel.

As the road heads ever further north, you scarcely realise at first that the rolling farmland of the south has moved into those boundless forests and that, gradually, the dark green gives way to the peat and tundra of Lapland, where the midnight sun gives the landscape a red glow in the late evening. This is the territory of reindeer, and the animals of the wilderness areas – bear, wolf and lynx – though their numbers have declined in recent years. In the northwest the ground rises to more than 1,000 metres (3,000 ft) as it reaches towards the Norwegian mountains. Along the west coast of the Gulf of Bothnia, the beaches and surprisingly warm waters are ripe for exploration.

Even the cities are interspersed with greenery. Parks and trees run between the houses and rocky knolls protrude above street level to make possible a church such as Temppeliaukio Church in Helsinki, scooped literally out of the rock, under a beautiful domed roof.

For a country of five million, Finland has produced an astonishing number of architects, artists, sculptors and designers – and it shows. In Helsinki, in particular, almost every corner reveals an intriguing detail: an elegantly carved façade on a block of flats, a statue, a curved window, or a small figurine full of humour that you nearly miss but laugh when you spot it. In older cities such as Turku or Porvoo, where the Swedish influence was strongest, some of the oldest buildings remain. Nowhere else in Scandinavia has so many cultural festivals or such an assortment of artistic events.

Even the seasons seem more distinct. In winter, it is time for snow and skiing and also for the great reindeer round-ups in Lapland. In summer, sea and lake are full of sails and swimmers. Between the two are a sudden bursting spring when everything turns green in a week, and autumn, full of reds and browns as the leaves swirl over the city squares. Finland is emphatically a land for all seasons. ❑

PRECEDING PAGES: Helsinki's skyline at sunset; sauna near the lakeland town of Jyväskylä; skiing at Saariselka in Lapland.
LEFT: solitary sauna at Ranssin Kievariin, near Tampere.

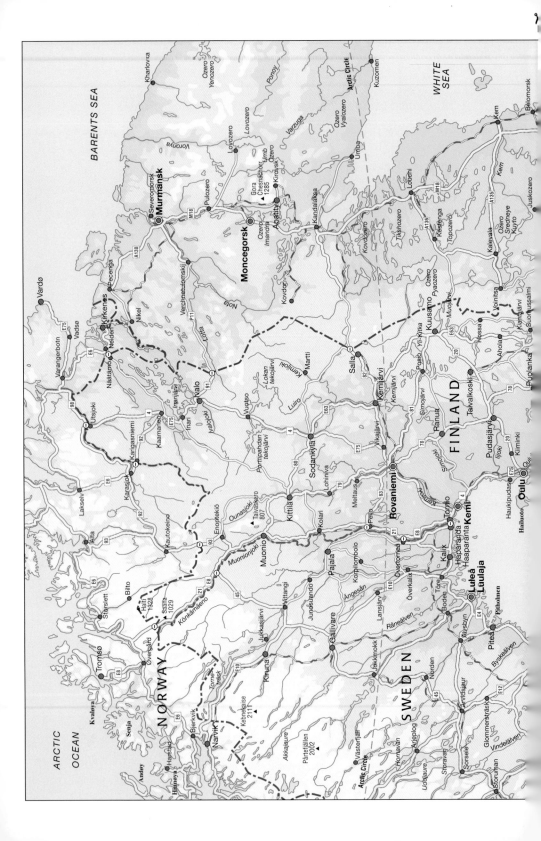

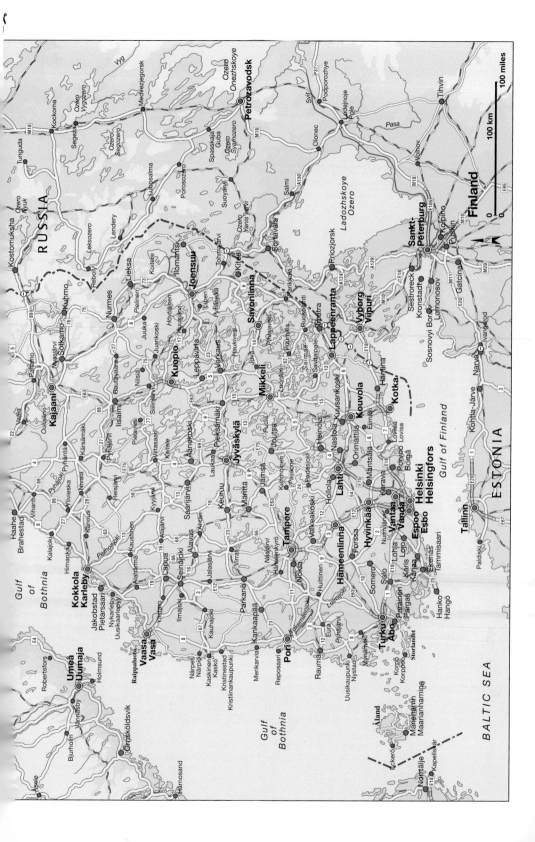

HELSINKI

*With its intriguing cultural mix of Russians and Scandinavians,
the tiny Finnish capital has a charm as fresh as the breeze that
blows over its harbour from the Baltic Sea*

Map on
page 154

Helsinki

Surrounding the city, the sea appears when you least expect it, its salty tongue lapping at the sides of metropolitan bridges and boulevards, pressing its way into residential areas, creating natural harbours and bays.

In summer, the sea glistens and preens under a tireless sun, driving the light-starved locals wild with its rays. Autumn arrives and, as darkness encroaches and the rains begin to fall, it starts to churn, creating a world of wet and grey where the borders between sea and land are no longer distinct. Only during the long cold winter does the sea finally rest, freezing into an endless expanse on which weekend promenaders can walk dogs or try out their cross-country skis.

To understand Helsinki is to accept that kitsch title "Daughter of the Baltic". It is to the Baltic that Helsinki owes its fortunes, its weather and perhaps even the massive, undulating nature of its architecture. It is also to the Baltic that the city owes much of its relatively short but difficult history.

PRECEDING PAGES:
Helsinki harbour.
LEFT: produce on
sale at the harbour.
BELOW: dome of
Helsinki Cathedral.

Helsinki's history

Helsinki was founded in 1550 by King Gustav Vasa of Sweden-Finland to compete with Tallinn in Estonia, whose port was controlled by the Hanseatic League. A first fledgling city was erected on the mouth of the Vantaa River at the innermost point of the Helsinki Bay – a little northeast of where Helsinki stands today. To fill it, Gustav Vasa simply ordered citizens from Porvoo, Ulvila and Rauma to move to the new town.

The new port of "Helsingfors" proved, however, to be not only unpopular but unlucrative as the shallow inner bay became shallower and impossible to navigate. It languished for nearly a century until a visiting governor general named Per Brahe recommended it be moved further towards the open sea. In 1640 a second site was designated on the section of present-day Helsinki called Kruununhaka, and the citizens again moved. On this new site Helsinki finally began to grow, though it still wasn't much more than an outpost for fishermen and farmers. Then the Russian Empire stirred against Sweden, and the town's small fortunes began to go downhill. After battling against the Great Famine in 1697, the Northern War from 1700 to 1721, and the Great Plague in 1710, Helsinki was reduced to ashes and the population to some 150 hardy souls.

Sweden's decision in 1746 to build Suomenlinna Fortress off the shore of Helsinki *(see page 177)*, to protect what remained of its Finnish territory, proved to be the city's saviour. Construction of the fortress drew attention to the port and brought it its first taste of wealth. Merchants constructed a handful of stone houses and, although streets were still unpaved, an interest in European cultural life took root.

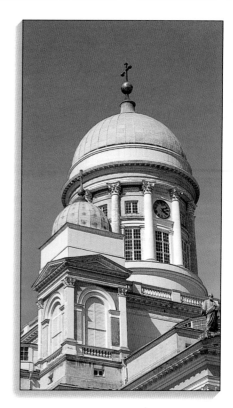

The city was given new life. Russian money and the talents of German architect Carl Ludwig Engel, whose Neo-classical work can also be seen in St Petersburg and Tallinn, were poured into the creation of administrative halls and a cathedral. As the city began to enjoy steady prosperity from around 1850, even workers' homes were mostly replaced with stone. By the year 1900, Helsinki was a new place. Half a century saw it grow from a small port with some 20,000 inhabitants and an equivalent number of cows and cabbage fields into a bonafide capital city. The population soared to 100,000, a railway was built, and gasworks, electricity and water mains all laid down.

At the same time, Helsinki became the seat of the nationalist movement and, with it, of a new self-consciousness. Native architects, such as Eliel Saarinen and then Alvar Aalto, emerged and, after independence in 1917, the more Finnish functionalism replaced Jugend (the German version of Art Nouveau) as Helsinki's predominant architectural style.

Unfortunately, nothing could completely protect the city from the massive Russian air raids of 1944 – nor from fervent, and not always lovely postwar reconstruction. But Helsinki's position on the sea resurfaced to help it regain and then increase its stature, not only as a major port but eventually also as the important site for shipbuilding and international meetings it is today.

Helsinki today

Modern Helsinki is a tranquil but still growing city with some 600,000 occupants – many of whom are only second-generation city dwellers. Gone are the marshes and wooden houses of yesteryear, but the faces of the fishermen who sell their catch from the docks are reminders of the city's recent urbanisation.

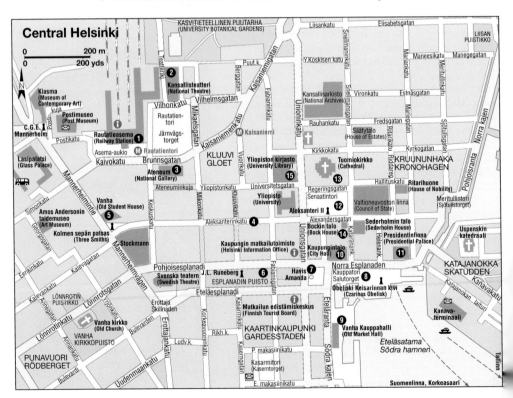

Helsinki isn't an overtly frivolous city but, whenever possible, the Finns have let their innate artistry flavour their capital. Statues stand proud on every other corner, and even the most functional of buildings can present themselves as a notable monuments to Finland's architectural history.

Map on page 154

Consider **Rautatieasema**, the **Railway Station ❶**. A busy place that connects Helsinki with numerous commuter cities as well as the rest of Finland, it also contains both a metro station stop and an underground shopping complex. At the same time, the station is a strikingly stylish, round-edged structure in pinkish granite with green trim, a black roof and a 48-metre (160-ft) green clocktower.

Designed by Eliel Saarinen in 1905 but not completed until 1919, it links two of Helsinki's most prevalent styles: National Romanticism and functionalism *(see page 79)*. It also incorporates work by several other well-known Finns. Thanks to Emil Wikström, pairs of solemn-faced, muscular giants hold translucent lanterns on either side of the station's impressive front doors. A large painting by Eero Järnefelt looks over the Eliel Restaurant inside.

Many road signs are shown in both Finnish and Swedish.

The railway station has today replaced the harbour as the metropolitan focus in Helsinki life. It is also a good reference point for making a city tour and, weather permitting, most places of interest to visitors are within walking distance of here. An extensive network of urban transport also uses the station as its base. The metro stops beneath it, many buses stop beside it and almost all trams stop in front of it.

Exploring the city

The first thing to do before beginning a tour of Helsinki, however, is to find your directional bearings. These are not immediately obvious because much of central Helsinki lies on a peninsula, jutting southward into the Baltic. Being by the sea, therefore, doesn't automatically mean you are in the south of the city. In fact, the peninsula has only a brief southern shore but extended longitudinal coasts on both its eastern and western sides.

BELOW: the guardhouse at the Presidential Palace.

Don't rely on names either, which can be deceiving, particularly if they belong to the time not so long ago when the city was much smaller. The "South" Harbour actually lies on the peninsula's eastern side. It is, however, south of Kruunuhaka – the city centre when it was built. Just keep in mind that the railway station is pretty much right in the middle of the peninsula; the tiny *Keskusta*, or centre, runs east-west below it; and the other sections of central Helsinki radiate out around them.

More confusing, probably, is a visitor's initial glance at the city. Helsinki doesn't follow any of the rules of European capitals. It isn't quaint; it isn't regal; it isn't even terribly old. Little more than a century ago, there were still animals wandering in the streets, and almost everything wooden predating 1808 was burnt to the ground. So don't be surprised to step out of the railway station and find yourself face to face with two monolithic commercial complexes side-by-side; one, modern and bedecked with neon signs, called *Kaivopiha*, and the second, nicknamed *Makkaratalo*, or "Sausage House", because of a long

tubular balcony winding about its façade. Helsinki is a pragmatist – and for good reason. But Helsinki can also be compelling, not in a flirtatious way but in a quintessentially Finnish way: reserved, modest, yet stylish and wry.

The **Kansallisteatteri (National Theatre)** ❷, to the immediate east of the station and at the northern head of the cobbled railway square, is impressive. This little castle in white granite with green trim and a red roof was conceived in national romantic style. Productions are in Finnish but the pensive statue of Aleksis Kivi, Finland's national writer, in front of it, transcends language.

Directly across the square from the theatre is the **Ateneum** ❸ (Kaivokatu 2; tel: 9-173 361; open Tues–Sun; entrance fee). Built in 1887, the Ateneum's gilt yellow-and-white façade might seem reminiscent of St Petersburg but it is the site of Finland's National Gallery of Art, one of the first manifestations of Finland's struggle for independence. The museum's collection of Finnish paintings, sculpture and graphic art covers the years 1750 to 1960 and includes works by such famous Finns as Akseli Gallén-Kallela and Albert Edelfelt.

The Ateneum lies on the east side of Makkaratalo. Wedged in between Kaivopiha and the north-south running **Mannerheimintie** (Helsinki's main thoroughfare and the longest street in Finland) is the handsome though slightly faded Seurahuone Hotel. Inside, the red-velveted, high-ceilinged Café Socis is a perennial favourite with locals and resident foreigners, especially late at night.

Shops and students

Behind these buildings stretch three blocks containing one of Helsinki's most important shopping districts. **Aleksanterinkatu** ❹ (better known as Aleksi), running parallel to the railway station, is the main thread of this area, but

BELOW:
Wikström's massive figures at Helsinki Railway Station.

intersecting streets also contain shops. Kaivopiha's fountain-crowned square has its own special shopping identity; outdoor racks sell postcards and novelties, and at weekends there are often street fairs and art markets.

Steps from this square lead up to Mannerheimintie and **Vanha (the Old Student House)** . Built in 1870, Vanha's own stairs are a favourite meeting-place for young trendies in leather jackets, and its interior now houses a "progressive" performance hall, smoky drinking room, exhibition quarter and library. Student organisations, as well as a cinema and ticket service, have been moved to the New Student House, on the other side of the Kaivopiha steps.

Vanha lies on the intersection of Aleksi and Mannerheimintie, and a trio of naked men with fine pectorals – the Three Smiths' Statue – dominate the triangular square beneath it. As soon as the snow melts in spring, musicians use this square to serenade the passing crowds, ice cream stands open for business and even some café tables appear.

Finland's largest department store, **Stockmann**, lies on the other side of Three Smiths' Square from Vanha. Beside it, on Keskuskatu, is Scandinavia's largest bookshop, Akateeminen Kirjakauppa *(see page 313)*. This is a great place to browse in, though an expensive one given the high price of hardback books in Finland. Upstairs is a stylish café designed by Alvar Aalto.

Place to meet

The bookshop faces another Helsinki landmark, **Esplanadin puisto (Esplanade Park)** . Planned by Ehrenström (also responsible for the 19th-century city plan), it was first laid out in 1831 and runs east-west between Mannerheimintie and South Harbour.

Traditional Finnish dolls are popular souvenirs.

BELOW: Helsinki's bustling harbour.

The **Svenska teatern (Swedish Theatre)**, an elegant semi-circular stone building dating from 1866, commands Esplanade Park's western head on Mannerheimintie. Back to back with it and facing into the long and narrow park is a family-type restaurant called Happy Days. Its terrace is always filled with boisterous beer drinkers in warm weather.

An old-fashioned promenade leads from here across the length of the park; between well-sculpted patches of lawn, past the central statue of J. L. Runeberg, Finland's national poet, to the Kappeli Restaurant at its eastern end. This park is still a very popular meeting place and is often the scene of animated fairs, such as the Christmas Fair in December or Night of the Arts in August. On May Day Eve it is given over to general lunacy. Kappeli is also an important spot for a rendezvous, though in recent years it has lost its sheen. A very different sort of place from Happy Days, tall lacy windows and a whimsical roof give it a Chekhovian, gazebo-like feel – the older parts of the café date from 1867. Like all self-respecting restaurants in Helsinki, Kappeli has a summer terrace. This mars its beauty but allows patrons to simultaneously enjoy fresh air, drinks and a range of musical performances (Jun–Sept) from the bandstand opposite.

Flanking the bandstand are two pretty little "ponds" graced by statues of cavorting fish boys and water nymphs. But they cannot compete with the **Havis Amanda fountain** ❼ on the small square that separates the eastern end of the park from the South Harbour amid a constant swirl of traffic and trams. The sensuous bronze Amanda created quite a stir when she was first erected in 1908. Surrounded by four sea lions spouting water, she represents the city of Helsinki rising from the sea, innocent and naked. On May Day Eve, at least, she gets something to wear – a white student cap – while a champagne-happy chaos of

BELOW: enjoying the sunshine in Esplanadi.

clustering human cap-wearers cheer. This square is also the site of an outdoor produce, handicrafts and flower market.

Two boulevards stretch east-west alongside either side of the park. Nowadays, the fine 19th-century stone buildings along Pohjoisesplanadi mostly house design shops like Marimekko and Aarikka, the latter featuring, among other things, Aarikka's distinctive wooden jewellery. Number 19 is an exception. The **Helsinki Information Office** and the **City Tourist Board** occupy its first floor. Both offer extensive selections of maps and brochures.

More venerable houses line the Southern Esplanadi, most of which function in some type of official or commercial capacity. The oldest is Engel's Empire-style former Council of State, dating from 1824. During the period of Russian rule, it was the palace of the governor general.

Map on page 154

Going to market

The **Kauppatori (Central Market Square)** ❽, across from Havis Amanda on the South Harbour, exudes a much earthier type of appeal. A busy market makes its home here year round, from 7am to 2pm Mondays through Saturdays and, again, from 3.30pm to 8pm during summer weekday evenings. Going to market is still an important part of daily routine in Helsinki, partly because agrarian life is a comparatively recent experience for many residents. Shoppers, baskets tossed over their arms, wander from stand to stand looking for the perfect new potato or bunch of dill.

Peninsular Helsinki has no less than four open-air markets. Of these, the Central Market is both the one most aimed at visitors and the most expensive, but locals on lunch-breaks from nearby shops and offices and housewives from

BELOW:
Kappeli Restaurant, a popular haunt in summer.

ART NOUVEAU

At first sight they are just buildings, but the elements are unique: interesting windows, heavy ornamentation, grey granite, natural colours and castle-like features. Some of the most famous tourist attractions in Helsinki are Art Nouveau – the National Museum, or the Hvitträsk House in Kirkkonummi. But Art Nouveau, or Jugend as it is called in Finland, is far more common in Helsinki than first seems to be the case.

Art Nouveau is also called National Romanticism. Its roots go back to the great epic *Kalevala*, which inspired the composer Sibelius and the artist Gallén-Kallela. Architects Gesellius, Saarinen and Lindgren soon followed suit, going back to the roots of Karelianism, forests, bedrock – the key elements of Finnishness.

One of the best areas to look for their designs is Katajanokka. Eira is another area – see Lars Sonck's hospital at Laivurinkatu 27. Lord Hotel (Lönnrotinkatu 29) by Lindahl and Thomé is typically Art Nouveau with a granite façade, as is their Otava House (Uudenmaankatu 10), Pohjola House at Aleksanterinkatu 44 (by Gesellius *et al.*) or the Tarjanne's National Theatre. Even Saarinen's railway station has hints of Art Nouveau. Arrive before your train leaves and take a look.

Home-grown vegetables are a popular buy at the Central Market.

the affluent southern suburbs still favour it. A multitude of ruddy-faced merchants gather to serve them and, after the ice melts, boat owners also get involved, tying their vessels to the end of the harbour and selling fish and root and other vegetables straight from their prows.

The north part of the market square is reserved for Finland's delicious fresh produce. Offerings very much follow the seasons and, in summer, become irresistible: sweet baby peas and mounds of deeply flavoured berries. No wonder that, by July, every Helsinki dweller can be seen clutching a small paper bag filled with something juicy and colourful. The coffee tent attracts locals and tourists; even President Ahtisaari has been known to stroll here from the palace for his daily constitution. Try one of the sweet rolls or warm meat pastries.

Further down, around the bellicose **Obeliski Keisarinnan kivi** – whose imperial, doubled-headed golden eagle was ripped off during the Russian Revolution and not restored until 1972 – the market turns away from food. Some of these stands proffer interesting goods and handicrafts, but if you are looking for authenticity you should know that most Finns stopped wearing fur hats quite a while ago. Women wearing high heels might also want to bear in mind that the spaces between the cobblestones are particularly treacherous here.

The water in this part of South Harbour is overrun by gulls and geese and not that clean, but don't let that stop you from sitting with the locals on its storied docks in the sun, and enjoying a punnet of Finland's fabulous strawberries.

However, if it is cold or raining, you might prefer to duck into the yellow-and-red brick **Vanha Kauppahalli (Old Market Hall)** ❾. Having traded for more than 100 years, the Old Market Hall is not only Helsinki's most centrally located *kauppahalli* but its oldest. It knows its advantage. The interior is polished to the gills, and the price of even simple *piirakka* can be high. As well as reindeer cold-cuts and rounds of Oltermanni cheese, you can buy ready-made snacks from an excellent Russian-style kebab stand or at the small market café.

BELOW:
a typical Helsinki shopping complex.

Civic triumphs

The Central Market sprawls like a spectre of the masses before some of Helsinki's most important administrative buildings. An austere row lies directly across at the end of Pohjoisesplanadi: the long blue City Hall, designed by Engel in 1833, with a Finnish flag flying above it; the sensible brown Swedish Embassy, importantly placed, and with a Swedish flag; the Supreme Court, dating from 1883; and the Presidential Palace.

The **Kaupungintalo (City Hall)** ❿ started out with a different purpose. Until 1833 it was home to the Seurahuone Hotel (now across from the railway station). Its first opening was celebrated by a masquerade ball, so that women could attend – although they had to leave by 4.30am.

The **Presidentinlinna (Presidential Palace)** ⓫ was designed in 1818 as a private home and turned into a tsarist palace by Engel in 1843. The Finnish president no longer lives here, but the new official residence Mäntyniemi, not far from Seurasaari, is occasionally open for visitors.

Helsinki's third major landmark, **Senaatintori (Senate Square)** ⓬, stands one block north of here, back along Aleksi. There seems to be something fateful about Senate Square. As early as the 17th century, the same spot housed a town hall, church and central square. It was flattened by the next century's continual battles, but the merchants made rich by Suomenlinna soon rebuilt it, erecting the city's first stone buildings about its southern perimeter. The 1808 fire destroyed everything wooden, but Russia straightaway commissioned architect C. L. Engel to rebuild the square as the municipal centre of their new city plan for Helsinki. Eventually, so many important institutions made their home here that Senate Square became a sort of national centre.

The square is still a very impressive spot. Encompassing some 7,000 sq. metres (8,300 sq. yards), it is covered by no less than 400,000 grey-and-red cobblestones of Finnish granite. Nowadays, the Senate Square functions principally as a byway. The main building of Helsinki University, which occupies the square's entire western border, has a new entrance at the back that lures student activity away. The current Council of State, directly opposite, receives few visits from the average citizen. The former Town Hall, on the south side, is used for entertaining official guests, and the flux of boutiques around it cater mostly for visitors.

But the city remembers. Senaatintori becomes the centre of activity on important occasions such as Independence Day in December, when the windswept square is a sea of candles held by students who march here from Hietaniemi Cemetery in the mid-winter dark. Locals gather again one month later to listen to the mayor's traditional New Year's Eve speech and watch fireworks, and again for May Day. The University often uses it for commemorative events.

Map on page 154

BELOW: gypsies selling traditional lace at the harbour market.

Statue of Tsar Alexander, standing proud on Senaatintori (Senate Square).

An extremely self-important statue of Tsar Alexander II, erected in 1894, stands in the centre of all this. At his feet, four additional figures tell the square's story: *Lex*, or law (facing the government palace); *Lux*, or light (facing the sun); *Labour* (facing the university); and *Pax*, or peace (facing the cathedral).

The **Tuomiokirkko (Helsinki Cathedral)** , up a bank of treacherously steep steps on the northside, is a point of pride for Finns, and the exterior – with its five green cupolas, numerous white Corinthian columns and sprinkling of important figurines posing on its roof – is certainly impressive. The interior, however, is startlingly severe. Apart from the gilded altarpiece and organ, only statues of Luther, Agricola and Melanchthon disturb its white symmetry.

Engel's triumph

A walk around Senate Square can also reveal a lot about Helsinki's history. The city's oldest stone building, dating from 1757, is the small blue-grey Sederholm House on the corner of Aleksi and Katariinankatu. Across the street is the **Bockin talo (Bock House)** ⓮, also 18th-century, which became the meeting place for Helsinki's City Council in 1818, as a plaque by its door proclaims. It also served briefly as the governor general's residence after Engel had it embellished with Ionic pillars and a third floor.

The rest of the square is pure Engel, making it not only a beautiful but an unusually consistent example of Neo-classical design. In 1832, the oldest part of the main building of Helsinki University (it was extended later to cover the entire block) was completed under the architect, on the western side of the square. Ten years earlier, he had designed the Council of State, along the entire eastern side of the square. The Finnish Government still has its seat here. Engel

BELOW: trams still ply the city's streets.

drew the plan for the cathedral as well, although he died 12 years before its completion in 1852.

Across Unioninkatu, the **Yliopiston kirjasto (University Library)** ⓯ is decidely ornate. Not only do white Corinthian columns line every inch of its yellow façade, but inside the splendour continues. In the central room, more columns (now marble with gold tips) support a dark-wood second tier, beneath a painted cupola ceiling. Yet this is still a working library, and visitors are expected to leave their coats at the door, sign in and, above all, respect the quiet. Nor are all the rooms open to visitors – look out for some prohibition signs. But don't let this discourage you from enjoying the public parts of this most beautiful of Engel's works, dating from 1844.

Outside the centre

After exploring Helsinki's *Keskusta* (centre), venture into one of the surrounding districts, each of which has its own very particular character, though borders are not always clearly defined.

One of the most attractive is **Katajanokka**, which lies on a small promontory sticking out into the sea a few blocks east from Senate Square. Katajanokka is connected to the centre by two short bridges where locals like to cast their fishing rods. A restaurant complex opened a few years ago, injecting new life into this area. After a snowstorm or on a brilliant spring day, its elegant streets are the picture of serenity. Unfortunately, the first thing you see crossing the Kanavakatu Bridge on to Katajanokka is one of Alvar Aalto's least successful efforts: the dirty white marble Enso Gutzeit Office Building (the "sugarcube"), dated 1962. Fortunately, Katajanokka has better sights to offer.

Maps
Centre 154
Districts
166–7

BELOW: façade of the University of Helsinki Library.

The **Uspenskin katedraali (Uspensky Cathedral)** , across the street at the top of a sudden grassy knoll, gives supreme proof of this. Russian Orthodox, built in 1868, dedicated to the Virgin Mary and undeniably glamorous, Uspensky makes a striking exception to Helsinki's general architectural style. Its red-brick conglomeration of cross-tipped spires and onion-shaped domes has undoubtedly helped convince many filmmakers to use Helsinki as a surrogate Moscow (for example, in *Reds* and *Gorky Park*). Uspensky's interior is also both impressive and atmospheric, with a glittering iconostasis. The cathedral opens daily (except Mondays in winter) but on Sundays for short periods only. Services in Church Slavic are held at least twice weekly.

Appropriately enough, a Russian restaurant called the Bellevue sits at the base of the cathedral, across from Katajanokka Park. The Bellevue, however, has a slightly unorthodox political history. The restaurant was founded the year Finland declared independence from Russia (1917). It also has on one of its golden walls a thank-you note received in 1990 from America's former First Lady, Barbara Bush.

The Russian motif is echoed elsewhere on Katajanokka, and flirtatious basilic motifs appear over many doorways. Red brick also gets more use, particularly in the recently built residences on the tip of the promontory. But central Luotsikatu is one street where Jugendian (Art Nouveau) style rules. Many of the buildings on this and nearby streets were designed by the architectural team of Gesellius, Lindgren and Saarinen at the turn of the 20th century and abound with little pleasures. Don't miss the charming griffin doorway at No. 5.

Turning north from Luotsikatu on to Vyökatu takes you to the northern waterfront. A narrow flight of stone steps leads down to an ageing gateway, which

BELOW: the ornate interior of Uspensky Cathedral.

until 1968 blocked the way to the **Merikasarmi (Naval Barracks)**. These long, yellow buildings have since been restored and now house the Finnish Foreign Ministry. Some have been reconstructed but follow Engel's original design. The public is welcome to stroll along the avenues that run between them.

The southern side of Katajanokka sees more public activity. This is where the huge Viking Line ships come in from Stockholm three times a day, disembarking crowds of passengers. Conversions have already been completed on the block of old warehouses at Pikku Satamakatu, beside the Viking Line Terminal and the so-called Wanha Satama now entertains a clutch of eating spots (including the cheerful Café Sucre), exhibition halls and stores. Two more warehouses nearby have also been earmarked for renovation but the Customs and Bonded Warehouse, however, should not change. Even if you don't have any business to attend to here, it's worth passing by to view its inventive Jugendian style, as designed by Gustaf Nyström in 1900.

The old city

Following Kanavakatu back west will return you to Helsinki's oldest district, **Kruununhaka** ⑰, whose name means "the Crown's Paddock" and not so many centuries ago was primarily a home for cows. Senate Square is at the lower end of this area, which is now favoured by the well-heeled and boasts a large collection of antique furniture, book and clothing shops and art galleries.

The tubular Sibelius Monument by Eila Hiltunen honours Finland's finest composer.

Central Helsinki's second oldest building lies in the southeastern corner of this district, at the juncture of Aleksanterinkatu and Meritullintori. The modest squat structure was erected in 1765 as a Customs Warehouse, but now houses everyday offices. Other venerable left-overs of an earlier age hover nearby, such as the deep red Lord Mayor's Residence at No. 12 Aleksanterinkatu (next to Helsinki's Theatre Museum) with its gorgeous blown-glass windowpanes, and the mid-19th-century, neo-Gothic Ritarihuone ("House of Nobility") situated one block north on Hallituskatu.

BELOW: striking architecture of the Katajanokka area.

A few particularly nice pedestrian streets crown the crest of hilly Kruununhaka. Solid stone buildings in yellow, brown, rust and grey cut into exposed rock cliffs, insulating the end of the district from the Siltavuori Strait flowing directly below.

They also shelter the city's oldest extant wooden buildings at Kristianinkatu 12, the **Ruiskumestarin talo (Burgher's House)** ⑱ (tel: 9-135 1065; open Wed–Sun; entrance fee). The Burgher's House was built in 1818, shortly after the Great Fire, by a wealthy merchant who unfortunately wasn't quite wealthy enough to use stone as a building material. A high wooden fence encloses it with a second mustard-coloured house and a weatherbeaten red shed, all cuddled round a small earth-floored courtyard filled with the pungent scent of wood smoke. In structure, the main house remains exactly as it was when first built, and its beautiful wooden floors are completely original. The furniture, however, has been assembled from different periods starting from 1860. To complete the period atmosphere, guides dress in old-fashioned garb.

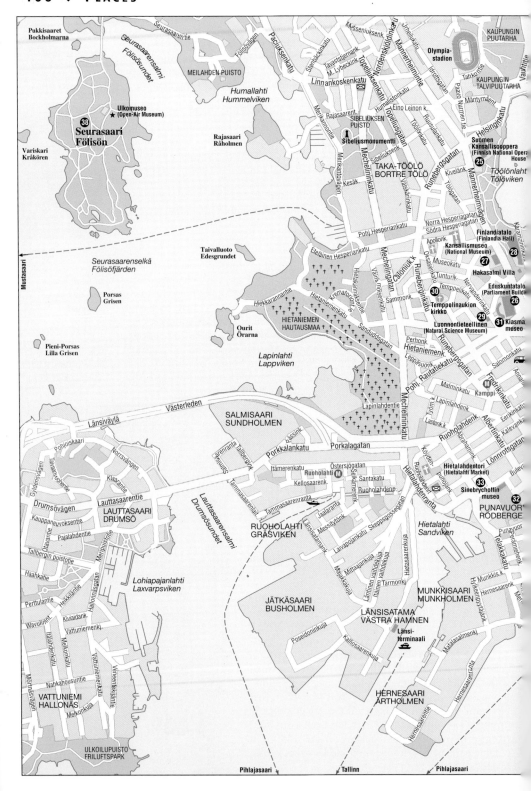

Pukkisaaret
Bockholmarna

Seurasaarensalmi
Fölisösundet

Seurasaarentie

MEILAHDEN PUISTO

Humallahti
Hummelviken

Ulkomuseo
★ (Open-Air Museum)

38

Seurasaari
Fölisön

Variskari
Kråkören

Rajasaari
Råholmen

Mustasaari

Seurasaarenselkä
Fölisöfjärden

Taivalluoto
Edesgrundet

Porsas
Grisen

Pieni-Porsas
Lilla Grisen

Ourit
Örarna

Hiekkarannantie

Hietaniementie

Kremarorrnie

HIETANIEMEN
HAUTAUSMAA

Lapinlahti
Lappviken

Länsiväylä

Västerleden

SALMISAARI
SUNDHOLMEN

Pohjoiskaari

Norrsvängen

Gyldensvägen

Javaranvoorrentie

Klaarantie

Drumsövägen

LAUTTASAARI
DRUMSÖ

Lauttasaarentie

Kauppaneuvoksentie

Pajalahdentie

Olavantie

Tallbergin puistotie

Haahkatie

Perttulantie

Wavulinint.

Heikkiläntie

Kiviaidank.

Hallonnäsgatan

Meripuistotie

Merikannontie

Lauttasaarensalmi
Drumsösundet

Lauttasaarentie

Lohiapajanlahti
Laxvarpsviken

VATTUNIEMI
HALLONÄS

Mörnäsvägen

Vattuniemenkatu

Nahkahousuntie

Melkonkuja

Iälahdenkatu

Melonkatu

Vattuniemenkj.

Veneentekijäntie

ULKOILUPUISTO
FRILUFTSPARK

Masseniuksenk.

Tavaststjernank.

M. Lybeckink.

Stenbäckinkatu

Paciuksenkatu

Fölisövägen

Nordenskiöldink.

Topeliuksenkatu

Mannerheimintie

Jäkärlänk.

Olympia-
stadion

KAUPUNGIN
PUUTARHA

Tahontie

Paavo Nurmen tie

Mäntymäki

Vauhtitie

KAUPUNGIN
TALVIPUUTARHA

Linnankoskenkatu ✉

Rajasaarent.

Eino Leinon k.

Tuulistonkatu

SIBELIUKSEN
PUISTO

Sibeliusmonumentti

Merikannontie

Meilahdentie

Ruusulankatu

Töölönkatu

Helsinginkatu

Suomen
Kansallisooppera
(Finnish National Opera
House)

25

Kesäk.

TAKA-TÖÖLÖ
BORTRE TÖLÖ

Mechelininkatu

Vaskiniitynkatu

Sibeliuksenk.

Runebergsgatan

Kivelänk.

Töölöntie

Mannerheimvägen

Töölönlahti
Tölöviken

Pohj. Hesperiankatu

Norra Hesperiagatan
Södra Hesperiagatan

Finlandiatalo
(Finlandia Hall)

Apollonk.

28

Eteläinen Hesperiankatu

Mechelingatan

Museokatu

Kansallismuseo
(National Museum)

27

Hakasalmi Villa

Caloniuk.k.

Runeberginkatu

Tunturik.

Temppelik.

Naryändenkatu

Museokatu

Eduskuntatalo
(Parliament Build)

26

Hietaniemenkatu

Sandudsgatan

Sammonk.

Varre.mösenkatu

Hiekkamäkentie

30

Temppeliaukion
kirkko

29

Luonnontieteellinen
(Natural Science Museum)

31 Kiasma
museo

Perhonk.

Hietaniemenk.

Runebergsgatan

Leppäsuonk.

Rautatiekatu

Salomonk.

Pohj.

Malminkatu

32

Kamppi

Fredrikinkatu

Annank.

Lapinlahdentie

Lapinlahdenk.

Lastenk.

Työnk.

Mechelininkatu

Albertinkatu

Eerikinkatu

Kalevank.

Abrahaminkatu

Ruoholahdenk.

Lönnrotsgatan

Bulev.

Porkkalankatu

Porkalagatan

Pässink.

Itämerenkatu

Jänerenranta

Tammasaarenlaituri

Tallbergink.

Itämerenkatu

Östersjögatan

Selkämerenk.

Ruoholahti Ⓜ

Santakatu

Kellosaarenk.

Ruoholahdenp.

Köidenp.

Hietalahdentori
(Hietalahti Market)

33 Sinebrychoffin
museo

PUNAVUOR.
RÖDBERGE

Sammarrantie

Tammasaarenlaituri

Tammasaarenranta

Jaalaranta

Messitytönk.

Länsimerenk.

Kalevankatu

Laivapojankatu

Skeppargossegstan

Hietalahdenranta

Hietalahdenranta

Pursimiehenkatu

Hietalahti
Sandviken

Punavuor.
Tehtaankatu

RUOHOLAHTI
GRÅSVIKEN

Laivapojankatu

Maakkakuja

Mittaajankuja

Länten valihdakuja

Itäinen vahdakuja

Itäinen Tarmonk.

Telakkakatu

JÄTKÄSAARI
BUSHOLMEN

LÄNSISATAMA
VÄSTRA HAMNEN

Poseidoninkuja

Kalliosaarenkuja

Länsi-
terminaali

Hy Munkkis.k.

Hernesaarenk.

MUNKKISAARI
MUNKHOLMEN

Matalasalmenkj.

HERNESAARI
ÄRTHOLMEN

Pihlajasaari

Tallinn

Pihlajasaari

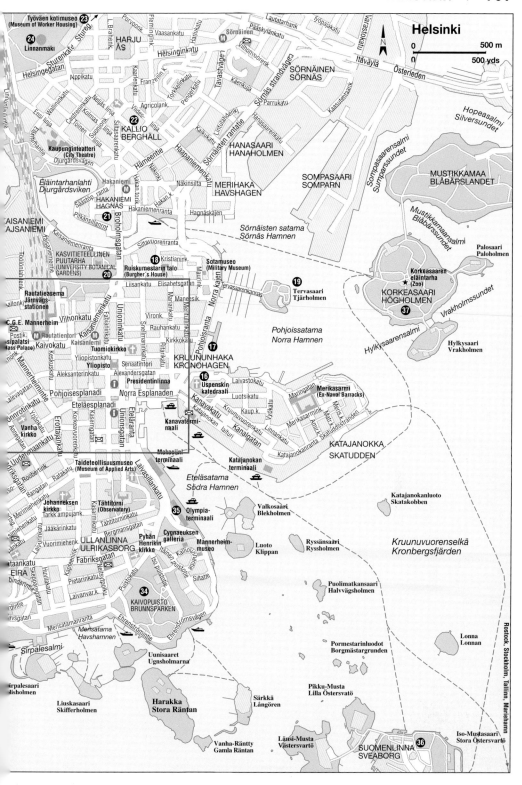

Helsinki

0 — 500 m
0 — 500 yds

Into Greater Helsinki

If it's a warm day, you may want to head east down to **Tervasaari** ⑲. This little island, now connected to Kruununhaka by a man-made isthmus, used to be the city's storage place for tar – an important early export (Tervasaari means "tar island"). Modern times have turned it into a nice park for summer sunning, with a dog run and laid-back terraced restaurant.

Although Finland has not won, strictly speaking, any of the wars it has fought, the **Sotamuseo** (**Military Museum**), on Maurinkatu 1, is worth seeing, especially as wars have been so tragic for the nation that eventually managed to defend its independence against Soviet aggression (tel: 9-1812 6381; open Sun–Fri; entrance fee).

Walking west now brings you down to Kaisaniemenkatu, the street that begins in front of the railway station and frames the west of Kruununhaka. An attractive park squeezes between it, the station and Kaisaniemi Bay.

Kaisaniemen puisto is a sort of multi-purpose park, with sloping stretches of grass, a variety of playing fields that turn into ice-hockey rinks in winter, an open-air restaurant and the **Kasvitieteellinen puutarha** ⑳ (**University Botanical Gardens**, Unioninkatu 44; tel: 9-191 8653; gardens open daily, 7am–8pm, greenhouses open Tues–Sun, 11am–5pm; entrance fee). Designed by a landscape gardener from St Petersburg in the 1830s, these gardens offer a very peaceful place for a stroll right in the middle of the town.

Blue-collar heritage

A long bridge separates the Kruununhaka area and the park from the tiny district of **Hakaniemi** ㉑ and larger Kallio, which were traditionally Helsinki's

BELOW: the Burgher's House, one of the city's oldest buildings.

"worker" communities. Indeed, Lenin briefly lived beside spacious Hakaniemen tori (Hakaniemi Square) before the Russian Revolution. Today, ironically, unemployed drunks largely lord over the area. From 7am until 2pm, Monday through Saturday, however, a no-nonsense market takes over the square and the Hakaniemi Market Hall on its edge. Both are noticeably more natural than those at the Central Market, and the hall has an upstairs devoted to dry goods including stands run by the ubiquitous Marimekko and Aarikka companies.

Kallio ㉒ was first built up in haphazard fashion during the early 19th century. It was eventually given a city plan and rebuilt after the fashion of St Petersburg, but you still need to know where to wander to find attractive areas. One of its prettiest blocks, Torkkelinkatu, rises above the whimsical Kallio Library on Viides Linja. The nearby Kallio Church is an important Art Nouveau structure in grey granite from 1912. Its bells ring a tune by Sibelius.

The northern border of Kallio hides the **Työväen kotimuseo (Museum of Worker Housing)** ㉓ (Kirstinkuja 4; tel: 9-146 1039; open May–Sept: Wed–Sun; entrance fee). This museum comprises four wooden tenements built by the city for its workers and used from 1909 until as recently as 1987. Household scenes have been recreated with great effect within eight apartments, using intimate knowledge of the former inhabitants. In flat C-6, for example, where an abandoned wife and her trouble-making illegitimate son lived, a bottle of alcohol stands in a traditional spot beneath the man's seat at the table. All the apartments displayed are single rooms that housed entire families. This meant that, by day, the beds had to be tucked away in some fashion, but, in flat 9-E in 1925, those of a poor widow and five of her six children are left unmade. Only the eldest daughter had already gone to work, folding her bed against the wall

 Map on pages 166–7

Helsinki has adopted the European love of pavement cafés.

BELOW: a 1920s room in the Museum of Worker Housing.

and leaving steel hair curlers on the table. This family's story is particularly poignant; after the woman's husband died (it is said by suicide), she saved and saved until she was able to buy a cross for his grave and, with no money left to hire a car, carried it on her back all the way to Malmi Cemetery.

Helsinki's amusement park, **Linnanmäki** ㉔, perches on a wooded hill a short walk north from here (access from Helsinginkatu or Tivolitie; tel: 9-773 991; open May–Aug: daily, noon–10pm; entrance fee). This isn't the raciest funfair in the world, but it is supposedly the most visited attraction in Finland.

Töölö Bay

Kallio lies north of the railway station along the east side of Töölö Bay. Several other of Helsinki's 50-odd museums lie on the bay's western side, in a neighbourhood called **Töölö**. Like Kallio, Töölö came into its own after the turn of the 20th century. Though it is not especially chic today, many of its streets offer priceless examples of Jugendian (Art Nouveau) architecture.

To get to Töölö from Kallio, you can follow a pleasant park around the bay's north end, over the train tracks. This way passes some important places for locals: the City Theatre, the City Conservatoire, the Olympic Stadium (beside which is an overly popular outdoor swimming pool) and the enormous, ultra-modern **Suomen Kansallisooppera (Finnish National Opera House)** ㉕ which opened in 1993 *(see page 81)*.

To take the alternative route to Töölö, start by walking one block west of the train station to Mannerheimintie, as far as the four-storey mall Forum Shopping Centre, with shops, fast-food restaurants, a bar and two cafés. Turn north, and one-and-a-half blocks further on a bronze statue of General Mannerheim on

BELOW: the Ilmatar and Sotka statue in Sibelius Park.

horseback presides over the busy intersection between Mannerheimintie, Arkadian, Postikatu and Salomon streets. Töölö lies directly over the traffic bridge from here. Beneath the bridge, the old Railway Yard has been converted into a fashionable art gallery and a clutch of international food and goods stores.

Map on pages 166–7

Architectural trio

The **Eduskuntatalo (Parliament Building)** ㉖, directly across the street, atop an important row of steps, is decidely less casual. Fourteen columns of grey granite mark its stern façade, built between 1925–30 after J.S. Sirén's design.

Statues of former Finnish presidents scatter the area between the Parliament Building and the **Kansallismuseo (National Museum)** ㉗. The Gesellius-Lindgren-Saarinen trio designed this museum in 1906 to reflect Finnish history in its very construction. Although National Romantic in style, the heavy grey building also incorporates snatches of old Finnish church and castle architecture. The main tower imitates that of the Turku Cathedral *(see page 208)*.

The museum's decoration and collection offer more on Finland. The stone bear by the entrance is the work of Wikström and the frescos on the foyer ceiling, depicting scenes from Finland's national epic the *Kalevala* are by Gallén-Kallela. The entertaining jumble of artefacts inside runs from early archaeological finds up to present-day items. The City Museum branch in the fine Hakasalmi Villa (tel: 9-169 3444) houses a special exhibition on Helsinki's history, and has one of the cosiest of Helsinki's many cafés on its front lawn.

Finlandiatalo (Finlandia Hall) ㉘, next door, is undoubtedly the most famous building in Töölö – if not all of Helsinki. Alvar Aalto designed it both inside and out, completing the main section in 1971 and the congress wing in

Streetside snack of Finnish pastries.

LEFT: *Attack* by Edvard Isto (1899). **BELOW:** detail of the Barbara Altar from Kalanti Church (both in the National Museum).

1975. It now houses the Helsinki Philharmonic Orchestra and is used for any number of concerts and events.

The striking white building was specifically devised to blend environmentally with the backdrop of Hesperia Park and Töölö Bay, especially in winter. Ironically, Finlandiatalo is having ecological troubles. The Carraran marble of its façade did not just grey; it warped disastrously from the Finnish winter. A new layer of similar white marble now replaces the old one, and it is anyone's guess how long that will last. Meanwhile, the hall has had a second, widely-known problem: the acoustics of the concert hall were poorly conceived and electrical experiments have been going on in an effort to try to improve them. Regardless, the hall serves as an indisputable bastion for modern Finnish culture.

A number of other important cultural spots cluster around the Parliament House. The Sibelius Academy, Helsinki's famous musical conservatory, is around the corner. Concerts are given by top students (tel: 9-405 4662 for information). Across the street at Pohjoinen Rautatiekatu 13 is the **Luonnonti-eteellinen museo (Natural Science Museum)** ㉙, whose numerous showcases and vivid dioramas offer a colourful lesson on Finnish wildlife. Its Neo-Baroque building is easily identified by the bronze cast of an elk on its lawn (tel: 9-191 7400; open daily; entrance fee).

Nestling, literally, into a small hill behind all of this on the winding streets of Töölö, is the ultra-modern church, **Temppelinaukion kirkko** ㉚. It is not only an architectural oddity – built as it is directly into the cliffs, with inner walls of stone – but it is also the site of many good concerts during the year. A service for English speakers is held here weekly (open daily, but on Sundays for worshippers only).

BELOW LEFT AND RIGHT: architectural glories along the beautiful Bulevardi.

Helsinki's new heart

The whole neighbourhood is evolving based on a plan by Alvar Aalto, which is finally being realised in perhaps ways the great designer would not have anticipated. In spring 1998 **Kiasma ㉛**, a new museum of contemporary art, opened its impressive doors, on Mannerheiminaukio, just across from the Parliament building and adjacent to Finlandia Hall, this remarkable machine-like structure by American architect Steven Holl is a symbol of a new Helsinki, whose city centre is shifting to this area. The curving asymmetrical building harmoniously interacts with its surroundings – the oddly-shaped windows afford good views of the key landmarks of Helsinki. The bold exhibitions vary from astounding to macabre (open Tues–Sun; entrance fee) .

A triangle of "functionalist" architecture has emerged with a new role in life: Kiasma, closest to the railway station, Lasipalatsi ("Glass Palace") across Mannerheimintie and the former Tennispalatsi ("Tennis Palace") at the other end of the bus station area. Lasipalatsi is one such functionalist structure that has been rejuvenated with utmost care to create a welcoming media centre with an Internet library, two TV studios (for live programming), a cinema, other media companies and fine cafés and restaurants. Tennispalatsi, formerly an eyesore for the aesthetically minded, was used during the 1952 Olympic Games, and now houses Finland's largest cinema complex (14 screens) and two museums. The bus station is poised for further development. Several new hotels are also opening in Töölö at the close of the 20th century, as further proof that this is fast becoming the city's new "heart".

In 1999 Finland chaired the European Union and in 2000 Helsinki not only celebrates its 450th anniversary but is simultaneously honoured as the European

Map on pages 166–7

A whole range of buskers take to the streets in the city's brief summer.

BELOW: the small boat harbour.

City of Culture – a monumental year for such a comparatively new and diminuitive capital city.

Gracious avenue

Another district in southwestern Helsinki worth exploring is **Punavuori** ❷, a plush area beneath Töölö towards the end of the peninsula. The main street here is Bulevardi, which begins at a perpendicular angle from Mannerheimintie (just a couple of blocks before its end) and leads down to Hietalahti shipyard. Drop in at Bulevardia restaurant (Bulevardi 34, tel: 9-645243) for lunch, dinner or a glass of wine on the summer terrace. It has been a favourite artists' hangout for decades.

Bulevardi is one of Helsinki's most beautiful avenues. Most of the buildings date from between 1890 and 1920 and were formerly home to Helsinki's turn-of-the-century patricians. Vanha Kirkko (The Old Church), however, between Annan and Yrjön streets, is a stray from Engel. Dating from 1826, it was the first Lutheran church to be built in the new "capital".

The former National Opera House lies a few blocks further west on Bulevardi. This delightful red building was erected in 1870 as a theatre for Russian officers and for decades it housed the national opera, until the building of the new opera house *(see page 170)*. The inside is plush and ornate, but much too small for classic opera productions. It functions better as a musical theatre and school.

As you reach the end of Bulevardi, you will come to the former Sinebrychoff Brewery, which was established in 1819 and is the oldest brewery in Finland. The Sinebrychoff Museum of Foreign Art (tel: 9-1733 6460; open Wed–Mon) is housed at Bulevardi 40, and includes Old Masters and miniatures. Don't miss

BELOW:
the strikingly
modern National
Opera House.

Map on pages 166–7

the **Hietalahdentori** ❸, best known for its flea market. The goods are usually just unwanted records and clothes, but this market is one of the best places in Helsinki to watch large numbers of locals in action during the day.

Bulevardi does, however, also harbour many fashionable art galleries and boutiques, which spill into neighbouring streets. Two blocks south and parallel to Bulevardi, the Iso-Roobertin pedestrian street has many youth orientated shops and restaurants.. Another two blocks further on, is the Johannes Church. This rather regal affair with important stiletto spires is the largest church in Helsinki and a particularly popular place for choral concerts, with excellent acoustics. Across the street, at Korkeavuorenkatu 23, the **Taideteollisuusmuseo (Museum of Applied Arts)** is an essential stop, as it is a showcase for Finland's famed skills in design, including Aalto furniture and Lapponia jewellery *(see pages 81–2)*. The museum is open daily, tel: 9-622 0540.

Neo-classical stone detail, near the Eira district of Helsinki.

In the same block is the **Suomen rakennnustaiteen museo (Museum of Finnish Architecture)**, at Kasarminkatu 24 (tel: 9-661 918; open Tue–Sun; entrance fee), which has an excellent archive of architectural drawings, and changing exhibitions focusing on Finnish architectural movements (including National Romantic, Neo-classic, Jugendian, Functionalist and Modern).

High-class life

Heading directly south from here you come upon Eira, perhaps Helsinki's most exclusive neighbourhood. On the southernmost end of the peninsula the coastline below Eira is lined by parkland. After the ice melts, small boats dock all along the coastline and half the world seems to be cycling by. While the sea is still frozen, you can actually walk out to some of the closer offshore islands.

BELOW: Helsinki's shopping area, Aleksanterinkatu.

Towards the northeast and the centre, this strip of green grows into Helsinki's best park: **Kaivopuisto ③**. In summer, the city sponsors numerous free concerts here and Kaivopuisto overflows with happy sun-bathing locals. Kaivohuone, a former spa in the park, is also one of the city's most popular places to meet and hear music. The recently refurbished nightclub features hot Finnish bands, but due to complaints about noise on its terrace, it can currently rock 'n' roll only on agreed evenings.

Embassies fill the well-heeled Ullanlinna district. Most noticeably, the Russian Embassy commands almost a block opposite St Henrik's, one of Helsinki's two Catholic churches. Above them rises **Observatory Hill** (the Finnish name *Tähtitorninmäki* literally means "star tower hill"). From here you can look down over the city centre and Katajanokka to the north.

The **Mannerheim-museo** (tel: 9-635 443; open Fri–Sun; entrance fee; guided tour obligatory) is tucked away between embassies at Kalliolinnantie 14. It was the home of General C.G.E. Mannerheim, perhaps the most respected figure in Finland's history *(see page 49)*. His achievements include a two-year expedition to Asia, when he travelled 14,000 km (8,700 miles) on horseback along the Silk Road. Some of his souvenirs from his lengthy travels are on display here.

Not far away is **Cygnaeuksen galleria** (Kalliolinnantie 8; tel: 9-656 928; open Wed–Sun; entrance fee), a tiny, exquisite wooden summer home of the poet Cygnaeus. Inside the house is a remarkable 19th-century collection of Finnish painting and sculpture.

Directly below to the east is the **Olympiaterminaali (Olympia Quay) ③**, stopping place for huge Silja liners and a reminder that the sea has brought prosperity to Helsinki, the "Daughter of the Baltic".

BELOW:
an 1842 stable in the Seurasaari open-air museum.

Helsinki's Islands

Literally hundreds of islands dot the Helsinki coastline. Some, like Lauttasaari and Kulosaari, have been so integrated by bridges and metro lines that they are almost indistinguishable from the mainland. Others are reserved for weekend cottages, reached over the ice in winter or by motorboat in summer.

Map on pages 166–7

Suomenlinna 🕉 ("Finland's castle") is undoubtedly the most important of the latter. In reality it consists of five islands, over which the ruins of a naval fortress and its fortifications are spread. Suomenlinna has played an integral part in Helsinki's life since its construction started in 1748, under Count Augustin Ehrensvärd. It is a unique architectural monument, which has been listed by UNESCO as a World Heritage Site.

Suomenlinna has a complicated identity. It began as a naval post, and still houses Finland's Naval War Academy, but it is hardly just a military enclave. A thriving local artists' community, which uses restored bastions as studios and showrooms, is more visible. Fishing boat repairers and restoration workers also live on the island.

Getting to the island is both cheap and easy. Water buses leave from Market Square every half hour, year round, and cost the same as a metro ticket. They dock on Iso Mustasaari and from here, a hilly path leads up through **Jetty Barracks** (Rantakasarmi), which now house art exhibitions and an interesting restaurant and microbrewery by the name of Panimo (tel: 9-668 200).

Continuing past wooden houses, the Lutheran church sometimes stages concerts. This part of Suomenlinna has permanent residents living both in new houses and formerly Russian-era military houses. This island also has three museums. The **Nukke-ja lelemuseo** (**Museum of Dolls and Toys**) (tel: 9-668 417; open daily in summer, Sat–Sun in spring and autumn; entrance fee) contains thousands of dolls and toys from the Helsinki region from the 1830s to the 1960s, collected during the last 30 years. It is a private collection, the achievement of Piippa Tandefelt, an energetic lady who also prepares apple pies for the museum café.

The large **Suomenlinna Museum** (tel: 9-668 120; open daily in summer, Sat–Sun in spring and autumn; entrance fee) is the main historical exhibition of the islands. A fine multivision programme is shown regularly. The building also houses the main information centre (tel: 9-648 1880) for Suomenlinna. The Military Museum exhibits heavy equipment. For anyone interested in big war machines, they are authentic artillery, and other machines, with roots in Swedish, Russian and Finnish war and defence history.

Crossing the bridge leads to the rambling remains of the **Kruunulinna Ehrensvärd** (**Ehrensvärd Crown Castle**) and gardens. The castle courtyard is the best preserved section of the fortress and contains the 1788 sarcophagus of the Count himself. His former home is now a museum, with old furniture, arms and lithographs (tel: 9-668 154; open May–Sept: daily; Oct–Apr: Sat–Sun; entrance fee).

The rest of Suomenlinna is split between residences and the fortress fortifications, which spread across Susisaari and the southernmost island of Kustaan-

BELOW:
Kaivopuisto Park.

TIP

One of the most popular eating places on Susisaari is the Cafe Piper, in a park just south of the Ehrensvärd Crown Castle. The cafe has a delightful setting, and offers al fresco dining with a view.

miekka. From the highest outcrop on this windswept last island, close to an atmospheric summer restaurant called Walhalla, it is sometimes possible to see Estonia, some 80 km (50 miles) away. The might of passing ferries, on their way to Estonia or Sweden, is a view that one could write home about *(see page 180)*. There is also the Rannikotykisto museo (Coast Artillery Museum), and the Vesikko Submarine.

Korkeasaari ⑨ (tel: 9-169 5969, open daily; entrance free) is another "tourist island" but has neither Suomenlinna's complexity nor its charm. Finland's only zoo completely dominates this rocky outcrop just a few steps away from the mouth of Sörnäinen Harbour. You can reach it by boat from Hakaniemi or from the Market Square. Helsinki Zoo, perhaps not surprisingly, specialises in "cold climate animals" although there's a very interesting enclosure, which is home to South American animals. However, if you want to learn about indigenous Finnish fauna, you'd probably do just as well at the Helsinki Zoological Museum *(see page 172)*.

Seurasaari ⑩ (tel: 9-484 712) is also strictly a visitors' island, but eminently more atmospheric. A pretty, forested place, its northeastern side has been made into an Ulkomuseo (Open-Air Museum), containing wooden buildings from provinces all over Finland. The transplanted houses on Seurasaari date from the 17th to 19th centuries and include farmsteads and a church. Bonfires are held near here to celebrate traditional festivities for Midsummer and Easter, during which local Finnish children dress up as "Easter witches". The other side of the island is a national park.

The island is connected to the Helsinki shore by a wooden footbridge – so no need for a boat. Just take either bus No. 24 from the centre or cycle along the

BELOW: old ships and historic buildings within Helsinki's harbour.

Meilahti coastal drive (which takes you past Sibelius Park and the silvery tubular Sibelius Monument) to the bridge. Admission to the island is free but, to enter any of the houses, you'll need to buy a ticket. Houses are open in June, July and August daily until 5pm, and two weeks before and after the season until 3pm.

Less well known are the smaller islands that form a string around Helsinki's southern peninsula. Across the "Olympic Harbour" are Luoto and Valkosaari, popular restaurant islands with romantic villas. A long pier outside Kaivopuisto *(see page 176)* offers a boat service to Särkkä, another island with a popular restaurant, and Harakka. Uunisaari is accessible at the southern end of the street Neitsytpolku. It's a popular recreational island with a beach, a sauna and a restaurant. The Finnish Sauna Society situated on the beautiful island of Lauttasaari offers wood-fired saunas and massage (tel: 9-678 677; open 11.30am–4pm for men, 4.30–8pm for women).

Helsinki's favourite island for swimming is undoubtedly **Pihjalasaari**. Literally meaning Rowan Island, Pihjalasaari actually comprises two islands, with a sandy beach, café and changing cabins on the larger island's western shore. Helsinki's only nudist beach is on the smaller island, which also hides wartime bunkers. Boats to Pihjalasaari depart in summer every 15 to 30 minutes just, outside Café Carousel in Eira.

The very special **Harakka** island is now a wildlife reserve but, up until 1990, was reserved for military purposes and is still absolutely pristine. A network of paths (marked by signposts giving information in Finnish and Swedish) circle the tiny island and visitors are asked not to stray from these paths or remove plants. You can reach Harakka by boat in the summer or, in winter, by crossing the ice from Eira *(see page 175)*. ❏

Map on pages 166–7

BELOW: boats plying the Baltic waters around the capital.

The Baltic States

As the Finnish economy started to grow stronger in the 1970s, affluent Finns and Swedes enjoyed more leisure time and discovered the 24-hour mini cruise and the opportunity to take a "quick" foreign holiday. For foreign visitors also, the ferries around the Baltic create an easy and unusual way to combine a visit to different countries.

The ships ply the Baltic sea lanes to and from Sweden, via the Aland Islands, and several sail under the Swedish flag. Any preconceived ideas about passenger-car ferries will vanish as soon as you board one of these magnificent ships operated by either of the top players, Viking Line (red) and Silja Line (white). They are fun, value for money, and cruise through the most beautiful seascapes in the world.

Some of the most popular ferry trips from Helsinki are across the Bay of Finland to the attractive cities of the former Soviet Union. Most popular of all is the two-day excursion to

St Petersburg: visas are not needed, accommodation is provided on the boat and there are no money worries; Russians would rather have your dollars, pounds or yen than their own devalued rouble. Largely built by European architects in the 18th century, St Petersburg is the least Russian of Soviet cities. Situated on 40 islands in the Neva river delta, its Italianate palazzi and numerous waterways draw comparisons with Venice and Amsterdam.

It is European art, too, that draws the crowds to the city's Hermitage gallery for, despite all the statistics – 1,057 rooms, two million items – the highlights of the collection are concentrated in the rooms devoted to western painting, from private collections nationalised after the Revolution: masterpieces by Rembrandt, Poussin, Cézanne, Van Gogh and Matisse.

St Petersburg is a rewarding city for walking and absorbing the street life. The city is particularly lively during the "white nights" of June, when everyone comes out to watch the lingering sunsets. A walk from the Hermitage, through the archway of the General Staff building, will take you to Nevsky Prospect, the city's main thoroughfare. Men still play chess here and street musicians perform. Also visit the enclosed market off Nevsky for a slice of daily life. The Kafe Literaturnoya (18 Nevsky) has a Viennese atmosphere: coffee and cakes, and occasional poetry readings or chamber concerts. Pushkin ate his last meal here in 1837, before fighting a fatal duel.

Arts Square, round the corner, offers music at the Philharmonia Bolshoy Hall and the Glinka Maly Hall, and opera and ballet at the Mariinsky Theatre. Gostiny Dvor (35 Nevsky) is the city's largest department store, where Russia's home-produced consumer goods sit alongside the increasingly popular imports from the west.

A trip to Petrodvorets, 28 km (18 miles) west of the city is a must. This is Peter the Great's answer to Versailles and he invited all the European rulers to attend its gala opening. The centrepiece of the Great Cascade is a statue of Samson tearing open the jaws of a lion which symbolises Peter's

LEFT: young Estonian girl in national dress.
RIGHT: medieval city of Riga, in Latvia.

victory over the Swedes in 1709. Equally revealing of his character are the trick fountains: be careful when choosing a seat – some will send up a shower of water.

Tallinn, the capital of Estonia, is the other ferry destination, and from here you can set off to explore all three newly independent Baltic states: Estonia, Latvia (capital Riga) and Lithuania (capital Vilnius). Tallinn lies directly opposite Helsinki, 80 km (50 miles) across the water, and large numbers of Finnish tourists (many of them former Estonian refugees who fled in the final years of World War II) visit the city – more, it has to be said, for the lively nightlife than for its beautiful medieval old town. Cobbled alleys ascend from the 14th-century castle and the Gothic architecture reminds you that Tallinn was once an important port of the Hanseatic League.

Riga, a city founded by merchants, has a very similar history. The 13th-century Roman-esque cathedral is lined with the tombs of bishops, knights and landmeisters. The organ is the fourth largest in the world, and most evenings you can hear performances of Bach or Mozart. In Vilnius, three things impinge on every visitor: the ubiquitous jewellery shops selling amber, for which Lithuania has long been famous; the medieval streets clustering below the castle and the festive atmosphere that prevails here now that the longed-for independence has finally come.

The increasing popularity of the trips and, in turn, the increased size of the ferries is, however, causing valid concern for the erosion of the shorelines, the islands of the inner archipelago and the seabed. Another environmental concern is the pollution caused by heavy traffic near ferry terminals. The ferries carry around 900,000 passenger cars, 30,000 coaches and 170,000 trailers a year. At the same time the ships are a vital link in Finnish-Swedish trade and one of Finland's lifelines to Europe. Much of Finland's foreign trade travels by ferry.

But on a still summer night, as pinpoints of light appear on islands beside the ferry's white wake, these issues are unlikely to trouble a passenger leaning over the deck rail and gazing out to a darkening sea. ❏

WEST OF HELSINKI

*Many of the artists and architects who created Helsinki's image
chose to reside in the city's western suburbs, which are also still
home to a few rural and traditional communities*

Map
on pages
194–95

The 19th-century search for a rural Finnish identity has left a selection of museums and buildings dotting the landscape of what are, now, glorified suburbs of the capital, albeit many with country settings. If you have the time to leave the city for a day, many of the places mentioned in this chapter are worth a visit and offer a different view to the city centre.

A garden "city"

Passing through Inkoo and Kirkkonummi, the next city of any size you'll come to is **Espoo ❶**. While Espoo is, strictly speaking, a "city", its main impression is of a huge, spread-out municipality. A bastion of wealthier Finns who work in Helsinki, Espoo is a strange mix of rural farm areas and genteel, leafy suburbs that give you, when taken in total, a large and colourful palette of Finnish residential architectural styles.

PRECEDING PAGES:
golden wheatfields.
LEFT: church
steeples on the
western road.
BELOW: an
agricultural life.

Espoo's Tapiola area is renowned as the planned garden suburb of the 1950s, in which leading architects of the age aimed to create a harmonious mix of housing, from flats to family houses, set around a central pool. Yet despite all the sleek newness, the area has been settled since 3500 BC, and Espoo's parish church dates from the 15th century. In addition, many artists and architects have made their homes in the area. Only a handful of wooden houses and scenic rapids now mark the original settlements, however the river paths are beautifully tended and lead to some surprisingly authentic Finnish countryside only moments away from Helsinki's centre.

Finland's national artist

At the beginning of the route from Helsinki to Turku is **Tarvaspää ❷**, the home of Finland's national artist, Akseli Gallén-Kallela *(see page 278)*. He was already well established when, between 1911–13, he built a studio-home around the Linudd Villa on the old Alberga Manor ground. The studio has been converted into the **Gallén-Kallela Museum**, at Gallén-Kallen-latie 27 (tel: 9-513 388; open daily in summer, closed Mon in winter, entrance fee).

Today, Helsinki reaches almost to Tarvaspää yet the latter is still set in forest and field (although next to a noisy highway). The studio was designed by Gallén-Kallela himself, whose forceful personality is etched throughout, along with his own hard physical work. Architect Eliel Saarinen, a close friend, participated informally in the studio project as technical adviser.

The museum,contains some 100 illustrations for the *Kalevala* which decorated the Finnish Pavilion at the Paris Exhibition in 1900. The paintings are on display at the Ateneum in Helsinki *(see page 156)* and

Turku Art Museum, where Gallén-Kallela's work sometimes features in temporary exhibitions. Also on view are paintings for his frescos in the Jusélius Mausoleum in Pori *(see page 238)*, which commemorated Sigrid Jusélius, the 11-year-old daughter of a Pori businessman. Working on these frescos was a poignant task for the painter because his own young daughter had died a few years earlier. There are also relics of his times in Africa, Paris and elsewhere.

The Gallen-Kallela Museum is a peaceful oasis, where concerts are occasionally held. It consists of a studio wing, tower and main building, with a coffee house and a terrace restaurant; guided tours are available by appointment.

To get there by car, leave Road 1 (E3) 200 metres (250 yards) past Turunväylä (Tarvontie). Almost at once, a road marked Tarvaspää takes you to the museum. Alternatively, travel on tram 4 and enjoy the scenic 2-km (1-mile) walk from the last stop, or take bus 33 from Munkkiniemi.

Art Nouveau in the woods

Another artistic mecca that it would be a shame to miss is Eliel Saarinen's home at **Hvitträsk ❸**, some 20 km (14 miles) west of Helsinki in Kirkkonummi municipality (tel: 9-297 5779; open Jun–Oct: daily; Nov–May: Tue–Sun; entrance fee; guided half-day tours by arrangement in summer). It can be easily reached by Road 1 (E3), taking junction 3 left for Jorvas, and follow the signs for Hvitträsk. It can also be reached by bus (number 166 from platform 62 at Helsinki bus station) or train (L train: Luoma and Masala or S train: Masala).

You would expect the studio home of three of Finland's most famous architects to be at one with its surroundings but Hvitträsk surpasses the term. The stone and timber buildings seem to blend into the forest, the great cliffs and

BELOW: self-portrait of Akseli Gallén-Kallela on display at Tarvaspää.

the lake (White Lake) that gives the house its name. Inside, architecture, interior designs and furniture all blend together. The partnership of Eliel Saarinen, Herman Gesellius and Armas Lindgren was responsible for many important buildings and, in all, the big, main studio, now a museum, saw the planning of 70 projects. Hvitträsk celebrated one of the architects' earliest triumphs, the Finnish Pavilion at the Paris World Exhibition in 1900. The dining-room ceiling, like the pavilion decoration, is Gallen-Kallela's work. Saarinen, who disliked long meetings, designed the hard black table and chairs; reproductions of his furniture designs are still on sale today.

The early working harmony did not always extend into the private life of the little community, however. Proximity, perhaps, turned the gaze of Saarinen's first wife, Matilda, towards his partner Gesellius and she simply crossed the garden and changed houses. Apparently bearing no grudge, Saarinen married Gesellius' sister, Loja, two years later. But the triumvirate broke up in 1906 and by 1916 Saarinen was working at Hvitträsk on his own.

In 1922, after gaining a major prize in a competition in New York, Saarinen moved to the United States, was made Dean of the Cranbrook Academy of Art and became as well known abroad as in Finland. He continued to visit Hvitträsk each year until his death in 1950, and his grave overlooks the lake.

The flat landscape and quiet, rural roads make the area ideal for cyclists.

Leased to Russia

The whole Kirkkonummi municipality was once a large rural Swedish-speaking area. However, at the end of World War II, Finland was forced to lease the Porkkala Peninsula in the south to the Soviet Union as a naval base, a situation that remained until 1955 *(see page 55)*. The Russian cemetery here, on a typical

BELOW:
Hvitträsk, once home to Finland's finest architects.

Map on pages 194–95

Soviet scale, is an ageless reminder of that time, when 7,000 Finns had to leave their homes at 10 days' notice.

Today Porkkala has a Finnish naval garrison in **Upinniemi**, with a remarkable Sea Chapel, designed by Marianne and Mikko Heliövaara, shaped like a boat with open sails and overlooking the sea. Some of the best bird migration routes pass over the Porkkala Peninsula and spring and autumn draw ornithologists galore to watch flocks of cranes, swans and geese. In summer, sailing boats and beach cabins dot the spectacular Baltic coastline.

Back on Road 1 and heading west, the area of lake and ridge is part of the Salpausselkä Ridge, formed at the end of the Ice Age. The next major stop is **Sammatti** ❹, just south of the road. Look out for the sign to **Paikkari Cottage**, (Paikkarin torppa), the home of Elias Lönnrot, who collected the old legends and tales for the *Kalevala (see page 95)*. The building is typical of a worker's home in 19th-century southwest Finland. Outside, Lönnrot's statue is by Halonen and Räsänen. Not far away stands Lammi House where the writer died.

At **Salo** ❺, some 115 km (80 miles) from Helsinki in the heart of the apple-growing Salojoki Valley, it is worth turning off the main road to go into the town centre, which has old houses and beautiful gardens, Uskela Church, another of C.L. Engel's works, and a fine valley view. Many of the world-famous Nokia mobile phones are manufactured in Salo *(see page 82)*.

Tyrant's carriage

At Piikkiö, only 15 km (10 miles) from Turku, turn right for the **Pukkilan kartano-ja ajokalumuseo (Pukkila Manor House Museum and Vehicle Museum)** ❻, where the rococo-style mansion is furnished as the home of a state official. The Carriage Museum in the former byre has 30 different carriages, including that of the Governor General Bobrikov, assassinated in 1904.

The town church dates back to 1755, built partly of stones from the ruins of **Kuusisto Castle** ❼. This medieval bishop's castle is worth a detour to the Kuusisto peninsula, just west of Piikkiö – take the road to Pargas (Parainen) and branch on to a secondary road to the ruins. The 14th century castle stood stoutly until Gustav Vasa ordered its demolition in 1528, but enough remains to have encouraged recent attempts at restoration.

Having come this far, you may like to continue to **Pargas (Parainen)** ❽, which has a beautiful view over the islands of the archipelago and is famous for its large limestone quarries. Pargas has one of the most stunning medieval greystone churches in Finland, Harmaa Kivikirkko, dedicated to St Simon. Built in the 1320s, it is unusual for the spreading brick columns that support the interior and contrast with the light blue trim of the pews. Notice, too, the panel paintings of Old Testament figures running around the porch where the organ sits. Pargas has a good marina, and a charming series of wooden buildings scattered around the church which form a kind of extended folklore museum; weaving still goes on here.

From here it is a short drive northwest to the old city of Turku *(see page 203)*. ❏

BELOW: a coat of arms shows the Swedish influence.
RIGHT: wildflowers bloom in Finland's springtime.

THE TRADITIONAL FINNISH SAUNA

An old Finnish proverb says: "First you build the sauna, then you build the house"; even today there's nothing so uniquely Finnish as a sauna

There are some things along the way which a traveller does not forget – and a real Finnish sauna is one of them. Although its origin is obscure, the sauna came to Finland over 2,000 years ago, and it is a rare Finn who admits to not liking one. Official statistics estimate that there are over 625,000 saunas in Finland, not counting those in private houses or summer cottages that dot the shoreline of the country's lakes *(see page 250)*. The actual figure could easily be over 1 million in a country of just 5 million people – but then, the sauna is a national institution.

BUSINESS AND PLEASURE

The sauna outgrew its rural roots long ago. Today, be it city or village, you will find public saunas, and it is safe to assume that every new apartment block has a sauna for its tenants. Many companies also have saunas for their employees.

A Finnish sauna is not a meeting place for sex, as it is in some countries; codes of behaviour are strict. Titles and position are, they say, left hanging in the changing room with the clothes. It is is not unusual for board meetings and government cabinet meetings to be held in a sauna – perhaps because it's "not done" to swear or raise one's voice. A sauna also leaves you relaxed yet alert.

▽ **FRIENDS AND FOLIAGE**
Tying up birch leaves for the sauna is a social event in summer.

▽ **MORAL CODE**
Despite the nudity, a Finnish sauna is a moral place. Generally, saunas are same-sex only; a mixed sauna is solely a family affair.

▽ **HOT GOSSIP**
There is more to the sauna than just getting clean. It is a happening – a time to meet friends or rivals, to talk and socialise.

HOW TO TAKE A SAUNA

There is no "right way" to take a sauna – temperature and style vary. The ideal temperature is between 80–100° C (175–210° F) although it can be a cooler 30° C (85° F) on the bottom platform, reserved for children. A common practice is to brush oneself with a wet birch switch, called the *vihta*. This not only gives off a fresh fragrance but increases blood circulation and perspiration.

How long you sit in the sauna is entirely up to you. When you have had enough, you move on to stage two: cooling off. A cold shower is the most common way but, if the sauna is by a lake or the sea, a quick plunge into the cool water is stimulating.

The final stage is to dry off, which should be done naturally, to avoid further perspiration. It is also time for a beer or coffee and a snack to complete the ritual.

△ **STEAM HEAT**
Water thrown over the hot stones creates a dry steam (*löyly*), which makes the heat tolerable and stimulates perspiration.

◁ **COOLING OFF**
In the winter, brave souls jump through holes in the ice or roll around in the snow – not recommended practice for people with high blood pressure.

◁ **SAUNA FASHIONS**
The sauna has become such an integral part of Finnish life, that there are even "designer" outlets specially geared towards sauna accessories.

▷ **ANCIENT USES**
In olden days in rural Finland the sauna was not just the place in which to get clean, but also where babies were born and sausages smoked.

SOUTHERN FINLAND

From Swedish-speaking farming communities to bastions built to protect the Finn-Russian border towns, the south coast has an atmosphere quite distinct from the rest of the country

Map on pages 194–95

To follow the south coast of Finland from west to east is to follow a route once travelled by Nordic kings and princes to St Petersburg. It is mainly flat, coastal country covered with farmland and densely grown forest. And, because proximity to the sea has always given extra value to land – in addition to the beneficial, warming effects of the Gulf of Finland – this area is heavily settled – in Finnish terms.

It is also heavily Swedish-speaking. From Pargas *(see page 188)* south of Turku at the head of the Turunmaa island chain, through Ekenäs (Tammisaari), Karis (Karjaa), and further east through a cluster of small villages on the approach to Kotka, you will hear a great deal of Swedish and read it as the first language on signposts. This is all part of the democracy of bilingualism in Finland: in any town with a majority of Swedish speakers, the Swedish name normally takes precedence.

Farms and fortresses

The landscape changes only very subtly from west to east. As most of Finland is above the 60th parallel, its southernmost reaches are the major farming areas. The land is low, and tends to be misty in the early morning and late evening. Although it is not as rich in lakes as the country north of here, it is sufficiently irrigated by local meandering rivers and streams.

The green of new wheat and the yellow of rape seed dominate in late spring; then the wheat matures and the wildflowers burst into bloom. The grassy strips at the roadside are first overrun with cowslip and lupin, a midsummer flower with tall purple, pink, and white spindles. When the lupin fades, *maitohorsma* takes over; also a tall, spindly flower, the splash of its magenta petals fill not just the road edges but entire forests and fields. Autumn is slightly more colourful in the west, where the linden adds its bright hue to the gold of the birches. The west is also hillier than the east. Set against this backdrop are clusters of old farm buildings, stained dark red; most larger coastal towns have old sections whose buildings are painted in an array of pastel shades. Manor houses in the region are painted a rich ochre or brilliant yellow.

The eastern portion of the coast, past Helsinki, is riddled with fortifications. For the Swedes, then the Russians, and finally the independent Finns, the Russian border has been a crucial dividing line. From 1944 to 1956, the Soviets had a military base at Porkkala, an elbow-shaped peninsula west of Helsinki.

The Finnish-Soviet borders still have a no-man's land running between them, and although travel between the two countries has become far easier and

LEFT: models of ships traditionally grace the windows of Loviisa's wooden houses.
BELOW: Hanko's church.

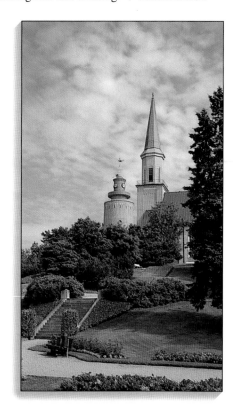

more popular since the break-up of the USSR, there is no mistaking the sterner attitude of the Russian customs guards and immediate deterioration of road conditions as soon as one crosses over the border to the east.

Exploring the islands

Richly vegetated but sparsely populated, the archipelago of **Turunmaa** ❾ is quieter than the Alands in terms of tourism (*see page 229*), and the islands are reached more quickly from the mainland. They are linked by a series of bridges and then ferries. Ferries also service some of the smaller islands that spin off south from the main chain. Local buses connect the larger towns.

Turunmaa's finest harbour is on the northeast spur of **Nagu**. An old wooden house overlooking the marina has been made into a guesthouse-style hotel, with a French brasserie and a chic restaurant, L'Escale, next door. Also to be found in Nagu is the Borstö Folk Museum and the 14th-century St Olof's Church (open Jun–Aug: daily).

As you approach Pargas (Parainen) from west or south you come to **Sattmark**, on the island of Stortervolandet. This tiny log cabin was once a sailor's quarters. It now serves light meals in its prettily furnished rooms and down on the dock that runs below and behind it.

Salo is the first large market town to the east on the mainland. Set off by a triad of churches – the Lutheran Uskela (1832), the Greek Orthodox Tsasouna at its foot, and the stunningly modern Helisnummen (Helisnummi Church) about 4 km (2½ miles) outside the town – Salo still has a very lively market, held every day except Sundays. Along the Uskela river there are some beautiful residential garden districts.

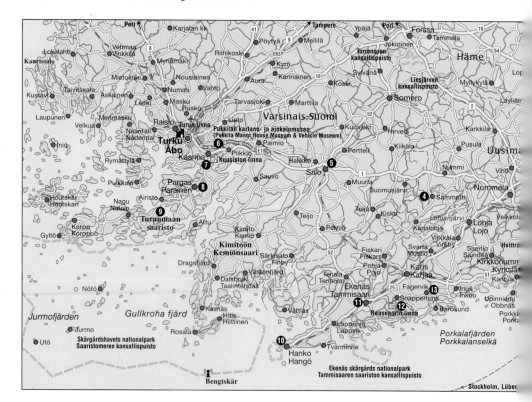

Marina life

Due south of Salo is **Hanko (Hangö)** , Finland's southernmost town. Known not only for its annual July regatta and its long beaches, Hanko has some of the most jocular architecture to be found in Finland. A long parade of turreted and deeply-eaved houses follows the stretch of beach – in varying states of repair.

Hanko's Linnoitusmuseo (Frontline Museum) outlines the town's strategic history, such as the destruction of the fortifications during the Crimean War (open May–Sept:daily except Mon; in winter, Sat, Sun and Wed afternoons only). Hanko was also the port from which 300,000 Finns emigrated between 1880 and 1930 to escape raging epidemics and famine. It is still a large customs port, with a lively summer milieu centered on its large marina, which hosts boats from dozens of foreign ports. On land, there is a parachuting school, public tennis courts, and a tall watchtower from which to view the busy sea lanes.

Ekenäs (Tammisaari) is the next main coastal stop along the route of kings. It is a finely laid-out old town, with cobbled streets named after different crafts trades, and is a great place for a stroll; some artisans still set up shop here in summer. Just to the south is the Tammisaaren saariston kansallispuisto, a national park, resplendent with marshes, forests and water birds.

There is an extremely active boating life in and around Ekenäs, and numerous outdoor concerts in summer: Ekenäs is considered by many as the major cultural centre of Finland's Swedish-speaking people. The Knippan boardwalk restaurant and the steeple of the old granite church (1680) are the town's main landmarks. There's also a pretty camping ground within walking distance. For an historical background on the town, visit Porvaristalo, the Ekenäs Museum on Gustav Wasas Gata 13 (tel: 19-263 3161, open daily throughout the summer).

Map on pages 194–95

TIP

Information on archipelago boat tours is available from the tourist information office at Bulevardi 10 in Helsinki (tel: 19-220 3411) or on the marina (summer only).

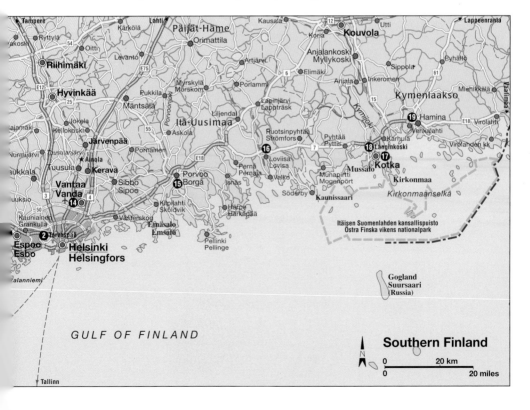

GULF OF FINLAND

Southern Finland

0   20 km
0   20 miles

Historic villages

A few kilometres eastward is **Snappertuna** (no connection with fish), a farming village of Swedish-speaking Finns and the town closest to the splendid 13th-century castle at **Raasepori** ⓬, enfolded in a wooded valley. Most of the fortification is in good condition and you can freely tour its ramparts and impressive interior spaces, refurbished in wood.

The Outdoor Theatre in the Raseborg dale stages dramatic and musical evenings, and if you visit in July you may catch a re-enacted medieval duel. (These tend to be comic rather than grave historic events; British factions are often featured.)

Further east beyond Snappertuna is **Fagervik** ⓭, the site of a tremendous old manor overlooking a protected sea inlet. Its granite and wood buildings make a fine backdrop for a picnic or horse ride. There are also good walking paths here; the so-called King's Road signposts point out landmarks.

North and east of Helsinki is **Vantaa** ⓮, another city with endless open space. The Vantaa rivermouth, a wide wash of water just to the east of the capital, is the home of the "*Vanhakaupunki*", or "old city", upon which Helsinki was founded in the 16th century *(see page 153)*.

Porvoo (Borgå) ⓯ is one of Finland's most important historical towns. The Swedish King Magnus Eriksson gave Porvoo a Royal Charter in 1346; from this point on it became a busy trading post and, ultimately, it was the place where the Diet of Porvoo (1809) convened to transfer Finland from Swedish to Russian hands *(see page 33)*. The striking **Porvoo Cathedral** (open daily, closed Mon in winter; entrance free), where this momentous event took place, dates back to the 15th century.

BELOW:
near Porvoo, the Alikartano Manor House is dedicated to the Finnish explorer, Nordenskiöld.

While its rich history made the town important, Porvoo's artists give it its real character. The **Edelfelt-Vallgren Art Museum** (Välikatu 11; tel: 19-580 589; open May–Aug: daily; Sept–Apr: Wed–Sun; entrance fee) occupies a 1792 merchant's house, formerly the Town Hall, on Rahtihuoneentori (The Town Hall Square). It features paintings by Albert Edelfelt – one of Finland's finest 19th-century artists *(see page 77)* – and works by sculptor Ville Vallgren, as well as a fine Art Nouveau furniture collection. The Albert Edelfelt Atelier in Haikko, 6 km (4 miles) south of Porvoo, also exhibits much of Edelfelt's work. The town is also alive with the work of current artists and writers.

For scenery, Porvoo also has few rivals: its trim riverbanks are lined with fishing cottages and the pastel-coloured houses of the old town provide a charming backdrop.

East of Porvoo, the landscape becomes more rural and less populated, with only the occasional village to break up the vast spread of wheatfields and forests. In summer, the grassy hillocks bristle with wildflowers. There are just two more towns and one sizeable city, all in fortification country. **Loviisa** ⑯, a pretty, provincial town with an esplanade headed by the New Gothic Church, is the smallest of these. A town museum tells the local history, including the role of the Rosen and Ungern bastions, built in the 18th century to protect the important trade route between Vyborg and Turku.

The frequency of rivers (originating in the great lake area immediately to the north) and Orthodox churches now begins to increase. After the old towns of Ruotsinpyhtää and Pyhtää is the broad Kotka Delta. At first sight Kotka can appear unappealingly industrial, yet on closer inspection it is one of the most beautifully situated cities in Finland.

Map on pages 194–95

Vast tracts of forest make up much of the landscape of southern Finland.

BELOW: bicycles are a good way of exploring the southern coast.

Delta fishing

It is around **Kotka** ⑰ that the Kymi river breaks up into five branches before rushing off into the sea, making for perfect salmon and trout fishing. The closest of the spray of islands along the coast can be reached by bridges, the rest by ferry. Kotka centre is based on an esplanade. One street to the northwest, at Kirkkokatu and Koulukatu, is the main Lutheran church, with tremendous brick buttresses; the imposing Orthodox church complex and park runs along Papinkatu. Kotka has frequent boat services to nearby islands, some of which have old fortifications. The pleasant Sapokka harbour has one of the finest parks in Finland; there is even a high artifical waterfall.

Apart from the Kotka islands, the **Kymenlaakso** (Kymi river valley) extends further inland, where there are gorgeous forest paths. Details are available from the Kotka tourist office at Keskuskatu 17, tel 5-234 4424.

The famous fishing lodge of Tsar Alexander III, is at **Langinkoski** ⑱ (signposted from Langinkoskentie; tel: 5-228 1050; open May–Aug: daily; entrance fee). The tremendous log building was crafted by the Finns for the Tsar; its furnishings are now preserved as a museum.

Several nature paths begin from Langinkoski – if you walk north for 5 km (3 miles), you'll pass Kyminlinna fortification, over Hovinkoski river through Kyminkartano (manor) to **Keisarin Kosket**. These "tsar's rapids" course around Munkkisaari Island, with its Orthodox chapel (Tsasouna). A pilgrimage of the faithful is made here every 14 August. The spot is also ideal for fishing and rapids shooting. On the bank is Keisarin Kosket Lodge, an Orthodox monastery site from 1650 to 1850, with café, boats, and cabins for hire; fishing licences are also sold (tel: 5-228 1050 for details).

BELOW: the Tsar's fishing lodge at Langinkoski, near Kotka.

In summer, **Kärkisaari**, just to the west of Kotka, makes for a lovely excursion. The former youth hostel here has been turned into one of the most stylish B&B locations in the country. The food, including the tasty pastries, are well worth sampling. The long swimming dock leads into the island-filled inlet of the Gulf of Finland. On the adjacent peninsula is Santalahti, with caravan and cabin facilities; the crescent-shaped beach has grassy knolls at the edge of a sandy bay.

The Kotka Tourist Board can point out nature-protected paths and rivers, as well as arrange other trips and activities (with guides, if needed).

Towards Russia

Kotka is only 70 km (45 miles) from the nearest Russian city, Viipuri (Vyborg) and 270 km (170 miles) from St Petersburg; all varieties of Finland-Russia trips can be arranged with the Kotka Tourist Board, but remember to plan overnight trips in advance so that your visa will be ready.

Hamina ⑲ is the last of the large Finnish towns before you reach the border. Its concentric plan is part of a huge fortification, and its military nature is also preserved by the presence of thousands of young Finnish men based here for national service. Pastel-coloured wooden houses contrast prettily with red brick barracks and magazines. Three old churches are to be found in Hamina, as well as several quaint museums. One of the large bastion sections has been turned into a covered concert venue. The acoustics of the "Bastioni" are excellent and the site awe-inspiring.

Further east lies **Vaalimaa**, the busiest border station on your way to Russia. Huge supermarkets sell goodies to Russians and Finns – more than 1 million people cross the border here annually. ❏

Map on pages 194–95

Old cannons on the Finn-Russian border are reminders of former tensions between the nations.

BELOW: the planned town of Hamina, with military fortifications.

WESTERN FINLAND

The western area of Finland is known by many as the "essential triangle", encompassing three major cities and various tributes to the industries and artists that have formed the modern nation

Map on page 204

In many countries, a city conjures up images of busy streets clogged with cars and tall buildings. A Finnish city certainly has its motor traffic but it is also a spreading area of lake, forest and green spaces between the buildings that sometimes feels as though it were in the heart of rural Finland. A round trip of some 500 km (310 miles) from the capital Helsinki to the west of Finland, takes in the three largest cities and is one of the best ways to get a feel of the country in a couple of weeks. Our route leads to Turku, the old capital in the centre of Swedish-speaking Finland, and then on to Tampere, the industrial capital, where water set the first 18th-century mills rolling.

Along the way are most of the elements, past and present, that make Finland what it is today. In the south, there are coasts and lakesides, some lakes so vast that it is difficult to decide whether they are lake or sea. Beautiful old houses restored as museums and hotels lie along the route, as do historic castles with magnificent banqueting halls and dungeons, and statues that reflect Finland's history, sometimes warring, sometimes at peace. Further north, the lakes become more frequent, and it is tempting to leave the car and travel as the Finns of old did, using waterways such as the Silverline route which winds through the lake system between Tampere and Hämeenlinna. You can go north by the Poet's Way to Virrat, and swim, fish or sail on lake or sea.

This is a good opportunity to get to know something about Finland's arts and culture, remarkable in a country of only five million, and see the Finns' famed skill in design at glassworks at studios that welcome visitors and offer distinctive articles that could only be Finnish. Above all, between the cities lies the long Finnish road through forests and old villages, to make it a tour filled with flowers and fresh air.

PRECEDING PAGES: misty headlands. **LEFT:** the *Sigyn* barque. **BELOW:** making lace at the Handicrafts Museum.

Turku

Turku ❶ is the "other" face of Finland, the view from the southwest, closest to Scandinavia and the rest of Europe, not just in trade but also in culture. Its atmosphere is a mixture of river and sea: the River Aura divides the modern city in two; the Baltic, curling round the river mouth, has countless islands in an archipelago that stretches southwest until it runs into the Aland Islands, halfway between Finland and Sweden *(see page 229)*.

It is also a city of paradoxes. Turku (Åbo in Swedish) feels like a capital even though it never held that title in a sovereign country but only as the principal city and home of the Viceroy in the Swedish-Finnish kingdom. It is Finland's oldest city and yet many of the buildings go back only to the Great Fire of 1827 which destroyed a town then largely made of wood. Islands, river and sea make Turku a summer

paradise, yet it is also the birthplace of Finnish culture and the country's religious centre.

The Swedes were the first known nation to arrive at the mouth of the Aura River when King Erik sailed in with an English bishop and an expeditionary force in 1155. As Bishop Henrik, the bishop later became the first Finnish patron saint. Even earlier, Finnish tribes from the southeast had settled and traded along the river valleys of southwest Finland, and sailors and merchants came and went to the first settlement, up-river at Koroinen.

The Swedes called their growing town Åbo and in 1229 Pope Gregory IX agreed to transfer the See of the Bishop of Finland to Koroinen. By 1300, a new cathedral downstream on Unikankare (the "Mound of Sleep") was ready for consecration, and Turku became the spiritual centre of Finland.

Around the same time, the solid lines of a castle began to rise near the mouth of the River Aura as the heart of royal power in Finland, where the Swedish governor lived and visiting dignitaries paid their respects. It was also a fighting

castle, standing firm under a winter siege in the mid-14th century in one of the bloody struggles for the Swedish throne. In all, the castle was besieged six times. In the 16th century, Gustav Vasa survived another winter siege and proclaimed his young son (later Johan III) as the Duke of Finland.

After Duke Johan returned in 1552, with his wife, the Polish princess Katarina Jagellonica, Turku Castle entered its most colourful phase of royal glory. Katarina brought glamour, in her Polish courtiers, her velvet and lace, and even her spoons, forks and knives, and introduced a splendid court life that was already common in most of Europe but had not yet reached Finland. In summer, the court visited the island of Ruissalo, just off the coast, as Finns do today. But this gracious life did not last. After Gustav Vasa's death, feuds broke out between his three sons, and the eldest brother, Erik XIV, besieged the Duke. The castle surrendered in three weeks and Johan and Katarina were bundled into captivity. Though later, as Johan III, Duke Johan gained his revenge on Erik whom he imprisoned in Turku Castle, court life never again achieved such heights.

Maps
Area 204
City 206

Exploring the old city

Today, the massive façades, honey-coloured under the sun, grey in winter, of **Turunlinna (Turku Castle)** Ⓐ (Linnankatu 80; tel: 2-262 0300; open daily; entrance fee) look towards the modern town centre, some 3 km (2 miles) away. Many of its rooms have been preserved as the Turku Historical Museum, with portraits of Duke Johan and his wife. The old chapel has regained its original role and the magnificent banqueting halls are the scene of civic celebrations.

Turku had the first university in Finland, founded by the 17th-century Governor General of Finland, Count Per Brahe. He travelled the length and

BELOW: impressive vaulted ceiling of Turku Cathedral.

*Panelled cabinet at
Turku Castle.*

breadth of his governorship and his name is commemorated in many towns and buildings. His greatest contribution to Turku, however, was **Åbo Akademi** ❸ which, after its ceremonial opening in 1640, made Turku the centre of culture and learning as well as religion. When Finland became a Russian Grand Duchy, the Tsar ordered the Academy to be transferred to the new capital to become the University of Helsinki but the Old Academy Building remains. In 1918, independent Finland created a second Akademi as Turku's Swedish-language university, and also founded the University of Turku.

After the Great Fire in 1827, market and town moved away from the cathedral to the west bank of the Aura, much of it designed and built to the plan of that industrious German, Carl Ludwig Engel, who visualised a city of rectangular blocks intersected by broad streets, a plan still clear in modern Turku. The way to start a walking tour is among the bright stalls, piled with fruit and flowers, in the market square. On one side, the Hotel Hamburger Börs is one of Turku's best, with busy bars, cafés and restaurants packing its ground floor. The hotel faces across to the green, cap-like dome of the Orthodox Church, an Engel design built in 1838 on the orders of Tsar Nicholas I. The yellow building to the southwest is the Swedish Theatre, also by Engel.

During the days of the Grand Duchy, the **Ortodoksinen kirkko (Orthodox Cathedral)** ❸ served a Russian community but it is now attached to Istanbul. Its present congregation of 2,000 includes converts and one or two families who moved from Karelia during the World War II resettlement. Inside, it has all the rich beauty one would expect, the dome held up by ornate pillars. Paintings tell the story of St George and the Dragon, and Empress Alexandra (wife of the Roman Emperor Diocletianus) to whom the church is dedicated.

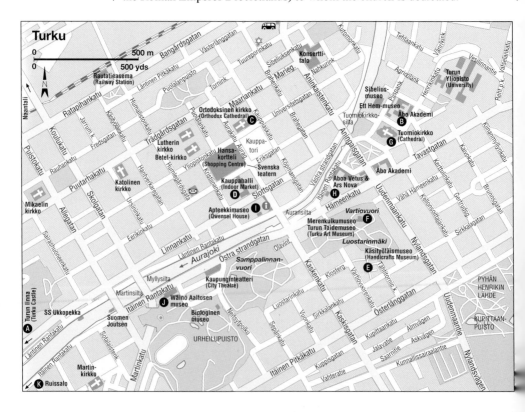

Shopping

A cluster of shops such as Pentik, Aarikka and Sylvi Salonen, along Yliopis-tonkatu (Universitetsgatan) to the west, is a happy hunting ground for gifts and mementoes, with a selection of handicrafts, wood and chinaware and other typically Finnish goods. Between here and Eerikinkatu (Eriksgatan) is the **Hansakortteli (Hansa Shopping Centre)**, enticingly weatherproof in a Finnish winter. Just across from Hansa, Mezzo is another indoor shopping complex with a variety of restaurants, cafés and shops.

More exciting is the 19th-century **Kauppahalli (Indoor Market)** , across the street in Eerikinkatu. There is something about the smell of a market hall that lures you in, a mixture of cheese, meat, fish, sweets and a tang of exotic spices. The stalls stretch along the entire length, with tempting arrays of *munkki*, a sort of doughnut, and *pulla*, a cake-like bread. At Turun Tee ja Mauste you can smell some of more than 200 teas before you buy and pick up oddities such as ginger tea for Christmas or tea spiced with cloves – good for cold weather, the Finns say. Nearby, a stall sells typical wooden tulips and leaves, painted in bright colours. Made by a sheltered workshop, they are half the usual cost.

Turning down Aurakatu towards the Aurasilta (bridge) you pass the **Tourist Information Office**. The bridge gives the first view of the numerous restaurant boats and the sleek white hull and complicated rigging of the *Suomen Joutsen*, the "Swan of Finland", which once plied the ocean between South America and Europe. Along the banks, people sit at open-air restaurants and, below the bridge, there is dancing every summer Tuesday from 6 to 8pm.

Over the bridge, on the right-hand side, there is a statue of long-distance runner Paavo Nurmi, Turku's most famous son.

Map on page 206

Paavo Nurmi (1897–1973) is said to have been the greatest long-distance runner of all time. He won a total of nine gold and three silver Olympic medals, and set 31 world records. He also carried the Olympic Torch in the 1952 Helsinki Games.

BELOW: guides in traditional dress at the Pharmacy Museum.

Historic buildings

The entrance to one of Turku's most interesting areas is just a short walk from here. This is Luostarinmäki (Cloister Hill), the site of an early convent. There's a certain rough justice in the fact that the only part of the wooden city to survive the Great Fire of 1827 was this hill, for it housed those too poor to buy houses in the 18th-century city and they moved here to build their own community. That escape has left an inheritance that, unlike most Nordic open-air museums, stands where it was founded and is not a collection of re-located buildings. The name, **Käsityöläismuseo (Handicrafts Museum)** ❸, (tel: 2-262 0350; open daily summer, Tues–Sun winter; entrance fee). is a slight misnomer because this old area is much more; the woman spinning today in the dark interior of a wooden house is a museum worker but she is spinning in the same way and in the same place as the early inhabitants, and the 18th-century costumes seem quite natural. There are traditional sweets, every sort of craft, tin, copper and goldsmith's, and a baker's which sometimes sells pretzels made in the traditional way. Seamstresses and tailors sew and the old way of life is revealed in the community houses where different families lived in the same building, sharing their kitchen and their bathhouse, or by the truckle bed of a university student who lived with a family, giving service in return for his keep. The main house near the entrance has an excellent self-service restaurant with good homemade food.

Coming down the hill, detour via the Observatory on Vartiovuori, another Engel building, now the **Merenkulkumuseo (Turku Art Museum)** ❼ until year 2004, when it will return to its former location on Puolalanmäki. Nearby is an anti-aircraft gun memorial from World War II, when ordinary Finns raised money for defensive guns – Turku bought nine.

Tuomiokirkko (Turku Cathedral) ❻ (open daily; entrance free), also on this side of the river, was the focal point of old Turku. Look down from the balcony for the best view of the high arches of the main aisle, with its side chapels. The balcony also has the Cathedral Museum (entrance fee), with valuable collections opened to the public in the 1980s after the most recent restoration. Among the most interesting chapels is the Kankainen Chapel where the stained-glass window by Wladimir Swetschkoff shows Queen Karin Månsdotter, wife of the luckless Erik XIV, who was eventually poisoned after his imprisonment.

Don't miss the statue of Mikael Agricola near the cathedral's south wall. The architect of the Reformation in Finland, he was born on a farm in Pernå east of Helsinki and took the name Agricola meaning "farmer's son" when he went to study in Rome. In the Cathedral Park Governor Per Brahe stands in a classically proud pose, not far from Åbo Akademi, a block or two to the north. The main buildings of the present Swedish-language university and the University of Turku are also nearby.

Not far away stands the magnificent **Rettig Palace**, formerly a secretive residence of Hans von Rettig, tobacco industrialist, shipowner and one of the richest men in Turku. After his death in 1979 the building was opened to the public. And what a building! Now called **Aboa Vetus and Ars Nova** ❿, the

An employee at the Handicrafts Museum wears traditional 18th-century costume.

BELOW: the *Icy Sea* memorial on Mill Bridge.

main house exhibits modern art and the garden has become a museum of medieval Turku (Itäinen Rantakatu 4–6; tel: 2-250 0552; open daily summer, Tues–Sun winter; entrance fee).

Along the river

In Turku you are never far from the River Aura and can cross and recross its five main bridges or take the little ferry that still carries pedestrians and cycles across free of charge.

For a riverbank tour, the first stop is **Apteekkimuseo (Qwensel House)** ❶, Turku's oldest wooden building, named after and built by Judge W.J. Qwensel, who bought the plot as long ago as 1695. Perhaps the best kept secret in town, the backyard of this house has a café with 18th-century decor and recipes. From the waterside, low bushes trace the name TURKU/ÅBO, and Qwensel House now houses the rare **Pharmacy Museum** (Läntinen rantakatu 13; tel: 2-262 0280; open daily; entrance fee), which keeps traditions alive by growing herbs in the backyard. A recent innovation, leaving from the front of the museum, is the horse-cab *Musta-Hilu* which provides a leisurely and unusual view of the city. (Children can also have the Koiramäki tour of the city in a special red and yellow bus with guides in costume. This daily summer tour is, as yet, only conducted in Finnish.)

Walking past Myllysilta (Mill Bridge), in Borenpuisto Park, the dramatic statue entitled *Icy Sea* is dedicated to Turku's seamen. August Upman (inscribed on the pedestal) was a pioneer of winter navigation. Past the next bridge, Martinsilta, the SS *Ukkopekka* was the last steamship to sail Finland's coastal waters. Depending on how far you care to walk, you can continue on this side as far as Turku Castle and the modern harbour areas that show how important the sea still is to Turku, with merchant tugs and tankers and the terminals of the Viking and Silja Lines.

On your way to the harbour at Linnankatu 74 is the Maritime Centre, also known as **Forum Marinum** (open daily Jun–Aug; one entrance fee covers all ships). The Maritime Museum and many of Turku's museum ships will find their final home here, including the smaller barque *Sigyn*, launched in Göteborg in 1887, and sailing as far as the East Indies and South America. Her last home port was the Aland Islands and her last voyage from there in 1949. *Sigyn* is unique as the last barque-rigged ocean-going vessel.

Heading back towards the centre you come to the austere outlines of the **Wäinö Aaltosen museo (Wäinö Aaltosen Museum)** ❷ (Itäinen Rantakatu 38; tel: 2-235 5690; open Tue–Sun; entrance fee). Designed by Aaltonen's architect son and daughter-in-law, the building contains much of his work including the massive statues of *Peace*, hands raised, and *Faith*, a mother and child. In a self-portrait, this private man placed a text in front of his face to hide his feelings. Outside the City Theatre is Aaltonen's statue of Aleksis Kivi, one of the first authors to write in Finnish.

The windmill on Samppalinnanmäki overlooking the river is the last of its kind in Turku. Here also, stopwatch in hand, Paavo Nurmi trained against his

Map on page 206

TIP

Numerous boat restaurants dot the riverside. At last count, there was a full dozen of them, each serving a variety of beers and fully packed on sunny summer days. In 1999 alone, three new boats were added.

BELOW: Pentti-Oskari Kangas, captain of the SS *Ukkopekka*.

own best times, and the polished granite stone on the slopes is Finland's independence memorial, unveiled in 1977 on the 60th anniversary. On this river walk, you will notice the waterbuses by Auransilta Bridge and below Martinsilta Bridge. A sightseeing cruise is the best way to get a feel for this water city.

Ruissalo Island

Boat services will take you several times daily to **Ruissalo Island** , also reached in a few minutes by crossing a bridge. It is a green and leafy island, a place for botanists and birdwatchers as well as cyclists and walkers. Ruissalo has the area's best beaches, including a nudist beach – something still rare in Finland, not because of any national prudery but because the Finns, with their lonely cabins on isolated lakesides, had not realised one might need permission to bathe without a swimsuit.

The island is also a surprise place for art lovers, for Ruissalo boasts one of the best art centres in Finland. The 19th-century **Villa Roma** is typical of the "lace villas" (so-called because of their latticed balconies and windows) built by wealthy merchants. Its owner, the Procultura Foundation (tel: 2-233 2740), shows summer exhibitions of top-quality Finnish art, from glass to painting to textiles. There are toy and home museums, and a café. A good restaurant is Honkapirtti, a Karelian-style pinewood building built in 1942–43 by infantry soldiers near the front during the Continuation War. In summer, the island is home to Ruisrock, the world's oldest annual rock festival *(see page 93)*.

One of the most civilised ways to see the archipelago is a supper cruise aboard the ss *Ukkopekka* which retains something of its steamship past and its original engine. As the passengers strive for window tables, the *Ukkopekka* moves

BELOW: the Convent Church in Naantali.

smoothly down the river and out to sea. The bearded skipper, Captain Pentti-Oskari Kangas, is everyone's image of a sea captain and a couple of musicians sing old Finnish sailing songs as the islands glide by. If the timing is right, a fisherman may sail out to the *Ukkopekka* with the fish he has caught and smoked that day. The steamship cruises to different islands and towns, including Captain Kangas' home town of Naantali, north of Turku.

Maps
Area 204
City 206

Naantali

Naantali is now a famous sailing harbour, packed with visiting boats. It is also a historic 200-year-old town, with old houses that are still lived in today. There is a beautiful greystone convent church, with a new organ that attracts famous organists, particularly during the June Music Festival when some 15,000 visitors crowd into the tiny town. At its start in the 1980s, the sceptics thought that little Naantali's festival "would die in 10 years". Now reaching into its third decade, it is proving them wrong. The harbour is also popular with artists, and galleries include the Purpura, which specialises in Finnish artists and supports an artist-in-residence scheme.

Naantali, around 20 minutes by the new road from Turku, could also be a detour on the way to Tampere, but the more direct routes leave the city on Road 40 (motorway at first). This leads to **Aura ❷**, some 30 km (20 miles) north, where from Road 9 you have a fine view of the Aurakoski (rapids). Road 9 continues northeast through rich farmland with a possible detour right at the Helsinki-Pori crossroads (Road 2) for a short drive to the Humppila Glassworks, where at a glass-walled demonstration forge you watch glass-blowers at work. The Glass Village at Nuutajärvi, a little further north on the left of the

Finland's president has a summer home near Naantali, at Kultaranta, whose gardens are open to the public. Many foreign dignitaries take a sauna in former President Kekkonen's unusual house above the rocky coast.

LEFT: the largest bell in Finland at Tampere's Orthodox Cathedral.
BELOW: the "prism" at the Sara Hildén Museum.

road, was formed around Finland's oldest glassworks from 1793, and is also well worth a brief stop. An alternative route, Road 41, slightly to the west goes through Oripää, a gliding centre, where the Moorish style building is the studio-home of sculptor Viljo Syrjämaa, and from Vammala, the road goes through the flat, fertile land of the Loimijoki valley. A 5-km (3-mile) detour on the secondary road to Ellivuori is well worthwhile; just north of Nokia are more magnificent rapids at the start of the waterway system that leads to Tampere.

Tampere

Citizens of Tampere call their city the Manchester or the Pittsburgh of Finland, depending on whether they are talking to someone from Great Britain or the United States, yet anything less like a classic industrial city is hard to imagine.

Tampere ❸ lies on a narrow neck of land between two lakes, great stretches of water so large that you feel you are close to a sea rather than way inland. Linking the lakes, the rushing waters of the Tammerkoski River first brought power, industry and riches to Tampere. Though it still provides some energy, the Tammerkoski is so clean nowadays that it attracts growing numbers of anglers, out for trout. At weekends, the two lakes are bright with rainbow sails and the white wakes of motor boats, packed with picnickers, track their course to one of the islands or to a summerhouse along the lakeside.

Despite a changing pattern of industry, Tampere has managed to retain many bygone factories and workers' houses without allowing them to turn into slums, and the tall red-brick chimneys that do remain are symbols of both past and present, for Tampere's factories are still high on the list of Finland's leading manufacturers and exporters.

BELOW: one of the Pirkka statues on the Hämeensilta Bridge.

THE INDUSTRIAL HEARTLAND

With its over-abundance of forests (two thirds of the country is covered with mostly pine and birch trees), it's hardly surprising that Finland should find itself at the forefront of international paper production, with the rise of the Industrial Revolution in the mid-19th century. It is still a thriving industry – more than 60 per cent of the paper produced in Finland is exported around the world – and factories lining the waterways are still a familiar sight, as is the distinctive, not altogether pleasant odour these factories pump into the air. But in these days of "green thinking" environmental concerns have begun to be raised, not just in Finland but the world over, about the preservation of the country's forest land, and increasingly recycled paper is being used and marketed as a more attractive and ecological option.

Tampere's other major industry in the 19th century was the production of textiles, set up by the Scotsman James Finlayson, but the city was also known for shoe-making, wood production and engineering among other processes. Today, industry is still at the forefront of Tampere life and, in keeping with its innovative past, it is at Finland's cutting edge of high-technology, including highly respected training institutions.

There are some 200 lakes in and around the city. The two largest, Näsijärvi to the north and Pyhäjärvi to the south, are the meeting point of two famous waterway routes. To the south, the Silverline threads its way though a labyrinth of lakes towards Hämeenlinna, passing Valkeakoski, another industrial town in a splendid rural setting, and stopping at the beautiful Aulanko Forest Park among other places *(see page 223)*.

The romantically named Poet's Way boat, SS *Tarjanne*, steers north through narrow, winding waters to Ruovesi and Virrat. The whole journey takes nine hours and gives a two-day taste of Finland's lakes, with an overnight stay at either Virrat or Ruovesi. A little further north, Ahtäri has one of Finland's best native zoos. The national poet, J. L Runeberg began his best-known work, *Tales of Ensign Ståhl*, in Ritoniemi Mansion at Ruovesi and, near the village, Akseli Gallén-Kallela *(see page 78)* built his first "Kalela" studio-home, which is open to the public.

Tampere was officially founded in 1779 by King Gustav III of Sweden-Finland but, since the Middle Ages, the Pirkkala area to the south of the centre had been settled by farmers, attracted by the waterways which made transport easy. From around the 13th century, when the Swedes granted them rights to collect taxes from the Lapp people, they prospered richly. These earliest *tamperelaiset* (Tampere people) are commemorated on the Hämeensilta Bridge in four statues by Wäinö Aaltonen, *The Merchant*, *The Hunter*, *The Tax Collector* and *The Maid of Finland*, characters who come from the ancient legends of the Pirkka. Also clear from the bridge is the tall chimney of one of Tampere's earliest industries, the paper-makers Frenckell from 1783. The old mill is now a theatre with two stages.

Maps
Area 204
City 214

Bronze statue by Wäinö Aaltonen on Hämeensilta Bridge, Tampere.

BELOW: the spectacular interior of Tampere Hall.

The Tammerkoski has largely lost its working factories, and hotels, shopping centres and museums have taken their place. The venerable and well restored Grand Hotel Tammer, the Cumulus Koskikatu and Hotel Ilves all have splendid views of the Tammerkoski rapids, and, from the top of the Ilves' 18 storeys, the panorama takes in the quay where the Silverline boats berth, the leisure craft, the red brick of the old factories and the magnificent stretches of lake. A minute or two away on the riverside, the **Verkaranta Arts and Crafts Centre Ⓐ** sells good-quality craftwork. Above it on the town side is the Tourist Information Office. Below the hotel, the Koskikeskus covered shopping centre has some 100 shops. There is also a Market Hall at Hämeenkatu 19.

Old memories, new buildings

Across a footbridge over the rapids, one of the oldest factory areas stands on Kehräsaari (Spinning Island). In the Independence (Civil) War, the victorious White Army crossed the Tammerkoski here to capture Tampere. Today, its factories and boutiques are grouped around cobbled courtyards. Nearby, the only factory still working on the river, Tako, makes carton paper. Keep an eye out too for the old factory chimney with a bomb shield on the top, a reminder that Tampere was bombed fiercely in the 1918 Civil War, when it was an important "Red" stronghold, and again during World War II with eight heavy raids.

Culture and education centre on Tampere, but it is modern culture and scientific and technical education. The architecture is also largely 20th-century, typified by the **Kirjasto (City Library) Ⓑ** (Pirkankatu 2; open Mon–Sat), an astonishing building said to be based on the open wings and spread tail feathers of a wood grouse, though you might see it more as a series of mushrooms.

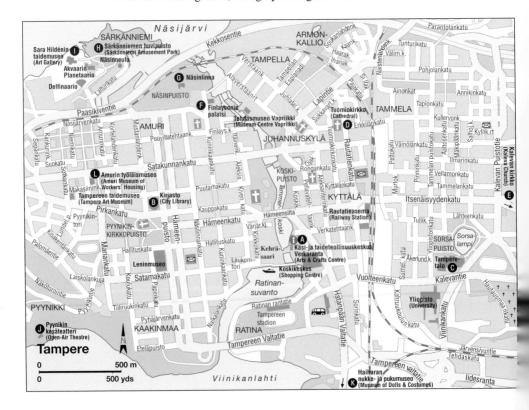

In the mid-1980s the library and the Tampere City Building Office won several awards for its husband and wife architects, Reima and Raili Pietilä. Finns are great readers and borrow, on average, 20 books each per year. Adults as well as children are intrigued by the Moomin Valley section that has the original fantasy characters, the Moomins, created by Tove Jansson *(see page 97)*.

Tampere's pride is the **Tampere-talo (Tampere Hall)** , a spectacular blue-white building designed by Esa Piiroinen and Sakari Aartelo in 1990. Light streaming in picks out the main foyer's fountains, which commemorate the Tammerkoski rapids as the source of prosperity. The main hall holds 2,000, a small auditorium 500 and, if you arrive on a festival morning, from the stage comes the sound of one of the choirs or orchestras in rehearsal. Lit for an opera such as *Parsifal*, the large hall is magnificent, and Tampere people are happy to tell you that their hall is bigger than Helsinki's Finlandia *(see page 171)*, and the acoustics are much better. The hall is used for conferences and congresses and there is a whole beehive of meeting rooms and a café, the Café Soolo.

Sugar snap peas are one of Finland's most popular home-grown vegetables and sold in all city markets.

Tampere's churches

Lars Sonck was only 30 when he won a national competition with his design for the **Tuomiokirkko (Tampere Cathedral)** , which was then St John's church, completed in 1907 at the height of the National Romantic movement. It stands in its own park at Tuomiokirkonkatu 3 (open daily; entrance free), a few blocks east of the river, and contains some of the best of Finnish art, including Magnus Enckell's altar fresco of the Resurrection and his circular window that forms a cross and wreath of thorns. Hugo Simberg painted *The Wounded Angel*, a shattered form carried by two boys, and *The Garden of Death* – despite its

BELOW:
the 16th-century
Messykylä church.

Finland's glassware ranges from the practical to the decorative.

name, not a gloomy picture. His note on the back of a working sketch reads: "A place where souls go before entering heaven." Around the gallery, his *Garland of Life* shows 12 boys carrying a green garland of roses, symbolising humanity's burden of life. This great church seats 2,000 and, softly lit, makes a beautiful setting for a Sunday evening concert, with every seat taken.

The **Kalevan kirkko (Kaleva Church)** ❺, east on the Kaleva road (open daily; entrance free), stands solid in the centre of a green park, like a silo rising out of a field. No wonder it's nicknamed "the silo of souls". Inside, the stark appearance changes to dramatic, with a soaring light that pulls your gaze upwards. A striking feature of this church, another Pietilä design from 1966, is the organ, its 3,000 pipes shaped like a "sail". Behind the altar the wooden statue is intended to be a reed – "a bruised reed He shall not break".

Tampere's oldest church is a rare example from the 15th century, **St Michael's** at Messukylä, around 5 km (2 miles) east along the Iidesjärvi (lake) on the old Lahti road (open daily May–Aug only; entrance free). The oldest and coldest part is the vestry that once stood beside an even earlier wooden church. A moment of high excitement in 1959 revealed extensive wall paintings, now restored, from the 1630s. The church's most valuable wooden sculpture is believed to be the royal saint King Olav of Norway, whose tomb in Trondheim became a place of pilgrimage during the Middle Ages.

Industrial heritage

BELOW: re-created room at the Workers' Museum.

Tampere's industrial history is also rich and, as though to prove how international the city was nearly two centuries ago, one of the most important industries, textiles, was founded by a Scotsman, James Finlayson. He arrived in 1820

from Russia to build a heavy engineering works at the north end of the Tam-merkoski, with the first water-powered spinning mill. When he sold to Rauch and Nottbeck in 1836 it grew to become one of the biggest textile factories in the Nordic countries, but in those early days Mrs Finlayson was not too proud to sell the mill's products in the market. James Finlayson was an industrialist in the Quaker mould and Finlaysons became almost a town within a city, with its own police, health programme and hospital, factory school, and a church: the yellow building with a wooden door near the factory complex. Visitors now find a completely refurbished area of bustling activity, with a microbrewery, the restaurant Plevna, a 10-screen cinema complex and museum devoted to the workers' movement.

The other main company, Tampella, on the eastern side of the river, started as a foundry in 1850. Recently renovated and renamed Vapriikki (from the Swedish word *fabrik*, or factory), the enormous edifice housed some of the EU meetings during Finland's presidency. The factory halls are transforming into a Museum Centre with the technology museum being the flagship.

After Finlayson returned to Scotland, the new owners continued the traditions and the name, and lived in a mansion house nearby, known as the **Finlaysonin palatsi (Finlayson Palace) ⑥** and built by Alexander von Nottbeck. It became a famous house, visited by Tsar Alexander II and his court, and there are portraits of both Alexander I and II on the central staircase, grand enough to feel you should be sweeping down it in full evening dress. The palace is now a club, with live music in the evenings. The restaurant serves food during the day and is also popular for art exhibitions and social functions. The surrounding park is open daily, admission free.

Map on page 214

BELOW: Iittala glassware is among the most respected in the country.

The greater part of Tampella has moved further out of town but, as many of its old buildings deserve preservation, the aim is to convert them to apartments, offices and similar uses. One former Tampella factory on a peninsula above Lake Näsijärvi is now the Lapinniemi Spa Hotel, the first of a style of hotels which concentrate on health, with massage and other treatments in an atmosphere of good food and comfort.

Another Nottbeck home was **Näsinlinna** , an old mansion on a hill in Näsinpuisto Park overlooking the lake, an easy walk from the Finlayson buildings. Don't miss Emil Wikström's Pohjanneito Fountain on your way through. To illustrate how knowledge and skill are passed from generation to generation, on one side a grandmother explains handiwork to a little girl, on the other a boy shows an old man how water power has made work easier. On top is the Maid of the North from the *Kalevala* sitting on a rainbow, spinning golden thread.

The Nottbeck house is now **Hämeen museo (Häme Museum)**, a collection of items from the the the old province of Häme. There are often exhibitions of traditional arts, such as *ryijy* rug-making, an ancient Scandinavian technique which probably arrived from Sweden. These rugs were not only warm and beautiful, they were practical too, serving as money to meet the tax collectors' demands.

Tampere's amusements

From Näsilinna, across the northern harbour entrance is an even higher viewpoint, the Näsinneula Observation Tower at the centre of **Särkänniemi Park** , with its Aquarium, Dolphinarium, Planetarium and Children's Zoo (tel: 3-248 8111; aquarium, planetarium and dolphinarium open daily; amusement park open daily early May–mid-Aug). A new attraction, white-water adventure

(*Koskiseikkailu*) has been carved into the rock with a little help from concrete: German-made rafts travel a long and potentially wet ride. The tower is the highest in Finland and there is no better way to get an overview of Tampere than from the open-air platform over 120 metres (400 ft) up or from the revolving restaurant above it. Looking immediately below, the funfair's scenic railways, roundabouts and ferris wheels look like a child's toys whirling and climbing on their metal girders. The restaurant is good and medium-priced; it takes 50 minutes to complete a revolution and is open until midnight.

If your tastes run to modern art rather than funfairs, or if you like both, don't miss the **Sara Hildénin taidemuseo (Sara Hildén Art Gallery)** in a beautiful building close by, which claims to have Tampere's best lake view. Sara Hildén was a businesswoman and art collector who specialised in Finnish and foreign art of the 1960s and 1970s, and there are also visiting exhibitions and concerts (tel: 3-214 3134; open daily; entrance fee).

Between the lakes, the western part of the isthmus rises in a raised beach to a tree-clad ridge which joins the lakes in a series of steps down through the woods. This is the Pyynikki Ridge, born 10,000 years ago during the last Ice Age round the old bowl of an ancient sea. It was once the home of the town's bishop, and its old viewing tower is a popular place for looking over both lakes and towards the **Pyynikin kesäteatteri (Pyynikki's Open-air Theatre) ⓙ** down near Lake Pyhäjärvi. In a remarkable example of lateral thinking, the theatre auditorium revolves rather than the stage – truly theatre in the round as the audience turns to face each new scene, with perhaps fairies from *A Midsummer Night's Dream* perched high in the trees. The theatre, open from mid-June to mid-August, is especially beautiful when the bird cherries are drenched in white blossom. There is also a restaurant and café.

Haiharan nukke-ja pukumuseo (Museum of Dolls and Costumes) ⓚ (tel: 2-222 6261; open Tues–Sun summer, Wed–Sun winter) moved recently from the Haihara manor house to the imposing Hatanpää manor, just south of Tampere's centre. The last owner, Gunvor Ekroos, built up a huge private collection of some 1,000 dolls, including one from 12th-century Peru, as well as puppet theatres and many exhibits that illustrate the history of play and old magic skills. On her death, the collection became the Haihara Museum Foundation with 5,000 dolls, and many more items that illustrate the life of the upper classes from the rococo era to modern times. An arboretum nearby is worth a visit.

Full circle

Further west is Pispala (Bishop's Village), now considered a very prestigious place to live. In fact, it was built two generations ago by factory workers. As a sign of progress, their children left and went to live in central Tampere but now the grandchildren of the original builders are eager to return and restore. The **Amurin työläismuseo (Amuri Museum of Workers' Housing) ⓛ** (Makasininkatu 12; tel: 3-3146 6690; open Tue–Sun, early May–mid Sep; entrance fee) shows how these houses would have looked between 1910 and 1970. There

BELOW: altar detail at Hattula Church.

are 25 houses and two shops, all giving the impression that the owners might return at any moment.

If you have the time to spare, the unusual **Lenin Museum** (Hämeenpuisto 28; tel: 3-276 8100; open daily; entrance fee) is also worth a visit. Exhibits document Lenin's stays in Finland after the failed 1905 revolution, including the occasion he met Stalin for the first time here in Tampere.

Whatever else you miss in this water city, do not miss a boat journey. If the Silverline or the Poet's Way take up too much time, try an excursion (City Information Office has details) or hop on a boat to Viikinsaari or another island. In half an hour you are on one of the beaches, you can birdwatch or botanise under cool forest trees, and picnic away from everyone else. Hard to believe that, strictly speaking, you are still in Finland's leading industrial city.

Back to Helsinki

Many of the elements that make up Finland – history, industry, agriculture, lakeland, forest, design and the arts – follow you along Road 3 from Tampere to Helsinki. The first stops are Valkeakoski and Sääksmäki, yet more of those Finnish industrial centres that contrive to place themselves in beautiful surroundings between two lakes.

In the Middle Ages, **Valkeakoski** ❹ was no more than a hamlet, later a mining village in the important parish of Sääksmäki; but, even then, it had the rapids that meant water power, first to grind corn and then to make paper. In contrast, the 19th-century National Romantic movement also brought artists to Sääksmäki, and these two ingredients still combine today. For a feeling of Valkeakoski's industrial history, go to the wooden outdoor

BELOW:
Sibelius's lakeside home, Ainola.

museum of **Kauppilanmäki**, typical of the early paper-mill workers' homes up to 1920. The workers' hall, with its union flags, was the centre of political thought as well as home to the community entertainment.

The old **Voipaalan kartano** (**Voipaala Manor**) on Rapola Hill has become an art centre. The museum was once the studio of the sculptor Elias Ilkka, who owned the manor and the farm where the Valkeakoski Summer Theatre performs. On the hill above is an ancient hill fort and a view of the church of **Sääksmäki** ❺, a short walk away. This early parish had an even older church but the present greystone building dates back to the 15th century. An accident on April Fools' Day 1929 resulted in a fire, but everyone thought the alarm was a joke. The church was restored in 1932 but some wall paintings by the windows remain from the old church, as do the altarpiece and two wooden statues.

Just over the bridge, detour right towards Toijala and then right again to **Visavuori** ❻, the studio home of one of Finland's best-known sculptors, Emil Wikström (1864–1942). Aged 29, he had just won a competition to design the frieze for Helsinki's House of Estates, when he designed his house on the peninsula overlooking the lake. Here he worked in the wood-lined studio, spending his nights observing the stars in his rooftop observatory (tel: 3-543 6528; open May–Sept: daily, Oct–Apr: Tues–Sun; entrance fee).

Of all Finland's well-known glassmakers, **Iittala** ❼ is probably the most famous, with austere designs, beautiful functional glassware, and *objets d'art* such as glass birds and fruit shapes so perfect that you immediately want to hold them – a practice not recommended in the museum which houses past and present designs by such eminent people as Alvar Aalto and Timo Sarpaneva, designer of the "i-collection" which became Iittala's trademark. Helped by an

Map on page 204

Gooseberries are part of the summer's yield in Finland.

BELOW: strawberry-picking is a favourite activity in summer months.

expert glass-blower who does most of the work, you can try your talents on a misshapen paperweight. Even better is the Iittala shop where seconds are often indistinguishable to the inexpert eye and less than half the price of perfect work.

There is no escape from modern history at the **Panssarimuseo (Parola Tank Museum)** ❽ (tel: 3-1814 4524; open daily May–Sept; entrance fee), set up by the Association of Armoured Troops and Veterans, survivors of the Finnish campaigns during World War II. Some Winter War tanks go back to 1910, and the Continuation War terrace has some captured Soviet tanks, their hammer and sickle replaced by the still-sinister swastika, after Finland found itself fighting on the same side as the Germans. For military historians this little known museum is fascinating, a tribute to the Finnish tank operators, but even the most casual visitor is intrigued by the armoured train in the woods above. The Finns had two of these mighty trains, adapted and armed with 76mm guns and machine-guns. To reach Parola, take Road 57, marked Hattula, off the main road, and then, just past the next crossroads, branch left again to Parola.

Continue back on Road 57 to **Hattulan Pyhän Ristin kirkko (Hattulan Church of the Holy Cross)** ❾, one of Finland's best known and oldest churches. It was built in 1320 beside the lake of Hattula when Catholicism had not long come to this region after the Swedes built Häme Castle, about 6 km (4 miles) further south. Inside, your eyes are immediately drawn upwards by the delicate colours of the intricate 16th-century frescos which cover ceilings and walls. They were later lime-washed and not re-discovered and restored until the mid-19th century. Today, Hattula has regained the atmosphere of a medieval church and its most valuable statue is a wooden St Olav, the 15th-century Norwegian royal saint (open daily 15 May–15 August; entrance fee).

The old army camp ground near the Tank Museum, with the Lion of Parola statue, recalls Tsar Alexander II's signing of the Language Charter in 1863, in nearby Hämeenlinna, to give Finnish equal status with Swedish.

BELOW: the town of Hämeenlinna.

Aulangon puisto (Aulanko Forest Park) , just off Road 3, is ideal for a break. The forest had a fortress long before the days of Christianity but the man who made Aulanko what it is today was Colonel Hugo Standertskjöld, in the 1930s the governor of Häme province. He had made his fortune as an arms dealer in Russia and returned to build a new manor and beautify the forest park with ornamental lakes, follies and the Observation Tower overlooking Aulankojärvi (lake). The Bear Cave nearby has an appealing family group of bears carved by Robert Stigell. Jean Sibelius, born in Hämeenlinna, is said to have commented on Aulanko: "I was thinking of these scenes from my childhood when I composed *Finlandia*." Aulanko is a stopping place for the Silverline boats and the modern hotel, with golf courses and tennis courts, the outdoor theatre and lake excursions attract a quarter of a million visitors a year.

Castle and composer

Hämeenlinna has two claims to fame: Häme Castle (tel: 3-675 6820; open daily; entrance fee) and the fact that it is the birthplace of Jean Sibelius.

In the early 13th century, when Earl Birger led the first Swedish foray into this ancient countryside, Swedish governors were ever-conscious of the closeness of Russia and obsessed with the need for defence. His first task was to build a square, walled defensive "camp" with towers at its corners, which still form the heart of the castle. Over the next 700 years, Häme was remodelled to suit the moods of kings and politicians, and Swedish, Finnish and Russian history is intertwined in the old red-brick walls. The castle area also includes the **Prison Museum** (tel: 3-621 2977; open daily) and the **Artillery Museum** (tel: 3-682 4600; open May–Sept: daily, Oct–Apr: Sat–Sun; entrance fee).

Silk threads in a rainbow of colours are part of the unique Silk Museum in the heart of Aulanko.

BELOW: the Silk Museum in Aulanko Forest Park.

Map on page 204

In Hyvinkää, in Rantapuisto Park, is Finland's largest statue, the gigantic yellow arches of the Triad Monument.

BELOW: in summer and autumn the markets are full of brilliant berries.
RIGHT: Naantali harbour.

Hämeenlinna itself was granted town status in 1639 by Count Per Brahe, but it was already an important settlement on the Oxen Trail between Turku and Häme Castle. This centuries-old route has served soldier, merchant and traveller alike, though pack animals and carts have given way to motor cars and the track has become a modern road. With its busy centre and shady park, Hämeenlinna makes an excellent base for touring.

Sibelius was born in December 1865 in the little timberboard house of the town physician, Christian Gustaf Sibelius. The three Sibelius children were musical and one room in the house, now the **Sibelius Home Museum** (Hallituskatu 11; tel: 3-621 2755; open daily; entrance fee) shows Sibelius's upright piano from some 20 years later and an old photograph of the young family trio performing at the Loviisa Spa Casino, where they gave summer concerts. The big dining room is now used for occasional recitals, and the house is full of memorabilia of the composer's childhood *(see page 91)*.

The **Suomen Lasimuseo/Finnish Glass Museum** (Tehtaankatu 23; tel: 19-741 7494; open May–Aug: daily, Sept–Dec, Feb–Apr: Tues–Sun; entrance fee) is the most popular place to visit in **Riihimäki ⑫**, just off Road 3 some 35 km (26 miles) south of Hämeenlinna. The building is an authentic glassworks from 1914, still active in the 1930s. The ground-floor exhibition traces the history of glass-making, from the early days of Finnish independence when the industry concentrated on mundane items such as window panes, to the 1930s which saw both the beginning of glassmaking as a fine art and, at the opposite end of the scale, more mass production. Recently, there has again been a partial return to individual glass-blowing and handmade glass, all shown in the upstairs collection of glass of every sort.

Lake dwellers

Heading south through Hyvinkää to Järvenpää, you are only 45 km (30 miles) from Helsinki. The area's Lake Tuusulanjarvi attracted late 19th-century artists away from their city haunts, to build studio-villas on the eastern side, just beyond **Järvenpää ⑬**.

The first of the artist-intellectuals were writer Juhani Aho and his artist wife, Jenny Soldan-Brofelt. Within a year they were followed by artist Pekka Halonen, whose work had already been inspired by the beautiful **Lake Tuusulanjarvi ⑭** and by the farming life around him, as was another incomer, portrait painter Eero Järnefelt, famous for his rural and folk scenes. When Sibelius and his wife Aino moved to the lake shores, the Halonens' home, Halosenniemi (open May–Sept: Tues–Sun), became a meeting point for convivial saunas, recitals and the drinking of Halonen's homemade rhubarb wine.

Ainola ⑮ was the Sibelius home for 53 years (tel: 9-601 966; open daily, summer only; entrance fee). Designed by Lars Sonck, it is still furnished as it was in Sibelius's time – the drawing room holds the composer's piano. Outside in summer, the garden is quiet and peaceful. Sibelius died at Ainola in 1957 at the age of 91; his wife died in 1969 at the age of 97. Underneath the apple trees their grave is a square flat stone, with always a few floral tributes close by. ❏

KÖKAR
LEMLAND
LUMPARLAND
MARIEHAMN
SALTVIK
SUND
SOTTUNGA
VÅRDÖ

THE ALAND ISLANDS

Separated from the mainland and inhabited by Swedish-speakers, the Aland Islands are nevertheless very firmly a part of the Finnish landscape and heritage

Map on page 230

The Aland Islands (Ahvenanmaa in Finnish) are a collection of granite-bound skerries spraying out to the west of the Finnish coast. Most people outside Scandinavia have never heard of them, though they are a part of a unique, autonomous political set-up that gives the 25,000 Swedish speakers here their own particular identity. They have had their own flag since 1954 and their own postage stamps since 1984.

Geography and culture

In 1917 the Alands were the western limit of the Grand Duchy of Russia that Finland then was, and the Russians began sending reinforcements to the islands. But, while Finland was celebrating independence from Russia in 1918–19, Alanders were petitioning to become part of Sweden. Although the League of Nations assigned the islands as a demilitarised, semi-autonomous entity to Finland (with Swedish as the official language), today's Alanders hold no grudge. Like mainland Finns, Alanders take tremendous pride in a Finnish athlete or team beating the Swedish competition. Yet they certainly don't think of themselves as ordinary Finns. Alanders have inhabited their islands for thousands of years, and have a strong ethnic culture and a formidable pride in their identity. The fact that they did not become associated with Sweden seems, if anything, to have nurtured even greater pride in their uniqueness.

From June to August, the archipelago is a place of breeze-ruffled inlets edged with tiny, sunkissed beaches of glacier-worn granite. Some are shaded by the shadows of umbrella pines. Fishing villages huddle at the edges of rocky promontories, dwarfed to child-size when one of the larger Sweden-Finland ferries, or even one of the grander private yachts, sails past. Winters here are sodden and windy and rarely cold enough for any real snow. Although the islands attract fleets of oversize sailing and motor yachts, and with them crowds of well-to-do boat owners, the feeling here is never élitist, merely restful.

The Alanders have scraped a living from the soil and extracted it from the sea for centuries. In the days before motorised sailing, it took about six weeks to journey over water to Helsinki, where Alanders traded sealskins and oil. They also profited from their local apples, herring and loaves of sweet black bread known as "*svartbröd*", which goes especially well with herring.

Today, Alanders earn their living in a slightly less gruelling fashion. Fifteen per cent are directly employed in tourism and another 15 per cent in tourist-related services. Seal hunting has dropped out of the picture, but farming, fishing and construction

PRECEDING PAGES: canoeing on the Aland waters. **LEFT:** coat of arms of the Aland district. **BELOW:** museum ship, *Pommern*.

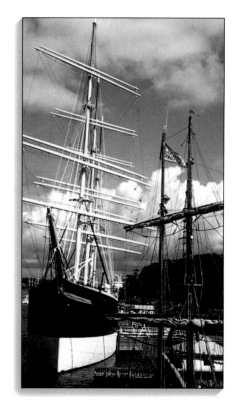

are still important. One unique Aland product you'll see is the Finnish potato crisp, made from Aland-grown spuds.

The grand-scale shipbuilding that once went on here has mostly died out, but a large part of Finland's merchant navy is still owned by Aland shippers, and Alanders have recently revived their traditional boat-building skills with three ocean-going, wooden sailing ships that you may be lucky enough to see in Mariehamn. The Finland-Sweden ferries provide hundreds of jobs, but some Alanders still work on merchant and freight ships, following the shining trails of the old Aland grain ships that plied worldwide routes as far as the Antipodes.

Alanders also continue to follow some extraordinary customs. Many of these centre on weddings: until very recently, brides from certain islands wore black and a few brides still wear the traditional high crown of birch leaves and wild-flowers. A real Aland wedding can go on for days. On a rotating biannual schedule, the Alands host another tradition, the international Island Olympics. Participants are mainly from British islands such as the Isle of Man, the Shetland and Orkney islands, and, from further afield, the Falklands. A decade ago Estonian coaches arrived penniless from the Baltic isle Saaremaa, and demanded US dollars to feed their athletes (they got food coupons).

With rare exceptions, the Alanders' life has not been the privileged world of the Swede-Finn gentry on the mainland. Despite the language differences, Alanders are more akin to the mainland Finn, with the same simple livelihoods – farming, fishing, forestry and shipping.

Mariehamn and around

An enjoyable way to visit the Aland Islands is by taking the Viking Line ship from Turku (*see page 203*) to Mariehamn, which provides a scenic cruise through the thousands of islands and skerries.

Mariehamn ❶ is the capital of the main island, Aland, and has 11,000 inhabitants; the original town on this site was called Ytterna, and some of its old

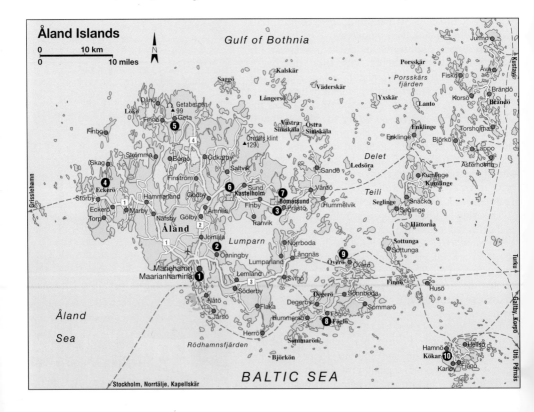

Åland Islands

Gulf of Bothnia

BALTIC SEA

buildings can still be seen in south Mariehamn. Mariehamn is the only town-sized settlement, but there are dozens of villages, many dating back centuries, such as **Onningby ❷** at Jomala, much favoured by painters, including the acclaimed Finnish artist Victor Westerholm, who had a summer house here. The smallest islands are either wholly uninhabited, or inhabited perhaps only by a single family.

The main ring of islands, connected by a ferry service, includes Aland, Föglö, Kökar, Sottunga, Kumlinge and Brändö. A splendid way to tour the islands is by bicycle and ferry. You'll find many Finnish and Swedish families doing so, particularly in July. From Aland, there is a daily bike ferry to **Prästö ❸**; you can hire bicycles from the Mariehamn harbours.

In Mariehamn west harbour is the four-masted museum ship *Pommern* – built in Glasgow in 1904 and still in its original state – which together with a visit to the nearby Maritime Museum will give you the lowdown on the archipelago's seagoing history (tel: 018 531421; open daily Apr–Oct; entrance fee).

On the cultural side is the **Ahvenanmanen museo**, located at Stadshusparken (tel: 018-25426; open daily, May–Aug; entrance fee), a museum and art gallery with exhibitions on prehistoric and Ice and Bronze Age Aland life. From more recent times are displays on folk customs and archaeological finds from the islands' many medieval churches.

The **Lilla Holmen Bird Reserve** (entrance free), below the east harbour, is an island park filled with roving peacocks and roosters,mixed in with Angora rabbits and guinea pigs (caged). There is also a café and short strip of beach. A more interesting excursion is made by foot or bicycle to the Ramsholmen Nature Reserve on the nearby island of Jomala.

A decorative maypole celebrates the start of spring on the Aland Islands.

BELOW: boats plying the waters near Mariehamn.

Mariehamn has a summer boat hotel, great for budget travellers (Botel Alida, tel: 18-13755). On smaller islands accommodation is in campsites, cottages or guesthouses. A tours and lodgings agency is Alandstrafiken (tel: 18-25155, fax: 18-17815).

BELOW:
Kastelholm Castle in the east Alands.

Eckerö

On the main island, the countryside stretches out for dozens of miles in all directions from Mariehamn, alternating between wide open fields and sea vistas to dense, pungent forests crowded with pines and birches. The scenery is particularly beautiful along the straits that cut into **Eckerö ❹**, straits which resemble rivers at their narrower points. Eckerö Harbour is set off by the cherry-red boathouses clustered along its bays and promontories. Due to its western exposure, you can watch the midnight sun in Eckerö from its evening dip towards the sea till its early dawn rising.

Several museums in Eckerö are worth a visit. The large Russian-era **Posthus (Post House)** has two small museums, both open daily in summer, which detail the dangerous voyages made by postmen delivering mail between here and Sweden. In mid-June the **Postrodden** or mailboat race leaves from Eckerö, a re-enactment of the once arduous journey to Stockholm to deliver post. Participants sail over in 18th-century costume, and stay at the old postal workers' hotel at Storby. At the attractive fishing harbour, **Jaktoch Fiskemuseum** (tel: 018-243 8299; open May–Aug: daily, Sept–Apr: Sat–Sun; entrance fee) has especially rewarding exhibitions on hunting and fishing,

Eckerö is closest to the Swedish mainland (Grisslehamn) and so is a popular car ferry departure point. The journey takes two hours.

Moving across the north to **Geta ❺** you'll find a tremendous landscape of shelves of granite laced with natural grottoes dug out aeons ago by glaciers and then eroded by the sea. There is a small café at the end of the Geta road; the grotto path is to the right. The teetering piles of stones that edge the path are said to be remains from old bread ovens.

East Aland

Saltvik, Sund, Lumparland and Lemland on the east side of the islands are farming areas. With its numerous, forest-fringed inlets and natural protection from the open sea, Lumparland Sound is a fine spot to fish or picnic, or arrange a cottage stay.

In Aland's northeast are the historic Kastelholm and Bomarsund fortresses. **Kastelholm ❻** in Tosarby Sund (tel: 18-43210; open last two weeks Apr: Mon–Fri; May–Sept: daily; fee for guided tours) was once the administrative centre of the islands, and dates from the 1300s. The Russians began fortifying it in 1829; ultimately the site was destroyed by fire, but it is now under extensive restoration. Adjacent are the Cultural History Museum and Jan Karlsgärden Open-Air Museum (open May–Sept: daily; entrance fee). Five km (3 miles) to the north of Kastelholm is the 13th-century granite church of Sund.

About 13 km (8 miles) east of Kastelholm is **Bomarsund ❼**, built by the Russians as a huge fortified area, surrounded by a stone wall and knocked out by British and French firepower during the Crimean War. The 1856 Peace of Paris that followed included Tsar Alexander's declaration that the islands would have no more military reinforcements. Alanders are, even today, exempt from national service in Finland.

Bird island

To the southeast of Aland lies the second most populated island, **Föglö** . The ferry takes about 30 minutes from Svinö (a bus from Mariehamn to Svinö takes about 40 minutes) and lands at the enchanting port town of **Degerby**, once an important vodka smugglers' destination as well as an important customs post. In the eastern part of the island is a natural bird reserve, inspiration for the three golden birds on Föglö's coat of arms.

Degerby's cross-shaped Maria Magdalena Church was once a key landmark for sailors crossing the north Baltic. It dates from the 12th century and was renovated at great expense in 1859. On the altar is a precious silver crucifix from the 1500s (excavated in the 1960s), preserved in a lucite casing. The church's sacristy holds an extraordinary collection of priests' robes.

The Maria Magdalena cemetery has many headstones carrying the name Perón; any Föglö resident named Perón is related to the family of the late Argentine president. One version of the unlikely story explaining this link claims that an Argentine seaman became involved in work at the Degerby customs station, found a Degerby wife, and never left.

Föglö has wonderful possibilities for touring by bike, with its empty roads and lack of any really steep terrain. From Degerby you can ride to **Overö** , the northernmost island in the Föglö group, in just over an hour, using a series of car bridges that stretch to the last strait before Overö. To cross this, you must go on board the cable ferry, which, like the inter-island ferries, is considered an extension of the road system and so is free.

Unless you decide to rent a private cottage along the Föglö straits, the only choice for accommodation will be the charming **Enigheten Guesthouse** at Degerby, a preserved farmhouse manor run by volunteers (tel: 018-50310).

The seafaring islands decorated their ships with glamorous models.

BELOW: medieval churches abound on the islands.

Archaeological treasures

Kökar  is a bare island and most of its vistas look towards the open sea. By the rocky coast at Hamnö is a fascinating medieval church, founded by Franciscan fathers and renovated in 1784. The soil around the church has yielded up rich archaeological treasures including a medieval graveyard, Estonian coins, and the church's original baptismal font, now located near the altar. Other finds are displayed in the stone chapel in the churchyard. Near the font is the memorial stone of the Franciscan-trained native son Stephanus Laurentii, who in 1496 was made Finland's first Doctor of Theology.

The **Kökar Museum** (open Jun–Aug: daily; entrance fee) has a collection of old photos whose written commentary has been hand-corrected by locals who perhaps recognise a wrongly identified grandparent. There are also farm tools, costumes and narratives about the Germans' failed attempts to shoot down Kökar's beacon tower during World War II.

The amenities here include only two food shops, one café, one bank and two taxis. However, there is a handsome old guesthouse, **Anton's** (tel: 018-55729), on a family estate with its own beach, campsite, and bicycle hire. ❏

Map on page 230

THE WEST COAST

Dotted with islands, the beautiful Gulf of Bothnia preserves its rich centuries-old maritime heritage and retains its harmonious blend of Finnish and Swedish culture and language

Map on page 238

The west coast of Finland is a fascinating mixture of past and present. There are plenty of reminders of days gone by: old wooden houses; museums that focus on the great days of sailing ships and the export of tar; and monuments to fierce battles when Sweden and Russia tussled over the body of Finland, caught fast between its powerful neighbours. The present is represented by modern industry which, fortunately, is usually well clear of historic town centres. The hinterland is either flat or gently undulating, largely an area of farms and forest with a sprinkling of lakes – in other words, typically Finnish.

As this is the part of Finland closest to Sweden, Swedish was the language of many communities on the southern part of this coast during the centuries when Finland was dominated by the Swedes. Even today, many still speak Swedish as a first language and some towns have both Swedish and Finnish names.

An industrial heritage

The first main town north of Turku *(see page 203)* on Road 8 is **Uusikaupunki (Nystad)** ❶, typical of this coastline. At the end of the 19th century, it boasted Finland's second biggest sailing fleet. An earlier high point came on 30 August 1721, when the Peace Treaty of Nystad ended the "Great Hate", a particularly bloody period in Russo-Swedish hostilities. The town's fortunes declined with the arrival of the steamship but revived with the coming of new industries in the 1960s. The Saab-Valmet car assembly plant offers tours and a motor museum exhibits rally-winning vehicles. The harbour is now used only by pleasure boats plying the archipelago; the old salt warehouses are now antiques shops and restaurants.

Nevertheless, maritime memories remain. The **Kulttuuruhistoriallinen museo** (Ylinenkatu 11; tel: 2-8451 5399; open Jun–Aug: Tues–Sun; entrance fee) is in the house of F.W. Wahlberg, a former shipowner and tobacco manufacturer. Vallimäki Hill has a pilot's cottage, in use from 1857 to 1967, which is now a small museum. The church, completed in 1629, received a vaulted roof in the 1730s and the 1775 steeple also served as a fire watchtower. Myllymäki Park is a reminder that many retired sailors became millers and the countryside was once dotted with windmills; four windmills and a tower remain.

Rauma ❷ is one of six Finnish towns founded in the Middle Ages and today is the largest medieval town in Scandinavia, listed as a UNESCO World Heritage Site. The 600 or so wooden buildings, painted in traditional pastel shades, are still private homes. Although the dwellings and shops are 18th- and 19th-century, the pattern of narrow streets dates back to the 16th century.

PRECEDING PAGES: windmills at Uusikaupunki. **LEFT:** inside Rauma church. **BELOW:** boats are a way of life.

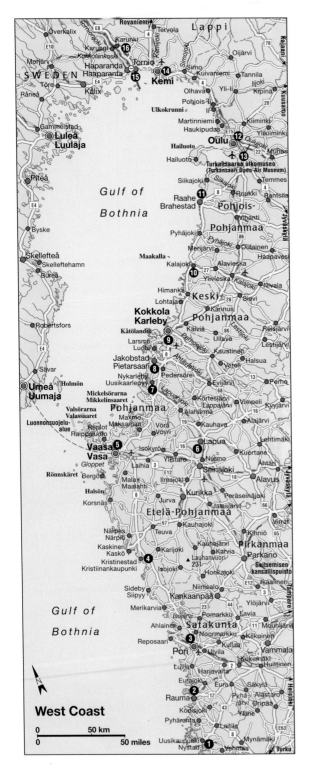

West Coast

0	50 km
0	50 miles

Like most west coast towns, Rauma expanded and prospered in the days of sailing ships and the **Marela Museum** at Kauppiaankatu 24 (open daily; entrance fee) is the home of a former merchant and master shipper, Abraham Marelin. Much of the interior – panelling, stoves and doors – is original and the museum has an interesting display of period costumes. Kirsti's, an early 20th-century sailor's home, provides another maritime connection, continued by the Rauma Museum in the Old Town Hall.

The museum's other main attraction is lace, for bobbin lace-making has been associated with Rauma since the mid-18th century. Nobody knows how lace came to the town, but by the 1850s it was a major industry and almost every woman in the town a skilled lace-maker. The bubble burst when lace bonnets went out of fashion, but since the 1950s there has been a revival, with a lace week in summer, and many Rauma ladies have acquired the old skill. Lace is sold in specialist shops.

Pori

Pori ❸, some 47 km (37 miles) north, of Rauma, was founded by Duke Johan of Sweden in 1558, as a port at the mouth of the Kokemäenjoki river. Since then the sea has receded and the land has risen, a phenomenon common to the Gulf of Bothnia coastline; so today Pori is 10 km (6 miles) from the sea. In the intervening years, the town burnt down nine times – something of a record even for Finland. The last conflagration in 1852 led to the stylish rebuilding of the present centre. With a population of 77,000, it is, above all, an industrial centre and port.

Post-1852 buildings include the Jennélius Palace, now the Town Hall, built in the style of a Venetian Palace. The Pori Theatre, completed in 1884, has been restored and is now looked on as one of the most beautiful in Finland. More off-beat is the strange **Jusélius Mausoleum** (tel: 2-623 8746; open May–Aug: daily, Sept–Apr: Mon–Sat;

entrance free) at Käppärä Cemetery, built by a Pori businessman in memory of his young daughter. Its interior is one of Akseli Gallén-Kallela's masterpieces (*see page 78*), restored by the artist's son in the 1930s.

The **Satakunnan museo** (Hallituskatu 11, tel: 2-621 1063; open Tues–Sun; entrance fee), dating from 1888, is the largest Finnish cultural history museum with over 60,000 items on display, plus an archive of 110,000 photographs and 10,000 books. The museum has a particularly fascinating section on Pori itself.

The **Porin taidemuseo** (Eteläranta; tel: 2-621 1080; open Tues–Sun; entrance fee), an art museum in a skilfully converted warehouse, is also worth a visit.

Kirjurinluoto Island in the river has a natural park with a summer theatre on which centres the great annual **Pori Jazz Festival**. Of all Finland's famous summer festivals (*see page 92*), Pori Jazz is both one of the best known and one of the earliest, with modest beginnings in 1966. It now lures in jazz musicians from many parts of Europe and beyond and, for a hectic week in July, this old town is alive with jazz day and night. An annual audience of between 40,000–60,000 bumps up the town's population by more than a half.

The 20-km (12-mile) peninsula leading from Pori to Reposaari (island) has a long sandy beach on the side away from the port and shipyard, Yyteri. It is one of Finland's best resorts, with a big hotel and congress centre. A new golf course has been created in response to a huge surge of interest in the game in Finland.

Beside the sea

Kristinestad (Kristiinankaupunki) ❹ was founded by the enthusiastic Swedish governor, Count Per Brahe, in 1649. A master of diplomacy, he gave the town the name of both his wife and Queen Kristina of Sweden-Finland.

Map on page 238

A former shipowner's home preserved as a Maritime Museum at Kristinestad shows the importance of local naval life.

BELOW: old and new on the Pori riverbank.

This Swedish influence is still noticeable and even today around 58 per cent of the population is Swedish-speaking and uses the town's Swedish name rather than its Finnish name.

Despite its illustrious beginnings, Kristinestad remained quiet until the 19th century, when it became the home port of one of the country's largest merchant fleets and a ship-building centre. The importance of this is shown clearly in the **Merimuseo** (Kauppatori 1; tel: 2-12859; open May–Sept; Tues–Sun; entrance fee), set in the house of former shipowner, S.A. Wendelin and displaying his maritime memorabilia. But, as elsewhere, the shipowners were caught out by the switch from sail to steam. The building of a railway in 1912 failed to halt the decline and many citizens emigrated to the United States.

Kristinestad is now a modest sort of place beside the water with an interesting townscape, including an impressive Town Hall by E.B. Lohrmann dated 1856. During Swedish rule every traveller into the town paid customs duty and the wooden customs house built in 1720 is now the tourist information office. Another customs house, at the northern end, is even older – built in 1680 – and the oldest street is the quaintly named Catwhipper's Lane. Ulrika Eleonora's Church (1700), named after another Queen of Sweden-Finland, was restored and reconsecrated in 1965. It is typical of a coastal church with votive ships, donated by sailors, hanging from the ceiling.

The **Lebellin kaupiaantalo** (Rantakatu 51; tel: 2-12 159; open Tues–Sun; entrance fee) is worth seeing. Labell was a Polish aristocrat and soldier who married the mayor's daughter and took her name. He lived in the Labell family home which had been gradually extended, with the result that its 10 rooms now represent a variety of styles spanning the 18th and early 19th centuries.

BELOW: farming life at Bragegården Open-Air Museum in Vaasa.

Vaasa and around

Vaasa (Vasa) ❺ is a marker along the coast and an obvious division between north and south. Its origins lie in Old Vaasa, established in the 14th century when the present site was below sea level. It has had a history of devastation by wars and fire, the last of which in 1852 left little but smouldering ruins.

Today, Vaasa (population 56,000) is a handsome town with wide, attractively laid-out streets and a large market square, a mixture of Jugendstil and modern architecture. Axel Setterberg designed the Orthodox church, which is surrounded by late 19th-century buildings of the Russian Grand Duchy, and the Court of Appeal (1862). The Town Hall (1883) is the work of Magnus Isaeus and is equally imposing. But for the best view of the town, clamber up the 200 steps in the tower behind the police station headquarters.

Vaasa is well endowed with museums reflecting the region's life, the most important being the **Pohjanmaan museo**, which covers local history and art (Museokatu 3; tel: 6-325 3800; open daily; entrance free Wed). The **Bragen ulkomuseo** (Hietalahden puisto; tel: 6-312 7166; open Jun–Aug: Tues–Sun; Jun–Aug; entrance fee), an open-air museum, shows how Ostrobothnian farmers lived at the end of the 19th century, and a strong culture is clear in several art museums and three professional theatres. The **Auto-ja Moottorimuseo** (Varastokatu 8, opposite the bus station; tel: 6-317 6271; open daily, May–Aug, 11am–5pm; entrance fee), has a private collection of vintage vehicles all lovingly restored, such as the glossy black 1939 American Pontiac.

This area is also rich in political history. In the Civil War of 1918 the whole area around Vaasa was a "White" stronghold. Nearby **Lapua ❻**, on Road 16 inland from Vaasa, was the birthplace of the anti-Communist Lapua Movement

Map on page 238

Traditional lace-making skills survive in Rauma.

BELOW: enjoying the sea life on the west coast.

which reached its zenith in 1930, when 12,000 people from all over Finland poured into Helsinki on the "Peasants' March", and forced the Finnish Government to ban Communism.

From an adjoining island linked by a causeway, ferries leave on three routes to Sweden, and there is **Wasalandia**, the town's colourful amusement park with the usual range of exciting rides (open May–Aug: daily; Sept–Apr: Sat–Sun; entrance fee). Nearby is an enclosed tropical "water world".

Offshore islands, which necessitate a short ferry crossing, add to the charms of Vaasa, as does the collection of old farm buildings at Stundars, 16 km (10 miles) from the town. North of Vaasa, the flat, farming country recalls parts of Sweden, with the Swedish influence being especially clear in the architecture.

Travelling north

St Birgitta's Church at **Nykarleby (Uusikaarlepyy) ❼**, built in 1708, is one of the most beautiful in Ostrobothnia. Its ceiling paintings are by Daniel Hjulström and Johan Alm, while the windows behind the altar are much more recent, painted by Lennart Segerstråhle in 1940. The 1876 Thelin organ is another prized possession. The town, founded in 1620 by Sweden's great warrior king, Gustav II Adolf, faces a beautiful archipelago.

Nykarleby also has its place in history. On 13 September 1808, a Swedo-Finnish force beat off an attack by a Russian army at the battle of Jutas just outside the town. The event is commemorated by a monument to Major General G. C. von Döbeln and in a poem by J. L. Runeberg, Finland's national poet. After this brief fame, Nykarleby did not develop to the same extent as some other coastal towns (today the population is 8,000). Though a narrow-gauge

BELOW: the fun park at Wasalandia.

railway line opened at the turn of the 20th century, it did little to promote trade and industry and closed in 1916. Today the 55-year-old steam engine *Emma* puffs along on summer weekends.

Pushing further north, **Jakobstad (Pietarsaari)** ❽ takes its Swedish name from a famous military commander, Jacob de la Gardie, and was founded by his widow in the mid-17th century. Much of the town was destroyed in the Russo-Swedish war of the early 18th century. Nevertheless, Jakobstad became the pre-eminent Finnish shipbuilding centre, producing ships that opened new trade routes around the world. In the 18th century, no shipowners were more powerful in the town than the Malms. One of the family was reputedly Finland's richest man, who, on his death, left 6½ million gold marks – a vast fortune in those days. **Malmin talo**, his house, is now a museum (open daily; entrance fee).

One of the town's best known sailing ships *Jakobstads Wapen*, a 1767 galleass, was designed by Fredrik Henrik af Chapman, one of the most famous naval architects of the 18th century. An exact copy of the ship has been completed from original drawings. Jakobstad also has Europe's oldest tobacco factory, its office block surmounted by what is claimed to be Finland's largest clock. In the older part of the town, proud owners have carefully restored some 300 or so wooden houses.

Kokkola

From Pietarsaari to Kokkola, take the attractive route called the "road of seven bridges", which runs from island to island across the archipelago.

Like Nykarleby, **Kokkola (Karleby)** ❾ was founded by King Gustav II Adolf in 1620, and went through the familiar cycle of growth, prosperity, decline

Map on page 238

BELOW:
Finns get their sea
legs early in life.

Fox pelts hanging up to dry in Oulo.

and a second period of expansion from the 1960s with new industries and a new port, established at Ykspihlaja (Yxpila) away from the town centre. Today it has a population of 35,600 of which 20 per cent is Swedish-speaking. One man, Anders Chydenius (1729–1803), had a decisive effect on Kokkola's development. He was a clergyman, Member of Parliament and one of Finland's first exponents of economic liberalism. At that time, the tar which should have brought prosperity to his town and coast had to be sold abroad through Stockholm, the then Sweden-Finland capital, which made most of the profits. Largely due to Chydenius's efforts, Stockholm's monopoly was broken and from 1765, one after another, the towns gained "staple" rights – the all-important freedom to sell and ship tar directly to foreign customers.

Kokkola's Town Hall was designed by C. L. Engel, who has left his mark on so many Finnish towns, but the town's most unusual trophy is in a small building in Englantilainen (the English Park). It relates to a bizarre episode in 1854 during the Crimean War. Beside the "English Boat", an inscription explains the "skirmish of Halkokari": "In 1854 in connection with the Crimean War, the British Fleet conducted raids along the coast of the Gulf of Bothnia. Two English frigates sent nine boats on a raid at Kokkola. Each was equipped with a cannon and a crew of about 30. After one hour's battle the enemy had to retreat. One boat ran ashore and was captured. Nine members of the crew were killed and 22 taken prisoner. In all, English casualties numbered between 100 and 150 men dead and wounded." The port has one of the largest harbours on the Gulf of Bothnia. Behind the old harbour and a beach is a memorial to the battle.

BELOW: the west coast thrives on its fishing industry.

On the 230-km (140-mile) north road between Kokkola and Oulu, there are only two places of any consequence. The sand dunes around the mouth of the river **Kalajoki** ⑩ have made the town of the same name into a holiday area with fishing, bathing and sailing. Further north is **Raahe (Brahestad)** ⑪ which, as its Swedish name implies, was founded by Count Per Brahe in 1649. Shipping used to be its dominant industry, but today it is the Rautaruukki Steelworks, fortunately outside the centre. In summer, guided works tours are popular and there are also summer boat trips around the offshore islands.

Tar city

Oulu ⑫, with a population of more than 110,000, is the largest city in northern Finland. It owes its existence to the Oulu river and King Karl IX of Sweden and its fortunes to tar, essential for wood sailing ships. After excessive Central European tar-burning in the 18th century led to a decline in the coniferous forests, the industry moved to the Baltic. Ostrobothnia was soon one of the most important areas for tar.

Making tar occupied the whole northern area; every village east of Oulu had its smouldering pits, and barrels by the thousand came down to the coast in long narrow boats, some 12 metres (40 ft) long. In 1781, Oulu merchants set up a Tar Exchange and in the 19th century the town was the leading tar exporter in the world. Prosperity ended abruptly in 1901 when the Tar Exchange went up in flames. The demand for tar disappeared with the sailing ships.

You can find old tar pits and tar boats at the **Turkansaaren ulkomuseo** ⑬, over a footbridge to a small island in the Oulujoki (river) 14 km (8 miles) east of Oulu, off Road 22. Established in 1922, this open-air museum has an interesting collection of 19 Ostrobothnian buildings, including a church, farm buildings and windmills. It is well worth a visit (tel: 8-5586 7191; open Jun–Sept: daily: entrance fee).

After the era of tar and sail, Oulu languished in the doldrums but the establishment of a university in the 1960s was a turning point. It attracted hi-tech companies to the area and led to the creation of the Finnish Technical Research Centre. This emphasis on the latest technology has been responsible for one of Oulu's notable attractions, **Tietomaa** (Nahkatehtaankatu 6; tel: 8-5584 1340; open daily; entrance fee), a science centre opened in 1988. The wealth of exhibits is not so much for looking at as for trying out. This hands-on approach appeals to both adults and children alike. Exhibits range from an aircraft simulator to a means of checking on the world's weather and population. In all, Oulu has seven museums, from those concentrating on geology and zoology to the oldest wooden house in the city (1737). The elegant **Oulun Taidemuseo** (Kasarmintie 7; tel: 8-314 3900; open Tues–Sun; entrance fee) has a permanent exhibition of Finnish contemporary art plus temporary exhibitions.

An 1822 fire led to a new city centre and cathedral, designed by Engel. The city also benefits from a number of islands linked by bridges, the Oulu river and some green oases, such as Hupisaaret Park. Visit *Koskikeskus* (Rapids Centre) on the mouth of the River Oulujoki, with 12 fountains and surrounding islands. The island of **Linnansaari** has castle ruins and there are recreational facilities on Raatinsaari and Mustasaari.

Map on page 238

BELOW:
Oulu's Ainola Museum in winter.

Towards Sweden

From Oulu to Kemi on the Swedish frontier, road and railway cross numerous rivers draining into the Gulf of Bothnia and the scenery undergoes a subtle change. This is no longer the west coast but the approach to Lapland.

Kemi ⑭ is called the seaport of Lapland or, rather optimistically, the "Pearl of the Gulf of Bothnia". Largely destroyed in World War II, the town is now a port and industrial centre. The open-air Kemin museo is in Peripuisto Park. The **Kemin Jalokivigalleria** (tel: 9-820 300; open daily; entrance fee) has a collection of 3,000 gemstones and copies of some of Europe's most famous Crown Jewels, including the Crown of the King of Finland – who never reigned. If you are this far north in winter, you can take an excursion (15 Dec–30 Aug: Thur–Sat) on an 1961 icebreaker, *Sampo*, which displays its remarkable power to force its way through ice up to 2 metres (6 ft) thick. You may also visit the annual Lumilinna (Snow Castle), a remarkable icy castle which houses exhibitions, a restaurant and even a few chilly hotel rooms!

Kemi lies at the mouth of the Kemijoki (river) and just on the border a little way north is **Tornio** ⑮, near the mouth of the Tornionjoki. As Tornio (population 23,000) ends, the Swedish town of Haparanda begins and, since its founding in 1621, this border position has made Tornio the scene of much bitter fighting, the last time during World War II.

Fortunately, the town's three major churches have survived and Tornio Church, with its separate bell tower, is one of the most beautiful in Finland. Completed in 1686, it is dedicated to the Swedish Queen Eleonora. Alatornio Church on the outskirts is a vast edifice, the largest in northern Finland and able to hold a congregation of 1,400. It is a splendid example of Jaakko Rijf's

BELOW: a traditional Finnish picnic on the rocky coast.

Map
on page
238

Neo-classical style. Tsar Alexander I ordered the building of an Orthodox Church in 1825. After Finnish Independence in 1917, the building lay empty until 1987 when it was restored, reconsecrated and re-opened to serve the 150 Orthodox Christians who live locally.

The fine **Aineen taidemuseo** (Torikatu 2; tel: 16-432 438; open Tues–Sun; entrance fee) houses the Aine Kuvataide Foundation art collection and an historical museum of western Lapland. On a fine day, the best place to get a view of the town is from the observation platform on top of the water tower.

Golf and fishing

Tornio Golf Club on the Finnish-Swedish border is the oddest in Europe. During a round of 18 holes, you play nine in Sweden and nine in Finland – and there's a one-hour time difference between the two. It opens from 1 June to 31 October, and it is a rare delight to play a night round in summer, thanks to the midnight sun. After the ninth hole in Finland – just after midnight – you will cross the border and continue in Sweden – yesterday!

Furry mascot at Kemi's spectacular Snow Castle.

If you travel 9 miles (15 km) north of Tornio off Road E78, you will come to **Kukkolankoski ⓰**, the longest (3,500 metres/3,830 yards) free-flowing rapids in Finland. At the highest point the fall is 18.8 metres (45 ft). They have been famous for fish since the Middle Ages. Today, as they balance precariously on a crude boardwalk out over the fast-flowing river, fishermen still use the old techinque of a longhandled net. At the nearby Café Myllypirtti freshly grilled and skewered white fish is the main item on the menu, an authentic taste to end the 1,000-km (600-mile) drive north along a coast that has always depended for its living upon sea, ships and river. ❏

BELOW: rocky shores near Kemi.

ENJOYING THE FINNISH SUMMER

Summer is the best time in Finland and those Finns who live abroad always return for the days of endless sun, fresh fruits and warm weather

On Friday afternoons in summer almost all the capital's dwellers leave Helsinki in the weekly rush hour. But once into the heartland of the country, the traffic eventually dissolves as it turns off at intervals on to what seem to outsiders like invisible dirt tracks. Thousands of these roads lead to yet more thousands of summer cottages. Here, Finns live their parallel lives.

LIFE AT THE SUMMER COTTAGE

Daily life at a *mökki* (summer cottage) is a mixture of Bohemian, Chekhovian and certainly Finnish. Families pay visits to relatives and friends; food is eaten and coffee drunk. Days are long and families often eat leisurely meals together, unlike in city homes where everyone is too busy. Cottage gardens yield salad vegetables and new potatoes, but the nearby *kyläkauppa* (village shop) is a steady source of bottled drinks and ready-made food. So important is the influx of summer visitors in small villages that in summer months sales (and population) may triple.

Finns don't stay at the cottage every day: aside from summer sports, such as fishing, cycling, swimming and sailing, summer festivals are always on the agenda *(see page 92).* Every town and village tries the same formula – pick a theme and build a reputation as a "must-do" event.

A summer in Finland is a totally different experience from winter snow; it is Finnish comfortable living at its best.

▷ THE SIMPLE LIFE
A good *mökki* should be rustic, yet equipped with modern amenities. Part of the attraction is the simple life but electricity is needed for appliances.

△ NATURE'S GARDEN
The vast tracts of Finnish forest provide berries and mushrooms for summer cooking, as well as trekking and canoeing adventures.

◁ PARK LIFE
For those who don't escape to the country, the cities' parks provide space to soak up the summer sun.

△ WATER IDYLL
Most of the 188,000 lakes are shallow; water temperatures over 20° C (68° F) are common – ideal for activities.

PAYING FOR A ROOM WITH A VIEW

Most Finns rent rather than own their *mökki* – a lakeside location is preferred but it is not cheap, and buying a nice house near water is impossible for most Finns. The cottages are usually inherited. "If I sold this cottage, I could easily move to a big house in Tampere," says a divorced woman in her late 30s. "But I would never forgive myself for selling this," she says, referring to her lakeside property with two tiny islands.

Less than an hour's drive from big towns such as Tampere, Finns may enjoy unrestricted freedom, with no noise and no pollution. The law requires that no new house is built on the lakeshore, so most cottages are hidden and the lakeview remains unmarred by unscrupulous investors.

However, wealthy urbanites masquerading as jovial countrypeople do not impress the locals – the cultural gap between town and country is widening.

△ **ROW YOUR BOAT**
The simple rowing boat has a variety of uses: leisurely fishing trips that may take half a day, or just for getting from one lakeside to another.

◁ **SUNSET PARTY**
After swimming and saunas, friends cool off on the pier, feeling the evening's breeze blowing, and admiring the colours of the nearly-setting sun.

LAKELAND

Finland's central region of lakes, surrounded by lush pine forests, is perhaps the most immediate image most people have of the country, and a tour of the waterways will not disappoint

Map on page 254

I f you could flood the whole of Scotland and dot it with some 33,000 islands and peninsulas, you would have the equivalent of the Saimaa Lake area alone. Add on the Päijänne system and you could cover Wales as well.

The Great Lakes of Saimaa and Päijänne in Central Finland are among the best known and most popular places to visit in the country and are the target for thousands of visitors who long only to be in, on, or beside them. But people do nothing to make this watery landscape appear crowded because there is so much of it – lakes and lakelets, smooth curving bays with yellow-grey beaches or ragged and broken shores, rushing torrents squeezed between high banks or flooding over hidden rocks, and rivers linking the different waters.

Where the land intervenes, Finnish engineers turned their skills as long ago as the 19th century to building canals to connect the stretches of water. Today, boats big and small can journey the length and breadth of both lake systems, calling at the small, strategically placed towns, where people have lived for centuries, and the even smaller villages, or stopping along the endless lakesides which have never been settled.

Sometimes, the land is flat beside the water or crunched up into ridges where rocks and trees point upwards. This varied landscape owes its beauty to the Ice Age when glaciers carved out the shape of lake and ridges, the most famous being at Punkaharju, an 8-km (5-mile) chain of ridges which winds between the lakes. Far inland, Saimaa has its own resident species of seal, the Saimaa marble seal, whose ancestors were trapped in the lake system long ago when the glaciers cut off the route to the sea.

There are two perfect ways to get to know the Great Lakes: from the water by passenger steamer or smaller craft, or by doing as the Finns do and renting a lakeside cabin, to fish, swim, canoe or simply sunbathe.

PRECEDING PAGES: sunset at Aurinko. **LEFT:** peacefulness in Lakeland. **BELOW:** water-skiing is a popular lake sport.

The Saimaa system

The famous Saimaa waterway was the historic buffer zone between the kingdom of Sweden-Finland and Tsarist Russia, at times changing hands with dizzying frequency. Subsequently it became part of the longest of any western nation's frontier with the Soviet Empire. The effects of these shifting borders are recurring themes as you travel the area.

It would be hard to visualise landscapes more fragmented or more liquid than the Saimaa waterway. A series of large and lesser lakes are linked by rivers, straits and canals, and framed by an amazing complexity of headlands, ridges, bays, islands and skerries, to form Europe's largest inland waterway system. Up to a quarter of the Saimaa region's total area of 70,000 sq. km (27,000 sq. miles) is covered by water.

Saimaa's waters provided natural highways for goods and people long before railways and, especially, roads probed into its remoter reaches. To a large extent, they still do. No lakeside home is without its rowing boat, usually with outboard engine. Tugboats hauling their floating timber trains, up to half a kilometre long, from forest to factory, are common sights.

Embryonic tourism dates from the 19th century as the well-to-do of Tsarist St Petersburg boarded the then new-fangled railway to explore the Grand Duchy of Finland on the neighbouring fringes of their empire. They went to take the waters in the handful of newly created spas, to marvel at such natural wonders as the foaming cascades of Imatra and to hunt and fish in the richly stocked forests and waters.

The best approach is via industrial **Kouvola** ❶, about 140 km (86 miles) northeast of Helsinki and a junction of road and rail routes into Saimaa. Although not the most interesting town in Finland, Kouvola's Kaunisnurmi quarters, formerly a railway staff colony, house quaint handicraft shops and

several museums. Kouvola is also a jumping-off point to the unspoiled lake regions of Iitti and Jaala, northwest of Kouvola. Jaala's UNESCO-listed World Heritage site Verla is a perfectly preserved cardboard factory.

There are much shorter ways to your destination of Kuopio but, to capture the spirit of Saimaa, ignore these and first head east on Road 6. About 80 km (50 miles) on, you reach Lappeenranta, South Karelia's main town.

Map on page 254

Finn-Russian control

Like almost every Finnish community, **Lappeenranta ❷** combines work and play. There is a great deal of industry and some excellent holiday facilities – for most kinds of watersports, for example. Its spa amenities have undergone a recent renaissance too, though their origins lie in the Tsarist 1820s. The town is the southern terminus for Saimaa's venerable lake fleet.

This was historically also a major military town, heavily fortified by the Swedes in the 18th century, only to be rebuilt by the Russians after they destroyed it. The Linnoitus (fortress) is the oldest and most interesting part, where you will find Finland's oldest Orthodox Church (1785), the **Etelä-Karjalan (South Karelian) Museum** (tel: 5-616 2255; open Jun–Aug: daily, Sept–May: Tues–Thur, Sat–Sun; entrance fee), with a fascinating exhibit on the old city of Vyborg, and the **Ratsuväkimuseo (Cavalry) Museum** (tel: 5-616 2255; open daily, summer only; entrance fee), detailing the history and distinctive red uniforms of Finland's proud soldiers. There are also a number of handicrafts workshops and quite a lot of military hardware.

The 19th century re-created in Lappeenranta.

Lappeenranta is only a few miles from the border with its large eastern neighbour; but it was not so in the days when Vyborg (Viipuri) and substantial portions of huge Lake Ladoga formed part of the Grand Duchy and (during its first decades) of the Republic of Finland. It was certainly not so in 1856 when the Saimaa Canal was completed, thus linking Saimaa with the Gulf of Finland through entirely Finnish territory and encouraging the development of a string of inland ports, Lappeenranta among them.

BELOW: a boat is an essential part of life in Lakeland.

Victorian travellers hailed the canal as one of the greatest engineering feats of the 19th century and, soon after leaving Lappeenranta, Road 6 crosses its watery slit or, rather, that of its successor. Post-World War II reparations transferred over half the canal into Soviet domains, after which it lay disused and in growing disrepair until the 1960s. After lengthy negotiations and the privilege of paying for its restoration, the Finns regained use of the canal, which reopened in 1968. It now handles around a million tons of cargo and over 30,000 passengers a year, providing an interesting "side door" into Russia; western visitors need visas except on day cruises from Lappeenranta.

Niagara of Finland

Despite the overwhelming predominance of lake and forest, parts of Saimaa's southern shores are undeniably industrial. Perhaps the most concentrated industrial area of Finland lies a few miles ahead, centred on **Imatra ❸**. This also has some claim as a famed beauty spot, and was described by one early 20th-century British visitor, with shameless exaggeration, as the "Niagara of Finland". Nevertheless, the very fine rapids of **Imatrankoski** were responsible for the presence of the grand old (now much-restored) Imatran Valtionhotelli, built to cater to the sightseers who flocked here, including many distinguished and high-born guests.

It was the eventual taming of the rapids, of course, which triggered off the industrial boom. Happily their full power and splendour can still be seen on certain days in summer; check with the local tourist office for there is no other good reason to linger here.

About 50 km (30 miles) on from Imatra, Road 6 passes within a few hundred metres of the Russian border; multilingual frontier-zone notices and watch towers did not quickly succumb to the best efforts of *glasnost*. Soon after, around Parikkala, the road turns north away from the border. Switching to Road 14, you soon come to one of Finland's best loved beauty spots.

Forests and lakes

Punkaharju ❹ is one of countless ridges bequeathed to Finland by the last Ice Age. In places it is just wide enough to carry the road; elsewhere it widens to carry magnificent pine and birch woods framing the ever-changing permutations of lake and sky, island and skerry, bedrock granite and the "green gold" forests. The light is ever-changing too, to combine all the main elements of essential Finnish scenery.

BELOW: Lappeenranta was a favourite with 19th-century Russians.

In addition to the narrow ridge, the Punkaharju islands include a large research forest (Tutkimuspuisto) and a protected nature reserve, associated with the superb Forestry Museum, Lusto. An architectural achievement in its own right,

Lusto has a complete exhibition on Finland's forests and anything associated with them – design, wilderness trekking, forestry industry and research (tel: 15-345 1030; open May–Sept: daily, Oct–Apr: Tues–Sun; entrance fee). Bicycles may also be hired here.

Tucked away amongst Punkaharju's ridges are well-equipped holiday centres and the **Kesämaa (Summerland) Leisure Centre** for family fun. One attraction in the area that definitely should not be missed is the Art Centre of **Retretti** (tel: 15-644 253; open daily, Jun–Aug: daily; entrance fee). Part of the centre is housed in caverns literally blasted out of the living rock to provide 800 sq. metres (8,600 sq. ft) of exhibition space and an atmospheric underground area. Artificial pools and waterfalls also provide stunning settings for changing exhibitions of Finnish art and design. An underground concert hall can cater for over 1,000 spectators. Olavi Lanu is the sculptor responsible for the striking human and other shapes that populate Retretti's surrounding pinewoods. The annual Retretti art exhibition, featuring four usually quite different, internationally acclaimed artists, is something of a media event in Finland.

In summer, a regular lake steamer sails between Punkaharju/Retretti and Savonlinna: the trip is a delightful mini-odyssey through the islands, taking over two hours compared with a 20-minute spin along the highway. Road travellers, however, should make a short detour on Road 71 to **Kerimäki ❺**, a typically scattered Finnish rural community harbouring the world's largest wooden church, built in 1848 with a congregation capacity of 3,500 people – larger than the town's population – and a 25-metre (82-ft) cupola (tel: 15-578 9111; open daily, Jun–Aug: daiy; entrance free). Classical music concerts are staged here in summer.

Map on page 254

The Imatrankoski rapids are an impressive sight.

BELOW: a boating regatta on the Saimaa system.

Savonlinna is a useful port for backpackers touring the country.

BELOW: Olavinlinna Castle is the dramatic setting for the Savonlinna Opera Festival.

Savonlinna

Savonlinna **6** – the name means "the castle of Savo" – sprawls over a series of interlinked islands. It is the most charming of Finland's main lakeland towns and the best base in Saimaa for making trips. It has the medieval castle of Olavinlinna, as well as spa facilities, excellent lake sports amenities, varied sightseeing and a great deal of culture. Castle and culture combine particularly successfully in the annual International Opera Festival, one of Finland's leading events, which takes place throughout July *(see page 92)*. Tickets for, and accommodation during, the festival should be booked well ahead (tel: 15-476 750; fax: 15-476 7540).

Olavinlinna (open daily; tours obligatory; entrance fee) occupies an islet a short walk from the town centre. With its massive granite walls, ramparts and shooting galleries topped by three great round towers (surviving from the original five), its Knights Hall and grim dungeon, it has everything you might expect from a medieval castle. Originally built by the Danish-born nobleman Erik Axelsson Tott in 1475, it was intended to be a main defence against the Russians, but so frequently did the eastern border shift that Olavinlinna often lay too far from the battlefield.

As an operatic setting the castle is simply splendid, whether it's for *Aïda* in Italian, *Faust* in French or *The Magic Flute* in Finnish. Opera-goers often come in their best finery and most are wisely armed with blankets, for Finnish summer nights are predictably cool. After the performance, with daylight fading at last, Olavinlinna is softly illuminated to provide a memorably romantic backdrop as you stroll back past elegant boutiques and coffee shops in the town, still open and welcoming.

Savonlinna itself developed from a small trading centre by the castle, its growth greatly hampered by wars and fires. The coming of steam and the opening of the Saimaa Canal gave the necessary stimulus, for the town's situation made it a natural junction for lake traffic that in due course spread to the four points of the Saimaa compass.

The days have long gone when the venerable Saimaa fleet was powered by wood-burning engines but, converted to diesel, a number of the attractive double-decked wooden vessels continue to ply Saimaa's waters. One of the sights of Savonlinna is the morning departure and evening return of these romantic vessels to the passenger harbour, right by the open-air market on Kauppatori in the centre of town. Another, near the castle, is the museum ship *Salama*, a steam schooner built in 1874, shipwrecked in 1898 and raised from the lake in 1971. The *Salama* is one of three converted old ships that form the inland navigation section of the **Savonlinnan maakuntamuseo** (**Savonlinna Provincial Museum**), on Riihisaari (tel: 15-571 712; open Jul–Aug: daily, Sept–Jun: Tues–Sun; entrance fee).

The northern route

From Savonlinna to Kuopio by lake steamer is a full day's journey, as opposed to a few hours by road, yet it is only by travelling on the lakes that you can fully experience the scenery: from forest and meadow through reed bed or granite shore, timber-built farms and summer cottages huddled along the lakefronts, to islands emerging suddenly from headlands; and watch the reflections tossed from huge sky to broad lake and back again in endlessly varying light and colour tones.

Map on page 254

BELOW: a cruise boat at Lahti.

The Päämajamuseo preserves General Mannerheim's headquarters as they were during World War II.

BELOW: Finland's summer may be brief, but it is full of wildflowers.

Road travellers have a choice of continuing west from Savonlinna on Roads 14 and 5 to Mikkeli and thence further west still into the Päijänne lake system *(see page 263)*; or staying with Saimaa to its northern limits beyond Kuopio. **Mikkeli** , a provinical capital, is a pleasant market community and also an historic army town. Mannerheim's Headquarters during World War II are now a museum, the **Päämajamuseo** (Päämajakuja 1–3; tel: 15-194 2427; open May–Aug: daily; entrance fee). Exhibits include a copy of London's *Daily Telegraph* from 18 December 1939, with the headline: "Finns smash two Soviet Divisions". Also open in Mikkeli is a wartime Viestikeskus Lokki (**Communications Centre**), located inside the Naisvuori Hill (open mid-May–Aug: daily). In summer, a joint ticket by the name *Kulkulupa* ("access permit") allows access to five local attractions. Some 5 km (3 miles) north of Mikkeli, the **Visulahti Family Leisure Centre** is set in a park populated by life-size model dinosaurs, an automobile exhibition and waxworks.

The recommended way to Kuopio is to leave Road 14 about 35 km (20 miles) west of Savonlinna and follow Road 464 via Rantasalmi, a particularly attractive and watery route. This joins Road 5 a little south of Varkaus. Varkaus itself is industrial (music specialists should note its **Mekaanisen Musiikin Museo** at Pelimanninkatu 8; tel: 17-558 0643 – unique in the Nordic countries), but the little town of **Joroinen** , 15 km (10 miles) to the south, is very typical of a smaller Finnish community. In contrast with its own modernity are the fine old farms and manor houses dotted about these fertile landscapes, some used as settings for the music festival which is arranged here each summer.

Road 5 is the direct way to Kuopio, 75 km (45 miles) north of Varkaus. West of Varkaus along Road 23 the pleasant rural community of Pieksämäki lies on Saimaa's western fringes on another approach route to Päijänne. Northeastwards from Varkaus, Road 23 leads to Joensuu in North Karelia *(see page 271)*, passing close by two major religious houses: the Orthodox monastery of **Valamon luostari** and the Convent of Lintula. On all three counts of history, culture and scenery these merit a visit, a recommended possibility being by special monastery cruises from Kuopio in summer.

The clue to the monastery's history lies in its name. Valamo is the large island on Lake Ladoga on which an Orthodox religious foundation was established in the Middle Ages, attracting a growing number of pilgrims over the centuries, though latterly its fortunes declined. During the Finn-Russian Winter War of 1939–40, the surviving handful of elderly monks was forced to leave and eventually accorded the present site of Uusi ("New") Valamo (tel: 17-570 111), originally an old manor house and outbuildings. One of these outbuildings was adapted as the monks' first place of worship, embellished by the precious 18th-century icons and other sacred objects which they had brought with them.

Valamon luostari has since experienced something of a renaissance. An injection of younger blood ensures its continuance; there is a fine new church completed in 1977, a cafeteria, a wine shop, souvenir shop and a modern hotel to cater for the growing num-

ber of visitors and pilgrims. The **Lintulan luostari** (**Convent of Lintula**) (tel: 17-563 106), a few kilometres away, has a similar but shorter history. The pious inhabitants of both contribute to their upkeep by working the land in these delightful lakeside settings though you may find the rather humbler aspects of Lintula more conducive to spiritual thought.

Map on page 254

Kuopio to Iisalmi

Kuopio ⑩ is a thoroughly nice town and one of Finland's liveliest, with a crowded summer calendar including the International Dance and Music Festival in June *(see page 92)*. Its daily market is one of the most varied outside Helsinki, and hard to miss as it fills most of Kuopio's central *Tori* (Market Place). Here you can try freshly baked *kalakukko* (fish and pork in a rye crust), traditional local fare that is definitely an acquired taste; or in due season you may be tempted by the varied edible fungi or succulent mounds of berries straight from the forests or bogs. There is a smaller market on summer evenings at the passenger harbour (east side of the town).

Like many Finnish country towns that developed in the 18th and 19th centuries, central Kuopio follows the grid-iron pattern, a chessboard of parallel streets more familiar to Americans than Europeans. This was designed to provide plenty of firebreaks between the then predominantly wooden buildings though, alas, it failed in its purpose all too often. Most of those that survived have been replaced by modern buildings but the **Kuopion kortellimuseo**, a few blocks south of the market place (Kirkkokatu 22; tel: 17-182625; open summer: dily, winter: Tues–Sun; entrance fee), preserves a number of original dwellings complete with authentic furniture, warehouses, and even gardens

LEFT: Kuopio's bustling market area.
BELOW: the annual wine festival in Kuopio.

Admiring the lake views from the Puijo Tower.

BELOW:
the daunting ski
jump in Lahti.

dating from the 18th century to the 1930s – a quiet oasis showing how much of small-town Finland used to look.

A little to the east of the market place the **Kuopion museo** at Kauppakatu 23 (tel: 17-182 603; open Sun–Fri; entrance fee) houses excellent regional collections of a cultural and natural history order in a castle-like building that is a typical example of Finnish early 20th-century National Romantic style. Among several famous Finns associated with Kuopio, statesman Johan Vilhelm Snellman worked and married here in the 1840s. The conjugal home at Snellmaninkatu 19 is also a small, but less detailed museum of the period (open May–Aug: dily; entrance free).

On the edge of the town centre, the **Ortodoksinen kirkkomuseo** (Karjalankatu 1; tel: 17-287 2244; open Tue–Sun; entrance fee) is unique in western Europe, housing collections of icons (many from the 18th century, some from the 10th century) and sacred objects brought here from Valamo and Konevitsa in Karelia and a few from Petsamo in the far north, all territories ceded to the Soviet Union. A little further on is Puijo hill topped by **Puijon torni**, over 75 metres (250 ft) high (tel: 17-209 558, open Jun–Jul: daily; entrance fee). The vistas from the tower's viewing platforms and revolving restaurant are beautiful, with lakes and forests merging into purple distances. Try and time your visit for an hour or two before sundown – the colours are out of this world.

By the time you reach **Iisalmi** ⓫, 80 km (50 miles) north of Kuopio on Road 5, you are almost exactly halfway between Helsinki and the Arctic Circle, and you are still – just – in the Saimaa region. Should you launch a canoe from Iisalmi's lake shore, it would be either level paddling or gently downhill all the way to the Gulf of Finland – over 400 km (250 miles) away.

Iisalmi is a pleasant small provincial town, birthplace of writer Juhani Aho in 1861 (the family home is a museum on the outskirts of town), and site of one of Finland's innumerable battles against the Russians (1808; the Finns won this one, even though they were outnumbered seven-to-one).

Evakkokeskus, a Karelian-Orthodox Cultural Centre at Kyllikinkatu 8, displays valuable relics recovered from territory now in Russia, along with 80 models of churches and chapels since destroyed there. You can dine at Kuappi, "the smallest restaurant in the world", or, if it's full, at Olutmestari, the nearby beer hall with an attractive terrace in summer. Iisalmi's Olvi brewery has an excellent brewery museum upstairs.

Map on page 254

The Päijänne system

Päijänne is Finland's longest and deepest lake – 119 km (74 miles) long as the crow flies, though many times that if you follow its wondrously intricate shoreline. At opposite ends of the lake system are two of Finland's more substantial towns, Lahti and Jyväskylä. The watery topography between the two defeated the railway engineers, but they are linked to the west of Päijänne by one of Europe's main highways, E24, and to the east of it by a network of slower more attractive routes. Alternatively in summer there is the leisurely 10½-hour waterborne route.

Further removed from troublesome historical border areas than many regions of Finland, this central district has been subjected less to conflict and change. Tourism also reached it later, though it has made up for it since, capitalising on the lovely well-watered, deeply wooded landscapes. Sports, education, industry and architecture are among its major themes.

BELOW:
Hollola Church.

TIP

Lahti is home to the world's only skiing museum, which includes exhibits on Finnish Olympic medallists and a video about the development of the sport.

BELOW: the popular view of Finland – endless lakes and forests.

Lahti ⑫ lies 103 km (64 miles) north of Helsinki on Road 4 (E75). It straddles part of one of Finland's more distinctive topographical features, the extensive ridge system called Salpausselkä, which is regularly the setting for major world skiing championships. Here, too, is the **Lahden Urheilukeskus**, the town's sports center, with some of Finland's best winter sports facilities including three ski jumps (50-, 70- and 90-metre, open daily for visitors). It is the venue for the annual Finlandia Ski Race and the Ski Games *(see page 315)*.

From the viewing platform on top of the highest ski jump, the town spreads at your feet. Beyond, the gleaming sheets of Vesijärvi (lake) are linked, by the Vääksy Canal a few miles to the north, to the much greater waters of Päijänne. Lahti is a modern place, one of its few older buildings being the Kaupungintalo (Town Hall,1912) designed, as were so many Finnish public buildings of the period, by Eliel Saarinen. Three blocks to the north is the market, a lively morning spot, and two blocks further north, at Kirkkokatu 4, the highly individualistic **Ristinkirkko (Church of the Cross)**, built in 1978 (open daily). This was the last church in Finland designed by Alvar Aalto, powerful in its simplicity and a fine main venue for the Lahti Organ Festival every summer.

The **Lahden Historiallinen museo** in Lahti Manor, an exotic late 19th-century building at Lahdenkatu 4 (tel: 3-814 4536; open daily; entrance fee), has very good regional ethnographical and cultural history collections, as well as unique art and furniture collections. For living history, though, go a few kilometres northwest to the area known as Tiirismaa. Here is south Finland's highest hill (223 metres/730 ft), some of her oldest rocks and the tourist centre of **Messilä** combining an old manor house, crafts centre and Summerland fun park. Sixteen km (10 miles) further on (not actually in Hollola) the 15th-century

greystone Hollola Church has some good wooden sculptures and is among the largest and finest of about 80 churches surviving from that period in Finland. Near it are a good rural museum and some excellent coffee houses.

Map on page 254

Fishing and bird-watching

From Lahti it's only 35 km (21 miles) northeast on Road 5 to the pleasant little town of **Heinola ⑬**, on the way passing Suomen urheiluopisto, the top Finnish Sports Institute at Vierumäki. Taking the popular summer lake route, it is an astonishing – and lovely – 4½ hours by steamer, 3½ hours by hydrofoil. A glance at the map reveals the contortions needed for lake traffic plying this route, first negotiating the Vääksy Canal north into Päijänne, and later squeezing southeast through narrow straits into the wider waters that lead to Heinola.

There are more narrow straits at Heinola, where the scurrying waters of **Jyrängönkoski** (rapids) provide good sport for local canoeists and for fishermen casting for lake and rainbow trout. You can also try for the latter, with rather more likelihood of success, from the teeming tanks of Siltasaari Fishing Centre by the rapids where, for a few Finnmarks, you can rent a rod and have your catch smoked to eat on the spot or take away.

Heinola blossomed into yet another spa town in Tsarist times. There are a number of wooden buildings dating from the turn of the 20th century, including a Chinese pavilion on the ridge-top park, now a restaurant, redolent of a more leisurely age. Not far away, the pond of Kirkkolampi is a focal point of the well-arranged **Kirkkolammen lintutarha** – bird sanctuary and hospital – with four aviaries (open daily, entrance free). The town's main church, an octagonal wooden building from the early 19th century, has a separate bell tower designed by that prolific architect, C.L. Engel.

From Heinola, Road 5 continues northeast to Mikkeli in western Saimaa. From here you could branch north on to Road 4 (E75) for Jyväskylä, but there is a slower and more attractive way. For this, leave Lahti north on Road 24 and after 25 km (15 miles), soon after crossing the Vääksy canal at Asikkala, branch right on to minor Road 314. This soon carries you along the several miles of Pulkkilanharju (ridge), another relic from the last Ice Age which vies with that of Punkaharju for narrowness and magnificence of lake and forest views. You continue by a series of asphalted but lesser roads via Sysmä and Luhanka, twisting along or across the complex succession of headlands, bays, capes and interlinked islands that make up Päijänne's contorted eastern shore. At **Luhanka ⑭**, the Mäkitupalaismuseo (Peltola Cotters Museum) throws light on the unenviable lot of the 19th-century "cotters": smallholders who effectively mortgaged their working lives to wealthy landowners in return for a scrap of land whose lease could be revoked at the owner's will.

To rejoin Road 9 (E63) at Korpilahti for the final leg to Jyväskylä you can now use an enormous bridge across Kärkistensalmi, one of Päijänne's many narrow straits. Road 24, of course, provides a more direct main road link all the way from Lahti to Jyväskylä in 174 km (107 miles). A particular beauty spot inside a

BELOW: Jyväskylä outdoor market.

Map on page 254

One of many Alvar Aalto buildings in Jyväskylä.

BELOW: selling local fish at Jyväskylä.

national park, a little off this route is the long, slender island of **Kelvenne ⑮**, about 60 km (37 miles) north of Lahti, with its lakes, lagoons and curious geological formations. You can reach it from Kullasvuori camping area at Padasjoki. Road 24 also bypasses Jämsä and joins Road 9 to the south of the town, avoiding the industrial district of Jämsänkoski.

Language and architecture

Jyväskylä ⑯ (population: 75,000) has contributed much, as an educational centre, to the country's cultural development: at a time when the Finnish language was still regarded by the Swedish-speaking ruling classes as the "peasants' language", the first Finnish-language secondary school opened here in 1858, and a teachers' training college opened a few years later. It now also has a lively university whose campus is the work of Alvar Aalto. Indeed it was in Jyväskylä that this renowned architect embarked on his career, and there are no fewer than 30 major buildings by him around the area, as well as the **Alvar Aalto museo** (7 Alvar Aallonkatu; tel: 14-624 809; open Tues–Sun; entrance fee) which has exhibits on his architecture and his furniture designs.

As with many Finnish towns whose older buildings have been largely lost, Jyväskylä is predominantly modern and it has a popular congress centre. From the observation platform of the Water Tower on the ridge running through the town you can gaze across it to the lakes. There are sports facilities on the same ridge and even more out at Laajavuori, a winter and summer sports centre on the northwest outskirts of town. Jyväskylä caters for most sports but is internationally best known as the venue for the 1,000 Lakes Rally in August, which draws 400,000 spectators to Finland's premier motor racing event. In June, the Jyväskylä Arts Festival chooses a different theme each year, examining its every aspect in seminars, exhibitions, concerts and theatre performances.

For a glimpse into the region's past, go to the excellent **Keski-Suomen museo** (tel: 14-624 930; open Tues–Sun; entrance fee), next to the Alvar Aalto Museum. Or, with a little more time, head 32 km (20 miles) west on Road 23 to **Petäjävesi** and **Keuruu,** a further 28 km (17 miles). Both have charming 18th-century wooden churches in typical central Finland rural settings – the one in Petäjävesi is listed by UNESCO as a World Heritage site. Road 23 continues west to Virrat at the northern end of the Poet's Way route *(see page 213).*

North of Jyväskylä, Road 4 (E4/75) continues through yet more forested lake-strewn landscapes harbouring a growing scattering of holiday and leisure centres. After 35 km (21 miles) Road 13 forks left to Saarijärvi, focal point of a pleasant holiday area. Just before it, turn south on Road 630, then shortly east to **Summassaari ⑰** where a Stone Age village has been reconstructed. A short distance beyond Saarijärvi in **Kolkanlahti ⑱** is the elegant 19th-century house, now a museum, where Finland's national poet, J. L. Runeberg, worked as a tutor in the 1820s.

Back on Road 4 (E4/75), before long you bypass Äänekoski, of no particular interest, as the highway leads ever northwards towards the Arctic Circle. ❏

Canoeing

One of the more testing annual events on the European canoeing calendar is the Arctic Canoe Race which takes place every summer north of the Arctic Circle from Kilpisjärvi to Tornio along 537 km (334 miles) of the border rivers between Finland and Sweden. Another is the six-day 700-km (430-mile) Finlandia Canoe Relay each June, usually through the complex Saimaa system.

With 187,888 lakes (at the last count) and innumerable rivers to choose from, it's surprising that canoeing has only become popular in Finland in recent years. There is now, however, a growing range of packages whereby you can canoe well-tried routes of varying lengths, the cost based on whether you are part of a group or by yourself, the hire of canoe, paddles, provision of map and/or guide, with the option of camping equipment or farmhouse accommodation.

A particularly well-tried series of routes forms an overall 350-km (217-mile) circuit beginning and ending at Heinola. This needs 10–15 days but can also be fragmented into more manageable two- to five-day sections. Another, along 320 km (200 miles) of the Ounasjoki river in Lapland from Enontekiö to Rovaniemi, features sections of true Arctic wilderness; the rapids are mainly Grade I but it's possible to portage round the most daunting of these. Yet another follows a 285-km (200-mile) lake-and-river route taken by the old tar boats from Kuhmo to Oulu.

If you're attracted to the idea of pioneering across the lakes the possibilities are legion. Any of the 19 road maps which cover the entire country on a scale of 1:200 000 will be sufficient for general planning, but absolutely essential for more detail are the special inland waters charts, for example, for Saimaa on a scale of 1:40 000/1:50 000.

It's not until you are in your canoe, however, that navigation problems become clear. From the low level of a canoe one island of rock and pinewood looks very like another. Across wide expanses of water there are few helpful landmarks. You will then appreciate those other vital aids to canoeing the Finnish lakes: a compass and a pair of binoculars.

The greatest inconvenience – at times amounting to hazard – you are likely to encounter is wind. Squalls can blow up quickly and, across these expanses, waters are soon whipped up into turbulence. Head for shelter at the first sign.

Camping may prove more difficult than you might expect in seemingly empty landscapes. Much of the shoreline is either rocky or fringed by reed beds. Once landed, finding space enough between trees can be a problem even for a small tent and, where a clearing does exist, it has probably been created to accommodate a cottage or farm. The right to pitch your tent anywhere has been abused by some foreigners and is no longer promoted, so seek permission to camp whenever possible.

But, of course, there is often no one to ask. It is one of the joys of canoeing in Finland that you may travel for days without sign of humanity other than a tugboat hauling its train of timber, or a fisherman. ❑

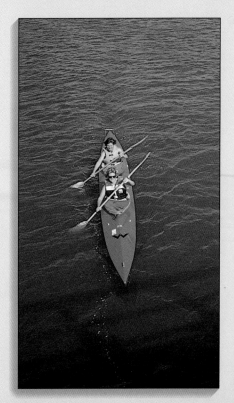

RIGHT: Kayaking the rapids and waters of Finland's lake regions is a popular sport.

KARELIA AND KUUSAMO

The ancient, rural communities of eastern Finland are considered the cultural heartland of the country, the region of myths and legends immortalised in the epic poem, the Kalevala

Map on page 272

Helsinki

Eastern Finland, which stretches broadly to the eastern frontier, is a changeover zone between the great Finnish Lakelands area and Lappi or Lapland. Few people live in this wild territory but the character of Karelia and its distinctive Orthodox churches have charm, tradition and colour.

Finland's most famous and perhaps most photographed scenery stretches below the lofty summit of the Koli Heights above Lake Pielinen, which also has good winter skiing. The "Bard and Border Way" takes the traveller to the frontier sights, including battlegrounds from World War II. Hiking in the wild, shooting the rapids and winter sports are the specialities of this region.

Festival centres

Joensuu ❶ at the mouth of the River Pielisjoki is the "capital" of North Karelia. It has a relaxed and welcoming air, for the majority of the inhabitants are Karelians, people who have a well-earned reputation for good humour and ready wit, traits particularly in evidence at the bustling marketplace.

At the end of June each year, Joensuu plays host to the Festival of Song, centred on the Joensuu Song Bowl, which has a stage large enough for an 11,000-strong choir. The **Pohjois-Karjalan museo** exhibits articles from prehistory, history and the folk culture of this part of Karelia. The museum (tel: 13-610 0670, open daily; entrance fee) is housed in a new tourist centre, Carelicum, opposite the market square at Koskikatu 5, which also has a tourist information office (tel: 13-267 5223), a souvenir shop, a café and other cultural venues. There is also the **Taidemuseo**, (Kirkkokatu 23, tel: 13-267 5388; open Tues–Sun; entrance fee) with an icon collection and Finnish paintings from the 19th and 20th centuries. The **Yliopiston kasviti-eteellinen puutarha** – University Botanical Gardens (Heinäpurontie 70; open Tues–Sun; entrance fee) feature a range of plant species and a butterfly section. In many places in Joensuu, you will find restaurants serving Karelian specialities, such as the Restaurant Puukello, on the island of Ilosaari at the rapids, which offers Karelian roasts and pies with salted fish.

Before turning north, go as far east as you can in Finland to **Ilomantsi ❷**. Take Road 6 south out of Joensuu and then Road 74 east for the 70-km (50-mile) drive. Ilomantsi was the scene of heavy fighting in World War II, and in the village of Hattuvaara to the northeast the **Taistelijan talo (Warrior's House)** marks the spot where fighting ended in 1944. Trips to the easternmost point of Finland (and the EU) are arranged via Hattuvaara. On a more peaceful note, since the 14th century Ilomantsi has also been a stronghold of the Orthodox Church and the main

PRECEDING PAGES: relaxing in the wild. **LEFT:** whitewater rafting at Kainuu. **BELOW:** wild flowers gathered as decoration.

church is dedicated to St Elias. Easter is the most impressive festival, but the area is full of old rites and rituals.

For more light-hearted music and colour, it would be hard to beat the village of **Rääkkylä ❸**, a few miles south of Joensuu on a secondary road along the southern end of Lake Pyhäselkä. Its renowned folk band has won the national championship and many other awards and some of the young musicians play that most Karelian of instruments, the kantele, a stringed instrument similar to a zither.

Shooting the rapids

Heading north from Joensuu, take Route 6 out of the town towards Eno. Where the road divides, take the right fork eastward (Route 73) which leads along the eastern shore of Lake Pielinen to **Lieksa ❹**. The roads through this countryside are tarred and well maintained but they are neither broad highways nor motorways and sometimes seem little different from the minor roads and lanes that lead off into the forest. But usually driving is simple, with main routes numbered and villages signposted.

The **Ruuankoski rapids** are a sight not to be missed from Lieksa. For some 33 km (21 miles) the Ruunaa plunges through six sets of foaming rapids and drops around 15 metres (50 ft) on the way. Equipped with lifejacket and waterproofs, shooting the rapids is safe under the careful supervision of a proficient guide.

Lieksa, one of the many forest centres in Finland, is less than 20 years old and has a population of only 19,000 (and a few bears) in an area larger than London. The **Pielinen museo (Pielinen Outdoor Museum)** has numerous buildings from different ages which document the settlement of the surrounding area – the oldest is from the 17th century (tel: 13-520 2402; open May–Sept: daily; entrance fee). The town's attractive church was built in 1982 by the husband and wife team Raili and Reima Pietilä.

At Vuonisjärvi, 29 km (18 miles) from the centre is **Paateri**, the studio of Eeva Ryynänen, a well-known wood sculptor who has decorated the area with her work, including a spectacular wooden Wilderness church (open late May–early Sept: daily; entrance fee). **Kaksinkantaja**, 38 km (24 miles) from the centre, has an exhibition of bear skulls and stuffed animals by Väinö Heikkinen, a famous bear hunter (open Jun–Aug: daily; entrance fee). Heikkinen, however, only speaks Finnish.

Lieksa may not be the most prepossessing of towns, but it is an important centre for visitors to this part of Finland's wilderness, which stretches as far as the Russian border. Capercaillie, elk, bear, reindeer and even wolves roam these dense pine forests. The best way to get an idea of its sheer size is from the viewing platform of the town's 47-metre (150-ft) tall water tower.

"Never go hiking on your own," is the warning motto of this region, and inexperienced walkers in particular should take guided tours, which can be arranged for individuals or groups. Most walks involve camping and the local shops in Lieksa can provide all the equipment and maps that are needed. Expeditions include the "Bears' Walk" along the Russian border, lake fishing in summer, and ice fishing in winter.

Trout, landlocked salmon (a relic of the Ice Age), coarse fish and bream all swim in these unpolluted waters. Join a guided fishing expedition if you would like to try your hand at catching them. A package will include the services of a guide, transport, accommodation and licences. Otherwise, you can buy a fishing licence from any local post office, or a regional fishing licence from a tourist office. Lieksa's main tourist office is on the town's main street, Pielisentie (tel: 13-520 2400; open daily).

Map on page 272

Exhibits at the Museum of North Karelia, Joensuu.

BELOW: a typical Karelian house.

Karelians

If Finland has a soul, that soul lives in Karelia. When Finns have gone to war, it has concerned Karelia. A Karelian theme runs through most of the music of Sibelius and his *Karelian Suite* reaches sublime heights of elegy and patriotism.

The Karelians were one of the earliest of the Finnish communities. They are evident in Bronze and Iron Age discoveries and their true origins are lost in myth and legend. The *Kalevala*, that great epic saga of ancient life in the far north, is really about the Karelians. This long poem, which in the 18th and 19th centuries became the cornerstone of the struggle for national culture, tells how with magic and sword the northern heroes fought for survival against the powers of evil. It recounts weddings, rituals, bear hunts and journeys into the mysterious Otherworld, and finally the heroes' joy as they celebrate in song the salvation of the land of Kalevala from its enemies. Although the *Kalevala*

depicts a pre-Christian period, the last poem predicts the decline of paganism, with the maid Marjatta giving birth to a son. The son is baptised and becomes king of Karelia.

The Karelians emerge into recorded history as a people living in the area of forest and lakes stretching from the present-day southeastern Finnish-Russian border to the White Sea. The Karelians came under Russian influences, although in no sense did they become russified. Slash and burn was their way of converting the impenetrable woodland into productive fields and they used the ash as a fertiliser. With these techniques came the production of grain and the need to dry it through steam heat, adapted first for grain-drying and then for relaxation. Thus, the sauna was born.

Orthodox religion is also a feature of the Karelian people, although it is accorded the title Greek Orthodox rather than Russian. There are 60,000 adherents and many churches in southeast Finland today. Karelian dialect, however, has almost died out.

The terrible Winter War of 1939–40 was fought to save Karelian land and has become the Finns' great *cause célèbre* but it was only one war out of some 200 which were fought for Finnish Karelia. As a result of the settlement forced on Finland at the end of the Continuation War, some 400,000 Karelians had to be re-settled in the 1940s. The Karelian Isthmus was lost, along with all of East Karelia, now settled by Russians. Since then, people of Karelian origin can be found in all parts of Finland. They tend to be lively and talkative, in contrast to the more taciturn nature of other Finns.

True Karelia today exists only as a fragment of its former self. The border has all but cut it out of the Finnish body politic, its people have dispersed. A line roughly parallel to the border from Lieska down to the Isthmus delineates modern Finnish Karelia. Yet even in this small region something distinctive remains. Perhaps it is their delicious food, or perhaps it is the grandeur of the forest. But the Karelian legacy is more than a lost homeland. Sauna, saga and Sibelius – these are the Karelians' true memorials. ❏

LEFT: Young Karelians generally dress in national costume only for festivals these days.

The national landscape

From Lieksa, the same Road 73 leads to **Nurmes ❺** in about an hour, keeping close to the shores of Lake Pielinen. First mentioned in documents in 1556, Nurmes only became a city as recently as 1974. Nicknamed "the town of the birch", Nurmes sits on a ridge between two lakes at the northern end of the Pielinen lake system; it is a beautiful town, with wooden houses built in authentic early-Karelian style.

Map on page 272

Bomba House is a traditional Karelian house at Ritoniemi, about 2 km (1 mile) from the town, surrounded by a recently built "Karelian village" which provides visitors not only with comfortable accommodation but also with delicious meals of local specialities. Bomba House's menu includes an assortment of local pies, the tiny fish vendace, cold smoked whitefish, warm smoked lamb, hearty meat casseroles, fried wild mushrooms, baked cheese with Arctic bramble jam – all designed to get the taste buds working overtime.

It would be a pity to miss Finland's most gracious way to travel and Nurmes is the place to leave the car and take a leisurely steam boat ride down Lake Pielinen to that famous beauty spot, the hills of **Koli**. The lake scenery is wonderful, and you may meet Finland's largest inland waterway ferry as well as numerous other boats, big and small.

Traditional Bomba House in Numes, a typical Karelian village.

The Koli Hills rise halfway down the western side of the lake, the highest **Ukko-Koli (Old Man Koli) ❻**, reaching 347 metres (1,100 ft). Scramble up to the top (there are steps) and spread out below you is a view that has inspired some of the greatest artists, including Albert Edelfelt and Eero Järnefelt, whose paintings immortalised Koli around the turn of the 20th century and did much to stimulate the national awakening of the time *(see page 77)*. Sibelius, too, wove the Koli Hills into his symphonies and, looking down, it is not hard to understand why this countryside is always called Finland's "national landscape". The legend goes that Sibelius loved the area so much that he had a grand piano carried to the top of this hill to celebrate his marriage.

BELOW: salmon leaping upstream.

The wilderness way north

Finland's wilderness way north has three of the country's glories – sauna, salmon and scenery, the last embodied in its national parks although not confined to them. You will meet these three great assets at almost every turn in Finland but never so frequently and in such abundance as in the region that starts north of Nurmes, roughly along the line of the Oulu waterway – lake and river – that almost bisects Finland, and stretches north to Rovaniemi and Lapland proper *(see page 287)*.

To many however, the biggest attraction of this area are the traditional saunas. There is purportedly one sauna for every four people in Finland and visitors will find them everywhere – in hotels, private homes, on board ships, at motels, holiday villages and forest camps. Every Finn is proud of the sauna, the one word which the Finnish language has offered to the rest of the world, and nothing better complements the end of a long northern day in the open air to refresh and revitalise body and soul *(see page 190)*.

On the stove or in the stream there is only one really classic fish in this area and that is the Atlantic salmon. Though Finland has no sea border with the Atlantic, thanks to the Ice Age, this region, like others, retains an Atlantic legacy in the salmon that swim in the large natural landlocked lakes and in the smaller stocked waters.

National parks are protected areas where nature is left as untouched as possible but some amenities are provided for visitors; marked trails, camp sites, and cabins are set in the larger parks, with hotel accommodation just outside the parks proper. With so much unspoiled territory, it may hardly seem necessary for Finland to designate national parks but it has 25, some of the best along this wilderness way north.

From the east of the country, the natural way in to the area is from Nurmes on Road 75 to Kuhmo, or via Road 6 north, either turning right on to Road 76 just before Sotkamo to reach Kuhmo or continuing left on Road 6 for Kajaani on Oulujärvi (lake) to the west. From the west coast the natural route would be from Oulu *(see page 244)* along the waterway connecting the Oulu river, lake, Kajaani and Kuhmo.

A natural world

Even before you reach the Oulu area, if your choice is Road 6 north you might like to detour to the remote national park, **Tiilikkajärven Kansallispuisto ❼**, near Rautavaara. After Valtimo, some 25 km (16 miles) north of Nurmes, turn left on to Road 5850 towards Rautavaara, and some 50 km (32 miles) on you come to the park. It was established to conserve the uninhabited area of Lake Tiilikka and the surrounding bogs.

BELOW: Orthodox Archbishop Paavali blesses the opening of Bomba House near Nurmes.

Map on page 272

Another national park, the **Hiidenporttin Kansallispuisto** ❽ is southeast of Sotkamo and best reached also from Road 6. Turn right off Road 6 onto Road 5824, and some 25km (16 miles) on you come to the park on the left. This is a rugged area, with the narrow Hiidenportti Gorge, a large rift valley with rock sides dropping some 20 metres (70 ft) to the floor of the gorge. Both the park and the neighbouring Peurajärvi hiking and fishing area have designated trails, marked with orange paint, and camp sites. At Peurajärvi, permits are sold that allow anglers to catch one salmon each. Though you could wriggle through a complicated series of minor roads on the Sotkamo route from here, unless you are feeling adventurous, it is probably easier to go back to Road 18.

The Kuhmo region is famous for its herds of rare forest reindeer, some 500 of which roam the forests in winter.

Both in and outside the parks, the further north you go, the more likely you are to find reindeer. These semi-domesticated animals are the main source of income for many people living in these parts and it is very important to take special care on roads when reindeer are around.

The Finnish frontier

Kuhmo ❾ is a frontier town surrounded by dense forests in the wilderness area of Kainuu. The largest municipal area in Finland, it covers 5,458 sq. km (2,100 sq. miles). Close to the Russian border and remote and empty though the area is, Kuhmo has established an international reputation through the annual Kuhmo Chamber Music Festival, first held in 1970 *(see page 92)*. Fifty km (30 miles) east in Saunajärvi is the Winter War Memorial marking Finland's desperate 100-day struggle in 1940 against overwhelming odds. Travel agents in Kuhmo arrange trips across the border to Russian Karelian villages, but visas are required and take at least 10 days to arrange.

BELOW: the lynx is one of the wild animals that lives in the Karelian forests.

At one time this whole area was devoted to making tar, by a lengthy process of cutting, leaving and then burning forest trees to extract the sticky liquid that formed the basic ingredient. Once it was in barrels, peasants loaded their small boats for the slow journey down through lake and river to the port of Oulu where, in a rare symbiosis, shipbuilders bought it for their own craft and entrepreneurs shipped it abroad. In the 19th century Finland was the biggest exporter of tar in the world.

A fascinating recreated **Kalevala Village** in a wooded park on the outskirts of Kuhmo displays numerous local folk traditions (tel: 8-655 4500; open Jun–Aug: daily; entrance fee). The aim is to give modern-day visitors some idea of Finnish culture as it was immortalised by the folklorist Elias Lönnrot and artists such as Akseli Gallén-Kallela. The result is a "living" demonstration of the daily culture of ancient times as portrayed in Finland's epic poem, the *Kalevala (see page 95)*.

The village also serves as the scene for numerous events based on other folk literature, including plays, celebrations and performances by theatre groups. Guided tours teach visitors about primitive hunting and fishing skills and how tar was made in the Finnish wilds. The village has models of ingenious traps to catch birds and animals, including bears, and examples of how the old fishing families and peasants lived. The large Hotel Kalevala serves a tasty buffet lunch during the holiday season (tel: 8-655 4100).

North of Kuhmo, near the village of Lentiira is Lentiiran Lomakyla, one of the most welcoming and comfortable holiday village chalet complexes by the lake. With a wood-fired sauna and cold beer included, this must surely be Finnish tourist hospitality at its very best (tel: 8-650 141).

BELOW: Karelia abounds with berries in summer, such as these bilberries.

AKSELI GALLÉN-KALLELA

Akseli Gallén-Kallela (1865–1931) is considered by many to be Finland's national artist. After studying at the Finnish Society of Fine Arts, Kallela made his debut in the 1880s to popular acclaim, with his realistic images of everyday Finns. Between 1884–8 Kallela lived in Paris and painted images of Parisian bohemian life, but he was soon to be drawn back to his native country. Kallela had become fascinated with Elias Löhnrot's epic collection of poetry, the *Kalevala* and wanted to capture in paint its mythical heroes. Returning to Finland, Kallela devoted his time to researching themes from the *Kalevala.* In 1890 he married Mary Slöör and they honeymooned in Eastern Finland and Karelia, the regions of the folk poems. The *Kalevala* paintings were to become the best-known of Kallela's works. From 1911–15 he was the chairman of the Finnish Artist Society and from 1919–31 he was the vice chairman of the Kalevala Society. However, Kallela was also a keen traveller. In 1909–10 the family lived in East Africa (present-day Kenya), and Kallela painted some 150 works, and gathered collections of ethnographic and zoological material. In the 1920s, they lived in the United States for three years, during which time Kallela created studies for the *Great Kalevala*, sadly unfinished.

Political past

A long straight road through some of Finland's darkest forests leads west out of Kuhmo to Sotkamo and then onwards to **Kajaani** ❿, the area's main town, on the eastern edge of Oulujärvi (lake) and once the collecting point for barrels of tar ready for their journey to the coast.

Kajaani was founded in 1651 by the Swedish governor-general Count Per Brahe in the shelter of an existing fortress designed as a bastion against Russia. But in 1716, the fortress fell and the whole town was razed during the disastrous war between Sweden and Russia. The town still has the ruins of the 1604 castle. The Town Hall is yet another designed by the well-travelled German architect, C. L. Engel, who was responsible for so much of early Helsinki *(see page 162)*. The old tar boat canal and the lock keeper's house by the river Kajaani are still visible. Famous residents have included Elias Lönnrot, who at one time lived in Kajaani, and the town is also known as the home of Finland's longest-serving president, Urho Kekkonen.

The Tsar's Stable in **Paltaniemi** ⓫ is a relic of a visit by Tsar Alexander I. Also in Paltaniemi is the birthplace of the poet Eino Leino, and the city has a Cultural and Congress Centre. Heading some 20 km (12 miles) from the centre, Ruuhijarvi Wilderness Village has peaceful fishing grounds and old hunting lodges which are open all year.

The road from Kajaani to Oulu hugs the shores of Lake Oulu, plunging first into thickly wooded hill country. Before entering Oulu, the route goes through Muhos which has the second-oldest church in Finland, dating from 1634. Oulu continues the tradition of tar making and the Lakelands town still lights tar pits on midsummer's eve.

Map on page 272

As the landscape becomes more Arctic, so, too, does the wildlife.

BELOW: tundra takes over the landscape near the Arctic Circle.

Map on page 272

Distances are long in this scantily populated area where Finns come to walk and fish and look at nature. The only other main centre, Kuusamo, almost at the Russian border, is some 360 km (225 miles) northeast across the breadth of the country along Road 20. Before Kuusamo, if you feel like a detour, turn left at Pudasjärvi and take Road 78 for 90 km (55 miles) to **Ranua ⑫**, which claims the world's northernmost zoo. Next to it is a piece of Santa Claus nonsense called the Murrr-Murrr-Linna (Castle) and featuring Santa's animal workshop.

Rushing water and wind

Kuusamo is marvellous wilderness country, with tundra as far as you can see in any direction, forest, racing rivers with water foaming through gorges and canyons, some bare, others a dense dark green. The main sound in these parts is a mixture of rushing water and wind high in the pines. There are dozens of rapids, some suitable for canoeing, others for fishing. The Oulanka-joki and Iijoki (rivers) are excellent for family canoeing trips, but the Kitka-joki calls for experienced canoeists only.

There are literally thousands of excellent fishing spots in both rivers and lakes. The "Russian" brown trout rise in the rivers from Lake Paanajärvi in greater numbers each year thanks to efficient tending of the fishing grounds. This is also berry country, with blueberries, raspberries, lingonberries and cloudberries all growing in great profusion on the Arctic tundra. The only snag is the number of mosquitoes: they multiply rapidly in the northern summer so take plenty of protection.

In both summer and winter, this vast unspoiled area is given over to recreation. In the middle, Karhuntassu Tourist Centre has been specially built to provide information on every activity, accommodation and most other aspects of the region, and there are other more distant centres. In winter, the area is excellent for skiing and the skidoo or snowmobile comes into its own. Snowmobiling is both an exhilarating and a practical way to get around this snowbound landscape, though many consider this modern convenience outweighed by its noise and fumes.

There are two national parks near here. The largest, **Oulangan Kansallispuisto ⑬**, to the north stretches over an largely untouched region of 270 sq. km (105 sq. miles), bordering the Oulanka river. It is a landscape of ravines and rushing torrents, sandbanks and flowering meadows. Karhunkierros, the most famous walking route in Finland, stretches some 100 km (60 miles) through the Oulanka canyon to the **Rukatunturi Fells ⑭**. A few kilometres will give the flavour of the trail but to cover the whole route, staying at camp sites or forest cabins en route, takes several days. In winter the area is given over to winter sports with some 28 ski pistes. A smaller national park, Riisitunturi, lies to the northeast of Oulanka, another untouched wilderness of spruce dominated by hills and bogs.

Almost imperceptibly on the way north, the landscape and culture have changed from the traditions of Karelia to the ancient ways of the Sami people. From here on, without doubt the land is Lappi. ❑

BELOW:
hunting and fishing are two sports often combined.

Hunting

The great bull elk of Finland, standing 1.8 metres (6 ft) high at the shoulder, gazes through the northern forest. Crowned by massive horns, this elk is not the sluggish, lumbering giant it looks. Silent as night, wary, elusive, fast and with highly developed senses, this titan of the tundra and one time co-habitant of the dinosaur tests man's hunting skills to the utmost.

The justification for shooting elk is the paramount need to protect both food and the young timber that is so important to Finland's economy. The elk breeds so well in modern Finland that an annual cull of around 50,000 animals is necessary. But while a hunter is justified, he is no pest controller. Justification is one thing; motivation is another. It is the thrill of the chase that brings the elk hunter with his .300 calibre rifle and his pack of dogs to the forest in October for the short elk-hunting season.

Sub-Arctic tundra make pursuit of the elk arduous and competitive, modern arms notwithstanding. The trees are dense, the cover is thick; trained dogs aid the hunter in his quest. An elk is big enough to disregard a dog. Sometimes the elk will take off, but not out of fear. A dog can hold an elk at bay simply because it is disinclined to move.

If the quarry moves, the dogs will hunt it mute by scent. The signal for the hunter who is following is the renewed barking of the dog, for this means the elk is standing still and the approach can begin. Now comes the most critical part of the day, for if an elk is tolerant of a dog, it is most decidedly intolerant of man. The ground is covered in material which, to quote an old advertising slogan, "snaps, crackles and pops". The hunter must proceed with light footsteps, and may have to crawl on his belly for the final approach. It is sudden movement that attracts attention and a day's effort may be ruined by one false move.

If culling is the justification behind elk hunting, it is also the *raison d'être* for wolf hunting. Wolves still prowl the border area of Finland and Russia. Once in Finland, wolves kill domestic reindeer, protected by a close season in the east and in the south protected year round.

Hunting wolves is a difficult affair but Finnish hunters use an ingenious method of encirclement, also found in other parts of Eastern Europe. From large spools strapped to their backs, the men lay a line of string with red flashes through the woods. It can take up to two days to set the lines but some curious instinct tells a wolf not to cross them; it's the opposite of a red rag to a bull. The helpers then drive the wolves to where the hunters are waiting. The guns now have some advantage, though the cunning and speed of wolves saves them from the bullet and only a few wolves are shot each year.

You can make hunting tours with guides in several parts of Finland, with elk hunting – lasting three or four days – the most popular. Hunting usually means living in a hut or cabin, invariably clean and bright. After many hours in the open, nothing could be better than the ritual of the sauna to give a sense of total well-being. ❑

RIGHT: Waiting for prey requires patience, skill and silence.

LAPLAND

Map on page 286

Synonymous with Christmas and bleak Arctic landscapes, it comes as a surprise to many visitors that Lapland is also a thriving region of agricultural and fishing communities

Helsinki

Two main roads bore their way northwards through the province of Lapland (Lappi). Road 4, sometimes called the Arctic Road, links Kemi with Rovaniemi before continuing northeastwards through ever more sparsely inhabited landscapes to cross into Norway at Utsjoki. The other is Road 21 (E78) which follows the Tornio Valley upstream from Tornio, continuing beside various tributaries that form the border with Sweden, eventually to cross into Norway near Kilpisjärvi. This is the river route of the Arctic Canoe Race and the road that accompanies it is also sometimes known as the "Way of the Four Winds", after the four points of the Sami traditional male headgear. Bridges and ferries provide links with Sweden.

Arctic landscape

Respectively the two routes cover 540 km (336 miles) and 457 km (284 miles). Either will show you superficially a great deal of Arctic countryside, but from neither will you glean anything but the faintest hint of what Lapland is all about. For that you must leave the main roads – preferably the minor ones too – and set out on foot or in a canoe or, in winter, a pair of skis. It's not even necessary to go very far for there are silent spaces to be found within a few hundred yards of the most modern hotel, which seem barely to have been touched since the last Ice Age, but of course the experience deepens with distance and duration. The vital need for proper clothing and equipment, however, can't be over-stressed: climatic changes occur with ferocious suddenness and, for all its magnificence, the Arctic wilderness can be a ruthless place.

As you progress northwards the trees become spindlier, the forests sparser, the habitations fewer, the hills more numerous and gradually higher until you reach the sweeping undulations of the bare-topped fells of northern and northwestern Lapland. Beyond the tree line vegetation crouches and crawls – dwarf juniper and willow and miniature birch clinging to the fellsides among the mosses and the lichens, the miniscule campions and tiny saxifrages. In summer take plenty of mosquito repellent; every paradise must have its serpent.

In 1944 the German army followed a scorched-earth policy as it retreated north into Norway, so any old buildings that survive are mostly away from the main roads. But despite the monumental changes wrought on the province by the second half of the 20th century *(see page 127)* at least some elements of an age-old way of life endure. One notable village that has managed to escape destruction and modern development is Suvanto, north of Kemijärvi, not far from Pelkosenniemi.

PRECEDING PAGES: reindeer herds. **LEFT:** spectators at Inari's reindeer races. **BELOW:** winter golf at Rovaniemi.

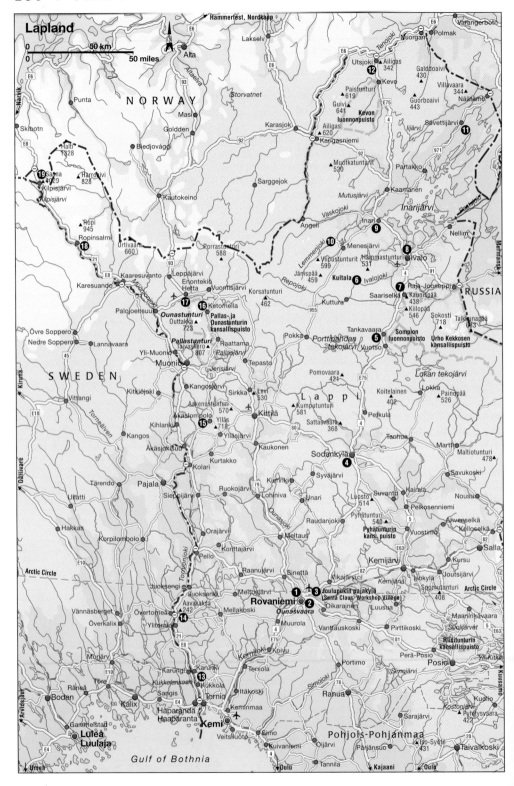

Map on page 286

Rovaniemi

From Kemi, Road 4 follows the valley of the Kemijoki in which a rash of timber-based industries has spawned a succession of communities. You reach **Rovaniemi ❶** within 115 km (70 miles). This, the administrative capital of Lapland, all but nudges the Arctic Circle and is the launching point for most trips into the province. The town, well placed at the confluence of the Ounasjoki and Kemijoki rivers, has been completely rebuilt since World War II, almost quadrupling its population (now about 34,500) in the process. In early summer timber is still floated down the Ounasjoki from the forests of central Lapland.

The reconstruction plan for Rovaniemi was made by Alvar Aalto who also designed the fine Lappia Hall complex on Hallituskatu, containing the Provincial Museum, a theatre and congress facilities and, next to it, the Library. The odd-looking **Arktikum House** (The Arctic Centre), half-buried underground and thus offering a sensation of Midnight Sun through the glass ceiling, has exhibits illustrating Arctic history and culture (tel: 16-317 840; summer: daily, winter: Tues–Sun;entrance fee).

Sami textiles reflect their lifestyles, such as their dependence on reindeer.

Also in the Arktikum building, the Provincial Museum gives a good introduction to Lapland's flora and fauna, Sami traditions and Rovaniemi's history, but you'll get a better feel of bygone living from the 19th-century farm buildings at the **Pöykkölä Museum**, by the Kemi river 3 km (2 miles) to the south on Road 78 (tel: 60-181 095; open Jun–Aug: daily; entrance fee). **Rovaniemi Art Museum** (Lapinkävijäntie 4; tel: 60-322 2822; open Tues–Sun; entrance free) has a collection of modern Finnish art. Not far from Lappia Hall the main Lutheran Church has a modern altar fresco, *The Source of Life*, by Lennart Segerstråle.

Rising up from the confluence of the Ounasjoki and Kemijoki are the wooded slopes of **Ounasvaara ❷**, now a well-developed skiing area and site of annual international winter games. It's also a favourite gathering place on Midsummer Night.

BELOW: when roads are few, locals take to the water.

Land of Santa Claus

Eight km (5 miles) from the town on Road 4, soon after the turn-off for Rovaniemi airport, **Joulupukin Pajakylä (Santa Claus' Workshop Village) ❸** straddles the Arctic Circle (Napapiiri). Its post office annually handles thousands of letters from children worldwide, and there are some good shops, a puppet theatre, art exhibitions, a glass factory, a few reindeer and, of course, Santa Claus *(see page 138)*.

Santa Park (tel: 016-333 0000; open Dec, Jun–Aug: daily, Jan–May, Sept–Nov: Sat–Sun; entrance fee) was recently opened in a man-made cave inside the Syväsenvaara Hill some 2 km (1 mile) south of the Arctic Circle. A miniature train takes visitors to the site, which was planned in co-operation with British theme park designers, and provides various fun rides for children.

A number of fell areas east of Road 4 in southern Lapland have been developed for winter and summer tourism. One of the best is centred on Pyhätunturi, about 135 km (84 miles) northeast of Rovaniemi. Another just north of it, is Luostotunturi, south of

For staying in
Saariselkä, contact the
Tourist Office at
Honkapolku 3,
(tel: 16-668 400;
fax: 16-668 405) or try
the Saariselkä Fell
Hotel, with fine rooms
and excellent Lappish
cuisine (tel: 16-68
111; fax: 16-668 771).

BELOW: snow
sculpture is a
popular pastime.

Sodankylä. At the **Scandic Hotel**, Luosto (tel: 16-624 400; fax: 16-624 410) you can stay overnight in a cosy log cabin with an Arctic-style built-in bed and blazing fire. Popular hiking and skiing routes span between these two centres.

You will have noticed the landscapes – predominantly forested – becoming progressively emptier. However, there are reindeer aplenty and the occasional elk, so do drive slowly; keep your eyes open and your camera handy – they say white reindeer bring good luck.

Sodankylä ❹, 130 km (80 miles) from Rovaniemi, is the first substantial place along this route, a long established community reputed to be the coldest in Finland. It is the home of the Midnight Sun Film Festival held each June. Next to its 19th-century stone church, its wooden predecessor is Lapland's oldest church, dating from 1689. Road 5 comes into Sodankylä from the southeast and minor roads wander off east and west to link tiny scattered communities.

Gold country

Northwards, there's little to detain you for the next 60 (100 km) miles or so until, a few miles beyond Vuotso, you reach **Tankavaara** ❺. Gold panning has been practised in various parts of Lapland for well over a century, and at Tankavaara there is an entertaining Kultakyla (Gold Village, tel: 16-626 158; fax: 16-626 261); its Kultamuseo (Gold Prospectors' Museum) not only chronicles man's historical endeavours to find gold, but for a modest fee gives tuition and allows you to pan for gold yourself for an hour, a day, even several days, in an authentic wilderness setting. At nearby **Kultala** ❻ (*kulta* is Finnish for gold) in trackless wilderness to the northwest, on the banks of the Ivalojoki, you can also see an 1870 goldwashing station.

About 40 km (25 miles) further north there is a great deal more self-catering accommodation, together with modern hotels, spas and sports facilities, centred on Laanila and **Saariselkä** ❼, an immensely popular winter sports centre among the élite of Helsinki's business life. Saariselkä's landscape marks a difference, scattered about the forests and slopes of a huge area of primeval fell towards the Russian border. It is an excellent area for skiing, and has plenty of wilderness huts. Much of this region is designated as a national park named after Urho Kekkonen, Finland's longest-serving president.

Ivalo and Inari

In another 23 km (14 miles) you pass the turn-off for Ivalo airport, Finland's northernmost. **Ivalo** ❽ itself straggles along the east bank of the Ivalojoki. It's the largest community in northern Lapland, with all the usual facilities, though in terms of Sami culture it is much less important than Inari. There is, however, an attractive little wooden Orthodox church tucked away in the woods, serving the Skolt Sami, a branch of the Sami people who formerly lived in territory ceded to the Soviet Union in 1944. They have different costumes, language and traditions to Finnish Sami, and some now breed sheep rather than, or as well as, reindeer. A number of Skolt Sami families live in Nellim, about 45 km (29 miles) northeast of Ivalo towards the Russian border.

Ivalo's Lutheran Church stands near the bridge which carries Road 4 over the Ivalojoki; then it's a further 39 km (27 miles) to **Inari** ❾ – much of it a delightful route along parts of the contorted shores of Lake Inari. Inari village is an excellent base for wilderness exploration; you can lodge at the traditional Hotel Inarin Kultahovi (tel: 16-671 221). Though smaller and rather more scat-

Map on page 286

Thick animal skin boots protect against the snow and ice.

BELOW: the colours of summer in Lapland.

tered than Ivalo, this is nevertheless the administrative centre for a vast if sparsely populated area, and a traditional meeting place for colourfully costumed Sami people for weddings and other festivities, especially during the church festivals of Lady Day and Easter.

Focus of many Sami festivities is the simple modern church near the lake shore. **Lake Inari** is Finland's third largest, covering 1,300 sq. km (808 sq. miles) and is dotted with about 3,000 islands, some of them considered sacred according to Sami tradition. It is a wild, lonely beautiful lake, the theme of numerous haunting songs and many legends. Boat trips and sightseeing flights are available during the summer to the holy Ukko island, particularly revered by the local Sami).

Inari's excellent **Saamelaismuseo (Siida Lappish Museum)** (tel: 16-665 212; open summer: daily, winter: Tues–Sun;; entrance fee) comprises a new museum building and an open-air section (*skansen*) with old buildings and equipment illustrating the traditionally nomadic way of life. There are also some exhibits on early Skolt Sami culture and modern Sami life. The Siida building also houses the Ylä-Lapin luontokeskus (Nature Centre for Upper Lapland), which sells fishing permits and assists in hiking plans for those wishing to explore the wilderness. From the museum a marked trail covering a return journey of some 15 km (9 miles) leads to a remote 18th-century wooden church at Pielppajärvi, one of Lapland's oldest surviving buildings. It's a beautiful spot that is also accessible by boat.

Be sure, however, to leave enough time for shopping at Inari's many fine handicraft shops that include a silversmith's shop and the acclaimed studio of knife-maker Petteri Laiti.

BELOW: drying reindeer meat.

SLEDGING

The easiest way to get across Lapland's vast, icy and largely flat landscape has always been on skis or sledges; the latter less exhausting for longer distances. There are many different types of sledging, but the most popular and readily associated with northern Finland is the dog sledge. Four or six husky dogs, hardy beasts naturally acclimatised to snow and ice, are harnessed to the front of a sledge, with passengers standing on the back runners. Unlike horses, the huskies are not readily controllable, so keeping the sledge stationary or stopping the sledge is done with a hook wedged deep in the snow. Once the hook is withdrawn, the dogs lurch forward.

Reindeer sledging, as epitomised by images of Santa and his sleigh each Christmas, is another method of getting around, with the advantage that these animals can cover longer and more snowy distances, although they journey slower than the dogs.

Many centres in Lapland now offer the chance of sledging excursions for tourists – contact tourist information offices in main towns for more details. It is essential that the right equipment is worn: thermals, waterproofs, hats and goggles are necessary to combat the dampness and icy bitterness of the snow.

Towards Norway

The minor Road 955 from Inari leads 40 km (25 miles) southwest to **Menesjärvi**, a Sami settlement from which one can continue by road then river boat or on foot up the wild and beautiful **Lemmenjoki Valley** ("river of love") to a remote gold prospectors' camp. The extensive national park area, though less isolated than it once was, is still a very lonely area of rocky canyons and primeval forest where you are wise to hire a guide. From Menesjärvi, Road 955 continues across Lapland to join Road 79 at Kittilä.

Around Inari and north of it, the road passes a number of attractive holiday centres, mostly of the self-catering variety. After 26 km (16 miles) you come to Kaamanen from which a minor road branches northeast 100 km (60 miles) to **Sevettijärvi** ⑪, the modern main settlement for the Skolt Sami. An interesting time to visit is during the Easter Orthodox festival. While there, visit the Sami graveyard, with its unusual turf-covered graves. Just a couple of kilometres north of Kaamanen you have a choice: to go north by minor road to Utsjoki, 94 km (58 miles) away on the border with Norway; or bear northwest along Road 4 to the Norwegian border 41 miles (66 km) away at Karigasniemi.

Either way, the landscapes get hillier, wilder and emptier. You will also pass the coniferous tree line, beyond which only the hardier dwarf birch survive on the lower fell slopes, their gnarled and weathered forms looking curiously biblical in this barren Arctic countryside.

The more beautiful route is the minor one to Utsjoki, passing a series of lakes close to the eastern fringes of the Kevo Nature Park, where Turku University runs an experimental station. **Utsjoki** ⑫ is an important Sami community – good for fishing and hiking – close to Finland's northernmost point. Its church

Hiking on the fells requires proper clothing and equipment but the scenery makes it worthwhile.

BELOW: northern flat bread has a distinctive taste.

(1860) is one of the few pre-World War II churches still standing in Lapland. The village and road follow the Utsjoki downstream to join with the Tenojoki, a famed salmon river.

Both Utsjoki and Karigasniemi are dominated by "holy" fells called *Ailigas*, the one dominating Karigasniemi reaching over 620 metres (2,000 ft). From these border points you can also join the Norwegian road system for a variety of routes eventually returning into western Lapland at Kilpisjärvi or Enontekiö.

Western Lapland

Your route through western Lapland is likely to begin at Tornio about 80 km (50 miles) south of the Arctic Circle *(see page 246)*. The earlier stretches of the Way of the Four Winds or Road 21 (E78) present a very different face of Lapland from the Arctic Road, for the lower section of the Tornio valley is much more populated, and served by Finland's northernmost railway branch to Kolari.

In its southern stages the road passes through a string of small communities mainly based, in these marginally milder and more fertile conditions, on agriculture and dairy farming. The Tornionjoki is also a good salmon river; at **Kukkola ⓭** look out for the Kukkolankoski rapids. About 70 km (43 miles) north of Tornio, beyond Ylitornio, is the 242-metre-high (794-ft) **Aavasaksa Hill ⓮**, the most southerly point from which the midnight sun can be seen, attracting considerable throngs for Midsummer Eve festivities. A few miles nearer Juoksenki, you cross the Arctic Circle. The scenery now gets wilder as you pass between Pello and Kolari. A little south of the latter Tornionjoki is replaced by a tributary, the Muonionjoki, at the Fenno-Swedish border.

BELOW: reindeer on the hoof.

Fell country

About 10 km (7 miles) north of Kolari a worthwhile detour by minor Road 940 to the right leads to **Akäslompolo** . This well-equipped tourist resort and skiing centre is scattered about the shores of a small lake set amongst magnificent forested hills and bare-topped fells; the highest is Ylläs, at 718 metres (2,355 ft), served by chair lifts. A marked trail follows the chain of fells stretching northwards from here, eventually leading in about 150 km (90 miles) to the Pallastunturi fell group. It's a glorious trail if you come properly equipped, with overnight shelter available in untended wilderness huts – these are even marked on the 1:200 000 road maps.

From Akäslompolo you can continue north along minor roads and in 31 km (19 miles) turn left on to Road 79. This is the main road from Rovaniemi, providing an alternative approach to western Lapland. After a further 10km (7 miles) Road 957 to the right is highly recommended as the best approach to Enontekiö. A further branch left off this route leads from Road 79 to the lonely hotel complex of Pallastunturi, magnificently cradled in the lap of five of the 14 fells which make up the Pallastunturi group (the highest being Taivaskero at 807 metres/2,647 ft).

From here the choice of fell walks includes the long-distance 60-km (37-mile) trail north from Yllästunturi across the fells to Enontekiö. Road 957 brings you to the upper Ounasjoki valley via the small community of Raattama to **Ketomella** where there's a car ferry across the river. Until fairly recent times this part of the valley was accessible only on foot or by boat or sledge, so a number of venerable farm buildings have survived, highly photogenic as they lean, tipsy with age. Along the entire route you get lovely views of first the

Map on page 286

Signposts won't let you forget quite how far north you've travelled.

BELOW: sparkling meltwaters at Windelhed.

Map on page 286

Pallas, then the Ounas fells. At the junction at Peltovuoma you turn west for Enontekiö and, eventually, Palojoensuu, back on Road 21.

Enontekiö

Enontekiö **17**, sometimes known as Hetta, is the attractively sited administrative centre of this extensive but sparsely populated area. The village sprawls along the northern shore of Ounasjärvi (lake), looking across to the great rounded shoulders of the Ounastunturi fells – the highest of which is Outtakka at 723 metres (2,372 ft). Once completely isolated, now it's accessible by air and road from all directions, with a road link north into Norway.

Most of Enontekiö's buildings are modern, including the pretty wooden church which has an altar mosaic depicting Sami people and reindeer. There's a good range of accommodation available, from camp sites to top-class hotels, all set up for the avid fishermen, hikers and canoeists for whom this makes an excellent holiday centre. It's also a main centre for the Sami of western Lapland, most of whom live in lone farmsteads or tiny communities in and around the area. Here, too, there are major traditional Sami gatherings at certain times of the year (see page 107).

From Palojoensuu, Road 21 continues northwest along the Muonionjoki and Könkämäeno valleys, the scenery becoming ever wilder and more barren. A little north of Kaaresuvanto you cross the coniferous tree line and pass the last of the spindly pines. At Järämä, 10 km (6 miles) further from the tiny settlement of Markkina, German soldiers built fortifications during a standstill in the Lapland War of 1944. Many of these bunkers have been restored and are now open to the public.

BELOW: if you are wrapped up warm enough, snow can be great fun.
RIGHT: snow skis are the most practical form of travel.

Lakes and mountains

A little south and north of **Ropinsalmi 18** there are good views respectively of Pättikkäkoski and Saukkokoski, two of the more testing rapids of the Arctic Canoe Race. The mountains reach ever greater heights; the highest, Halti, soars up to 1,328 metres (4,357 ft) on the Norwegian border at Finland's northwesternmost point.

More accessible and distinctive is **Saana 19**, 1,029 metres (3,376 ft) above the village and the resort of Kilpisjärvi. Kilpisjärvi is an excellent launching pad for wilderness enthusiasts. There is a lake of the same name whose western shore forms the border with Sweden, and a marked trail which takes about a day leads to the boundary stone marking the triple junction of Finland-Sweden-Norway. The Mallan luonnenpuisto, a nature reserve to the north of the lake requires a permit for entry, but once you are within it there is a pleasant 15-km (9-mile) trek.

The rest of these immense, empty, rugged, acres are as free to all comers as the elements – and as unpredictable. Never set off without proper equipment and provisions and, unless you are experienced in such landscapes, a guide; always inform someone where you are heading and when you expect to return. Simple advice, but it cannot be said often enough. ❏

INSIGHT GUIDES

Travel Tips

Insight Guides portray destinations in depth, providing the complete picture and the top photography

Insight Pocket Guides *focus on the best choices for places to see and things to do and include large fold-out maps*

Insight Compact Guides' portability makes them the perfect books to carry with you for on-the-spot reference

Three types of guide for all types of travel

INSIGHT GUIDES Different people need different kinds of information. Some want *background information* to help them prepare for the trip. Others seek *personal recommendations* from someone who knows the destination well. And others look for *compactly presented data* for on-the-spot reference. With three carefully designed series, Insight Guides offer readers the perfect choice. Insight Guides will turn your visit into an experience.

The world's largest collection of visual travel guides

CONTENTS

Getting Acquainted

The Place

Area: 338,000 sq km (130,500 sq miles).
Capital: Helsinki.
Population: 5 million.
Language: 93 per cent of the population speak Finnish; six per cent Swedish and one per cent other languages, including Sami.
Religion: Largely Evangelical Lutheran, with one per cent Finnish Orthodox and 12 per cent unaffiliated.
Time zone: Greenwich Mean Time (GMT) + 2 hours; Eastern Standard Time (EST) + 7 hours.
Currency: *markka* (Finnmark/FIM).
Weights and measures: metric.
Electricity: 220 AC (two-pin plug).
International dialling code: 358.

Geography

Finland is set on the Baltic Sea between Sweden to the west and Russia to the east. A tiny arm of Norway is flung over the top of Finland to join with Russia. About one-third of Finland's land mass is above the Arctic Circle, which defines the area known as Lapland, or Lappi.

Finland is 65 per cent covered by forest, 10 per cent by lakes, and 8 per cent by cultivated land (17 per cent conurbations, industrial use, etc.). The last Ice Age left a great deal of flat land but, towards the north, glaciers pushed ridged mountains into the landscape, creating the famous rolling hills or *tunturi* of Lapland. The highest peak is Haltiatunturi, at just over 1,400 metres (4,000 ft) above sea level. The lakes are concentrated in south central Finland.

Economy

Finland is a country that had modest agricultural and textile trades before the end of World War II. A few older companies founded in the 19th century, such as the family-owned Ahlstrom Oy, which began as metalworks and has now diversified into the paper and boiler industries, have survived into the 20th century.

Finland's obligation to pay war damages to the Soviet Union after World War II gave it the impetus to develop its modern industry because it was able to pay off much of its debt in manufactured goods. Pulp and paper products and machinery, the forestry industry, and a few electronics and engineering giants, such as Nokia mobile telephones and Neste oil refining, are now the lords of Finnish industry.

The rest of the economy is made up of service industries and agriculture. Although Finnish farmers are still very protected when it comes to government subsidies and over-production payments, farming is rapidly losing its appeal with the younger generations and, as a result, just 10 per cent of the population is now involved in the farming industry.

Government

Finland is a parliamentary democracy, with a president, a prime minister, and a 200-member, single-chamber parliament. The president is elected directly, while the prime minister is chosen by a conference of parties participating in the current government.

Coalition governments led by Social Democrats have dominated Finland's short history as an independent republic. In 1994 Martti Ahtisaari, a social democrat, was elected President for a six-year term. The unusual coalition government, consisting of Social Democrats, the conservative Kokoomus, the Greens, the Left-Wing Alliance and the Swedish People's Party, was formed after the 1995 election, and the same parties continued to rule the country after the 1999 election.

The Swedish-speaking Aland Islands, off the west coast, have an MP in the national Parliament (*Eduskunta*) in Helsinki. However the Alands are semi-autonomous, following a post-World War I League of Nations ruling, so have their own Parliament (*Landsting*), which administers regional matters.

There are 461 Finnish municipalities. The municipalities look after social services and welfare, as well as education.

People

Finland is the sixth largest land area in Europe. The population is sparse, however, with only 16 inhabitants per sq km (6 people per sq mile); in total there are five million inhabitants, about 40 per cent of whom live in rural areas. Approximately one million Finns live in greater Helsinki. The other cities' populations are sparse, however. There are approximately 100,000 foreign residents living in Finland.

Etiquette

In general Finns are courteous, particularly to foreign guests. However, they do not squeak "Sorry!" any time they brush past you on the street, not even if they tread on your toes. This is because the Finns have failed to come up with a normal word for "Sorry" or "Excuse Me". For graver offences or extreme politeness, there is the word *Anteeksi*, but for minor offences, a simple "Oops" is usually enough.

If you are going to a Finn's house for dinner, bringing a plant or flowers for the host or hostess and, if you plan to drink, a bottle of wine, is the norm. However, if you bring spirits to a casual gathering, it is not considered rude to bring an already opened bottle. This is in homage to the very high cost of alcohol in Finland.

Planning the Trip

Passports and Visas

Citizens of most western countries do not need visas to travel to Finland; a valid passport will suffice. EU citizens may enter with a valid ID card. The Nordic countries only stamp you in once for a three-month tourist stay, so if you arrive via, say Sweden, you won't need to be stamped at the Finnish border.

It is difficult for non-EU citizens to work in Finland; if you want to work, though, contact a Finnish Embassy or Consulate outside Finland well before you go. An employer's letter is usually needed in advance of the work permit being granted.

Customs

The following items are permitted to be brought into Finland.

Cigarettes/tobacco

Non-EU citizens over 16 years of age may bring in 200 cigarettes or 250 gm (½ lb) of tobacco products duty free. Europeans aged 16 or over can bring in 200 cigarettes or 250 gm (½ lb) tobacco products.

Alcohol

Any visitor aged 20 or over can bring in 15 litres of beer, 2 litres of other mild alcohol (drinks containing not more than 22 per cent by volume of ethyl alcohol) and 1 litre of strong alcohol (spirits). For visitors 18–19 years of age, the quantity limit is the same, but must not include strong alcohol.

In addition, visitors can bring in up to 1,100 markkas worth of gifts or items intended for one's own use. Food stuffs are limited to no more than 2.5 kg (around 5 lbs) of butter and 15 kg (33 lbs) of other foods; no more than one third of this may be edible fats.

Animal Quarantine

Pets vaccinated against rabies are in most cases allowed into Finland (pets must have been vaccinated at least 30 days and less than 12 months before entry). Be sure to double check these requirements and your vaccination certificates if bringing your pet is crucial because Finland is sometimes rabies-free, sometimes not, and these rules change from year to year.

Money

Finland's unit of currency is the markka (Finnmark or FIM), always referred to as a "mark". There are 100 pennies (p) in the markka. These include 10p, 50p, 1 FIM, 5 FIM and 10 FIM coins. Notes are available in 20, 50, 100, 500 and 1000 FIM denominations. Notes issued before 1980 and coins of 1, 2 and 20 pennies, will be changed only at Finland's bank offices until 31 December 2003. By then, Finland will have adopted the euro-denomination bank notes and coins, and any markka currency may be exchanged into euros at Finland's banks. There is no limit to how much foreign currency you bring in to Finland.

Shops and businesses operate a rounding-off system; if the cash register rings up 50 markkas and 74 pennies, for example, you pay 50 markkas and 70 pennies. If it rings up 50 markkas, 76 pennies, you pay 50 markkas, 80 pennies.

Credit Cards and Travellers' Cheques

Credit cards are very widely accepted in Finland; MasterCard/ Access, VISA, Diner's Club and American Express are accepted in all but the most humble establishments.

Traveller's cheques and common currencies can be exchanged easily in banks. Most Automatic Teller

Public Holidays

- New Year's Day (1 Jan)
- Epiphany (6 Jan)
- Good Friday (Mar/Apr – variable)
- Easter Day (Mar/Apr – variable)
- May Day Eve (30 April)
- May Day (1 May)
- Ascension Day (May)
- Whitsun (late May or early June)
- Midsummer (21–22 Jun)
- All Saints' Day (late Oct)
- Independence Day (6 Dec)
- Christmas Eve (24 Dec)
- Christmas Day (25 Dec)
- Boxing Day (26 Dec)

Machines (ATMs) will give local currency if your bank card has an international pin code (VISA, Cirrus, PLUS, MasterCard etc.).

What to Bring

The best advice on packing for Finland is to bring layers of clothes, no matter what the season. While it is famous for frigid winters – when gloves, long underwear, hats, woollen tights and socks, and several layers of cotton topped by wool and something waterproof are recommended – Finland is less known for its very sunny temperate summers.

In winter, bring heavy-duty footgear not only to keep out damp but to avoid the heartbreak of good shoes ruined by salt and gravel put down to melt the ice on the pavements. Spring and autumn are rainy, and summers are usually pleasantly dry and sunny, but occasionally wet.

Getting There

By Air

Finnair is the national carrier of Finland and operates international and national routes. Both Finnair and British Airways connect London and Helsinki with daily flights. Finnair (and many other airlines, including Lufthansa) fly direct between Helsinki and most

European capitals, and Finnair also links with several North American cities including New York. You may be able to find value-for-money package fares and charter flights from New York or London, but they are rare; watch newspaper advertisements for offers.

From Helsinki, Finnair and Air Botnia also fly numerous domestic routes to more than 20 cities, including several to North Finland airports, and have cross-country flights between some of them.

By Sea

The best routes to Finland by boat are from Sweden and Germany. **Silja Line** and **Viking Line** have daily routes between Stockholm and Helsinki. These ferries are luxurious with restaurants, saunas, swimming pools, tax-free shops and children's playrooms. Silja's refurbished Finn-jet boat makes the trip in summer to and from Germany in 24 hours.

It's less expensive to travel by ferry from Stockholm to Turku or Naantali in western Finland and then overland to Helsinki rather than by direct ship to Helsinki. Viking provides very cheap train or bus tickets for the overland trip; the ferry ticket is also cheaper as the voyage is shorter. One can also travel to Finland's Åland islands by boat from Stockholm or Turku – Viking has a daily service to Marie-hamn. Silja runs services between Vaasa and Sweden's Umeå but this service does not have tax-free sales so it may discontinue in future.

Silja Line
Tel: (0)9 18041.
Viking Line
Tel: (0)9 012 351/ (0)1942 262662 (UK).

By Rail

It's a long haul to Finland from just about anywhere by rail, because you inevitably finish the long rail trip north with a 15-hour journey by boat and train from Stockholm to Helsinki. From Britain, the handiest route is Sealink from Harwich to the Hook of Holland, overland to Copenhagen, then connecting train to Stockholm and boat/boat and train to Helsinki. Total travel time is about 45 hours. This is cheaper than an Apex flight only if you get a special fare rail ticket; residents of Nordic countries now qualify for Interrail tickets regardless of age.

Rail travel to north Finland requires completion by bus as Finnish rail lines only run as far as Rovaniemi and Kemijärvi (in winter to Kolari).

Disabled Travellers

For disabled people, travelling should not pose tremendous problems in Finland. Most newer buildings have access for disabled people, both in terms of ramps and lifts. Check the Finland Hotel guide which indicates by symbols which hotels have access and facilities for disabled people. With careful planning transport should also go smoothly; when ordering a taxi, specify your needs (wheelchair is "*pyörätuoli*"). Public transport may be a bit more problematic, although some city buses "kneel", making it easier to board. If you have queries related to disabled travel in Finland, contact:

Rullaten ry
Pajutie 7C 02770 Espoo
Tel: (0)9-805 7393
Fax: 855 2470.

There are agencies specialising in holidays for the disabled and one travel agency in Helsinki arranges a major tour, on request. The 7-day historical/architectural/cultural "Triangle Tour" of the three major cities (Helsinki, Tampere, Turku). It can be organised by contacting
Area Travel
Kaisaniemenkatu 13
00100 Helsinki
Tel: (0)9-818 383.

Travelling with Children

Overall, Finland is a family- and child-orientated society, and hence one that is generally safe for children. Public conveniences usually include baby changing areas and most restaurants can provide high chairs. Children are almost always accepted in all hotels. In Helsinki, the Tourist Board can provide a list of qualified child-minders.

Sailing around the Baltic

Visas have usually been required for travel to the former Soviet Union though, in the light of events, this may change. You can get visas in Finland from Finnish travel agents but it is safer to allow 10 working days for processing. Most western nationalities may enter Estonia, Latvia and Lithuania without a visa, and daytrips to Tallinn (Estonia) are extremely popular and recommended. There may be over 20 departures on an average summer day, so discounts are not unusual. Tickets are available at harbours on Katajanokka, Olympia-laituri and Länsisatama, Helsinki.

Kristina Cruises
Tel: (0)5-218 1011
Fax: (0)5-214 624)
Sell a summer St Petersburg trip, lasting three to four days, with lodging on board and guides for the city. Passengers without visas may go on this trip but, once in St Petersburg, they must remain with the guided tours.

For information on sea or other options for travel to the former Soviet Union, contact:
Kilroy Travels
Tel: 0171 680 7811
Fax: 0171 602 917.

More colour for the world.

HDCplus. New perspectives in colour photography.

Probably the <u>most important</u> TRAVEL TIP you will ever receive

Before you travel abroad, make sure that you and your family are protected from diseases that can cause serious health problems.

For instance, you can pick up *hepatitis A* which infects 10 million people worldwide every year (it's not just a disease of poorer countries) simply through consuming contaminated food or water!

What's more, in many countries if you have an accident needing medical treatment, or even dental treatment, you could also be at risk of infection from *hepatitis B* which is 100 times more infectious than AIDS, and can lead to liver cancer.

The good news is, you can be protected by vaccination against these and other serious diseases, such as *typhoid, meningitis* and *yellow fever*.

Travel safely! Check with your doctor at least 8 weeks before you go, to discover whether or not you need protection.

Consult your doctor before you go... not when you return!

SB
SmithKline Beecham
VACCINES

Produced as a service to public health

Practical Tips

Business Hours

In larger cities, stores are generally open from 9am–5pm, with late-night opening on Thursdays. In Helsinki, many shops now open until 9pm on weekdays and until 6pm on Saturday. Larger foodstores will usually be open 9am–8pm weekdays and 9am–4pm on Saturday. The only really late-opening places are in the tunnel under the Helsinki railway station, open weekdays 10am–10pm and weekends noon–10pm.

Larger shopping outlets, such as Stockmann's department store and the shops in the Forum shopping mall diagonally across from it on Mannerheimintie, Helsinki, are open weekdays 9am–8pm, Saturdays 9am–5pm.

Banking hours are 9.15am–4.15pm Mon–Fri. Some exchange bureaux open later, particularly at travel points such as the airport and major harbours, as well as on international ferries.

Media

Newspapers and Books

No one has yet been able to come up with a good explanation as to why papers published on the Continent cannot arrive in Finland on their day of publication. But, with the exception of the *International Herald Tribune*, which arrives on the afternoon of its publication date, you'll have to wait a day-and-a-half for British newspapers to get to Helsinki. The papers are sold at Helsinki railway station, in at least two bookstores (Suomalainen Kirjakauppa at Aleksanterinkatu 23, and Akateeminen Kirjakauppa at Pohjoisesplanadi 39, where you can also get books in English) and at the larger hotels in other cities, as well as at main airports.

Radio and Television

For news in English, you can tune in once a day to 103.7 FM in Helsinki. Transmission time changes with the season; ask the Tourist Board for an updated schedule or dial **Radio Finland** (tel: (0)9-1480-4321) for up-to-date information. You can also get information on broadcasts in other parts of Finland. You can also get news in English by dialling 040 in Helsinki. Many hotels subscribe to British or US cable news networks.

Postal Services

Post offices are open 9am–5pm. Services include stamps, registered mail and *poste restante*. The *poste restante* address is Manner-heimintie 11, 00100 Helsinki. It's on the railway square side of the post office and is open Mon–Sat 8am–1pm, Sun 11am–10pm.

When post offices are closed, there are stamp machines outside and in the railway station. Insert the necessary coin and you get the equivalent in stamps. The machines are orange and mounted on the walls, as are the post boxes.

Telephones

The Finnish telephone system is being overhauled and existing area codes are gradually changing. Callers from outside Finland should dial the international code, then the country code followed by the area code, omitting the initial zero (0).

The best way to call overseas cheaply is at the post and telegraph office in a main city. Look for the "*Lennätin*" section, which is for telecommunications. To make a regular direct call at Lennätin, use any booth with a green light and pay the cashier after your call. You must dial 00 to get a line outside of Finland, then the country code and number (for example, 00 44 for the UK; 00 1 for US numbers). If you want to reach an operator in your own country to make a reverse charge call, ask for the Finland Direct pamphlet, which lists the numbers. For the UK operator, dial (9)800 1 0440, US (9)800 1 0010/ATT. Dial 020222 for overseas call assistance from a Finnish (English-speaking) operator. The front of the white pages telephone directory also has directions for foreigners.

Don't forget that hotels usually add surcharges for telephone calls made from your room.

Mobile phones

Finland is a nation of mobile phone users. The most typical mobile phone system is GSM900, which covers practically all Finland. Roaming services are available with most existing operators around the world. US mobile phone operators do not use GSM at all, so to use your phone in Finland, the chip has to be removed and replaced with a GSM chip – enquire at your local phone store for more information. The two Finnish operators are **Radiolinja** (numbers starting with 050) and **Sonera** (040). A GSM1800 system is currently expanding, and may soon be available in major towns.

Doing Business

Doing business in Finland does not differ greatly from doing business elsewhere in Europe, with a few exceptions.

Business Hours: Everything is done earlier. Lunch is earlier (as early as 11am, with 1pm the outside limit), and many offices operate from 8am–4pm as opposed to 9am–5pm; in summer offices often close as early as 3pm.

Business Style: There is a marked lack of bombast. Finns tend not to dress anything up, but rather present things as they are, warts and all. In other words, they are terribly honest, and do not go in much for exaggeration of any kind, whether it relates to a person or a business deal. Hence, their way of selling things might seem a bit sub-dued compared to other countries.

Business Entertaining: You are as likely to be invited on a ski outing or sailboat ride as on a night out on the town. These days, Finns tend not to drink at lunch, but after hours drinking is still *de rigueur*, and as people on business accounts are about the only ones who can afford long spells of drinking, if you get an invitation, enjoy it while you can.

Business Etiquette: It is ill-advised to be late at business meetings; Finns tend to be very punctual and courteous, though quite formal. Handshakes are good for meeting business as well as casual acquaintances; most people here have business cards, and all have mobile phones, which they are delighted to use, so do not be put off by the fact that office hours seem short; there is almost always a cellular phone link to the person in question.

Holidays: Finally, try to avoid business in July and early August. The Finnish summer is short and sacred, and you'll find some offices nearly deserted of staff at these times. (Conversely, this is a good time for tourists, to whom hotels offer bargains to compensate for the lost business trade.) Other blackout periods are the spring skiing break in late February (Southern Finland) or early March (Northern Finland) plus two weeks at Christmas, and a week at Easter.

Health

You'll have little to worry about healthwise in Finland. However, you may have an uncomfortable time if you coincide with the mosquito season, which descends on the northern and central parts of the country in July and into August. Enquire in Finland about the most effective mosquito repellants from chemists, who know their own brand of insect best.

If you need medical treatment in Finland, it is generally free or dispensed at a nominal charge (100 markkas is the usual charge at most outpatient clinics, 140 markkas per day for a stay in a hospital ward). Almost any *Terveysasema* (health clinic) or *Sairaala* (hospital) will treat you;

you can also schedule regular appointments at a *Terveysasema* (listed as such in telephone directories). The Emergency section is generally called *Ensiapu*.

Visitors needing hospital care in Helsinki should contact:

Meilahti Hospital, Haartmaninkatu 4, Helsinki, tel: (0)9-4711 (for surgery and medicine);

Helsinki University Hospitals' Töölö Hospital, Topeliuksenkatu 5, tel: (0)9-4711 (orthopaedics specialists). In other cities, consult hotels for hospital emergency numbers.

A pharmacy is called *Apteekki*, and charges for prescriptions, but not outrageously. There is usually at least one pharmacy open in larger towns on a late-night basis. In Helsinki, the Apeekki at Mannerheimintie 96 is open 24 hours; tel: 02032 0200 for around-the-clock on-call numbers.

Emergency numbers

National emergency number: 112
Police: 10022
Helsinki House-Call Doctors: 0400-414 350
Emergency dental services: 736 166

Tourist Information

Finland has over 50 main tourist information offices, marked with an "i" for information. Summer tourist offices spring up along harbours and lakes where need dictates.

All-Finland information is available from the **Finnish Tourist Board**. In Helsinki, you can book hotels through the Hotel Booking Centre at Asema-aukio 3, 00100 Helsinki, tel: (0)9-2288 1400; fax: (0)9-2288 1499. A full listing of all tourist offices can be obtained at the Helsinki and Rovaniemi offices.

Tourist publications

Useful publications in Helsinki include *Helsinki Happens*, an English-language guide to cultural and tourist events, free from the tourist office and most hotels; *City*, a weekly newspaper featuring a

Main Tourist Offices

Finnish Tourist Board
Eteläesplanadi 4, 00130 Helsinki, tel: (0)9-4176 9300, fax: 4176 9301; postal address: PO Box 249, 00130 Helsinki.

Helsinki City Tourist Office
Pohjoisesplanadi 19, 00100 Helsinki, tel: (0)9-169 3757; fax: 169 3839.

Rovaniemi Tourist Information
Koskikatu 7, 96200 Rovaniemi, tel: (0)16-346 270; fax: (0)16-342 4650.

Tampere City Tourist Office
Verkatehtaankatu 2, FIN-33101 Tampere; tel: (0)3-3146 6800, fax: (0)3-3146 6463.

Turku City Tourist Office
Aurakatu 4, 20100 Turku, tel: (0)2-262 7444; fax 233 6488.

calendar of cultural events and restaurant listings; *Helsinki This Week* and brochures put out by the Tourist Board.

In the rest of the country, use local tourist offices.

Security & Crime

Vandalism is the only noticeable sign of crime in this safe country. Occasional pickpocketing is known on the Helsinki metro and main railway stations; it appears that alcoholics, on the hunt for money for their next drinking bout, are often the perpetrators. Be on your guard in these places.

Religious Services

The Lutheran Church is the state church of Finland, with over 90 per cent of Finns counted as Lutherans. There is a small Greek Orthodox population, and just two Catholic churches in Finland.

In Helsinki, services in English are held at the Temppeliaukio church, the church in the rock on Lutherinkatu (*see page 172*); there are both Lutheran and ecumenical services here. There is also one synagogue and one mosque in Helsinki, for those of Jewish or Muslim faith.

When you're
bitten by the travel bug,
make sure you're protected.

Check into a British Airways Travel Clinic.

British Airways Travel Clinics provide travellers with:
- A complete vaccination service and essential travel health-care items
- Up-dated travel health information and advice

Call **01276 685040** for details of your nearest Travel Clinic.

**BRITISH AIRWAYS
TRAVEL CLINICS**

New Insight Maps

Maps in Insight Guides are tailored to complement the text. But when you're on the road you sometimes need the big picture that only a large-scale map can provide. This new range of durable Insight Fleximaps has been designed to meet just that need.

Detailed, clear cartography

makes the comprehensive route and city maps easy to follow, highlights all the major tourist sites and provides valuable motoring information plus a full index.

Informative and easy to use

with additional text and photographs covering a destination's top 10 essential sites, plus useful addresses, facts about the destination and handy tips on getting around.

Laminated finish

allows you to mark your route on the map using a non-permanent marker pen, and wipe it off. It makes the maps more durable and easier to fold than traditional maps.

The first titles

cover many popular destinations. They include Algarve, Amsterdam, Bangkok, California, Cyprus, Dominican Republic, Florence, Hong Kong, Ireland, London, Mallorca, Paris, Prague, Rome, San Francisco, Sydney, Thailand, Tuscany, USA Southwest, Venice, and Vienna.

INSIGHT GUIDES

The world's largest collection of visual travel guides

Getting Around

On Arrival

Finland's main international airport, Helsinki-Vantaa, is connected by Finnair bus and local bus to Helsinki; fares are usually a little more on the Finnair bus. There is also a "shared" taxi stand at the airport; with a reasonable fare available to any destination in the centre of the city.

Public Transport

By Air

Finnair and Air Botnia both operate domestic flight services. Fares are relatively inexpensive; in July, fares are very cheap. It is a good idea to fly if, for example, you want to get to Lapland from the south without spending days on the road.

The Finnair Holiday Pass costs about US$500 and is good for up to 10 flights in 30 days; it's not valid on "Blue Flights", usually the most popular business travel times. The pass is available to any foreign resident who flies to Finland, and can be obtained from Finnair and some travel agents in Britain and the US; check with the Finnish Tourist Board nearest you. Finnair Holiday Youth Passes, to which roughly the same conditions apply, cost around US$250.

Also available are discounts for groups, families and senior citizens.

By Rail

The Finnish rail network is limited, but service is adequate in most cases and very good between major points like Turku and Helsinki. Finnrail passes are available for 3-day, 5-day, and 10-day periods; first-class passes also available. In

summer, a special *Loma-Lippu* (Holiday Ticket) is available for about 800 mk (7 travel days in a month) or about 400 mk (three travel days). One may start a "day" the previous day after 7pm, and continue during one "day" as far as the train goes if the departure time is before midnight.

For more information, contact:

Finnish State Railways
Vilhonkatu 13
PB 488, 00101 Helsinki
Tel: (0)9-7071
Fax: 707 4290.

Water Transport

Ferries and passenger boats in Finland play a strong role where international destinations are concerned (*see page 180*) but there are some lakeland ferry routes worth pursuing. There are the **Silverline** and **Poet's Way**, which begin in Tampere and cover much of the western lakelands, tours in the **Päijänne** region and over Finland's largest lake, **Saimaa**, in eastern Finland. Many other operators run trips on the lakes; for more information, contact the central or regional tourist boards (*see page 302*).

Helsinki's only real commuter

island is Suomenlinna, with ferries travelling back and forth roughly every half-hour (schedule depends on season). Most of these ferries are part of the public transport network of Helsinki. Other Helsinki islands closer to the coast are connected by road.

Silverline and Poet's Way
Tel: (0)3-2124 803
Lake Päijänne Cruises
Tel: (0)14-618 885
Roll Risteilyt
Tel: (0)17-262 6744)

Bus and Coach

Finland is greatly dependent on buses for transporting the bulk of its passenger traffic. There are coach services on 90 per cent of Finland's public roads (40,000 long-distance departures a day) which also cover the areas that trains don't, particularly in the north and in smaller places throughout the country. The head office for long-distance bus traffic is **Matkahuolto**, Lauttasaarentie 8, 00200 Helsinki, tel: (0)9-682701; fax: 692 2864.

There is no penalty for buying a ticket on the coach but you cannot get group discounts (for three adults or more on trips over 75

Getting Around Helsinki

Walking around Helsinki city centre is recommended, but if you want to travel by public transport, trams are the most efficient way to get around. Buy a **Helsinki Card** at the Tourist Office on Pohjoisesplanadi (also available from hotels and R-kiosks) for one, two or three days; with this you get free entry to museums and free transport on buses, trams, metro and trains, as well as assorted discounts at restaurants and concerts.

The 3T tram doubles as a sightseeing route; it covers a figure-eight around most of Helsinki. Catch it in front of the railway station, for example, between 6am and 1.15am. On buses and trams, you cancel your ticket in the same way; machines are on vehicles.

Bus and tram routes are usually not shown at the stops, only end destinations, so try to get journey advice before you go. Most run from 6am until midnight, but ask the Tourist Board about night buses in Helsinki and to Espoo and Vantaa.

Helsinki has a single metro line that runs east-west, serving local commuters in and out of town. It is fast and clean, but shuts down at 11.20pm so is not suitable for late-night travel. Services resume again at around 6am. Tickets, which are good for one hour including transfers to buses and trams, should be cancelled at the special machines at stations before the journey begins. Trains run at either 5- or 10-minute intervals.

km/47 miles) from the coach ticketseller. Senior citizens and full-time students (university and lower) are also eligible for discounts, but must purchase, for 30 marks, a coach card entitling them to this discount – at least 30 per cent. Bring a photo and ID. Accompanied children under four travel free.

Visitors can reserve long-distance coach seats (for a small fee) by calling Matkahuolto or visiting the main bus station, situated at the corner of Mannerheimintie and Simonkatu in Helsinki.

Driving

Finland's roads are not too plagued by traffic although they do get very busy between the capital and the countryside on Fridays and Sundays during the summer. There are few multi-lane motorways. Most are two-lane only.

Pay attention to road signs showing elk and reindeer zones. Collisions with these animals are usually serious. Use caution at all hours, but especially at dusk when elk are most active.

For winter driving, studded tyres should ideally be used from November to March and are strongly recommended throughout December at all times.

Foreign cars entering Finland should have a nationality sticker. In most cases, your own insurance with a green card will suffice in Finland, but check ahead to be sure. If you are driving a foreign car and are involved in an accident, contact the **Finnish Motor Insurers' Bureau**, tel: (0)9 19 251.

Don't risk driving while drunk in Finland. The limit is low (0.5 per cent blood alcohol) and the fines very steep; imprisonment is also possible in some cases. Taxis are available throughout the country, even in the backwaters; do as the Finns do and use them if you've been drinking.

Rules of the Road

Drive on the right, overtake on the left. All cars must use their lights outside built-up areas. Elsewhere,

lights must be used at dusk or at night or in bad weather (UK cars must sweep their lights right). Wearing of seat-belts is also compulsory.

Traffic coming from the right has right of way. Exceptions are on roads marked by a triangle sign; if this is facing you, you must give right of way; similarly if you are on a very major thoroughfare it is likely that the feed-in streets will have triangles, giving you the right of way. On roundabouts (rotaries), the first vehicle to reach the roundabout has right of way.

Speed limits are signposted, and range from 30 kmph (18 mph) in school zones to 100 kmph (62 mph) on motorways.

Taxis

Finnish taxis run throughout the country, with fares starting at around 19 markka. Helsinki city centre and the centres of other large cities, as well as most major airports, bus and railway stations, have taxi stands. Otherwise local telephone books list the number of the nearest dispatcher (under *Taksi* in the White Pages). Finding the closest one is worthwhile, especially in Helsinki, as taxis charge from embarkation point (plus an order fee). One can also hail a cab on the street, but this is a rarer way of getting a taxi in Finland than those above.

Bicycles

Finland is a good cycling country with its well-engineered cycle paths and gently rolling landscape. The number of outfits renting cycles has grown. Two major hire points are the youth hostel at Helsinki's Olympic Stadium and Ro-No rentals on both harbours of Mariehamn (*see page 230*) in the Åland islands (a popular summer cycling destination).

The **Finnish Youth Hostel Association** also offers planned route tours at good value prices (which can also include accommodation). Also ask the Finnish

Tourist Board (*see page 302*) about other firms that run planned cycling tours in the country.

Finnish Youth Hostel Association, Yrjänkatu 38B 00100 Helsinki. Tel: (0)9 694 0377 Fax: 693 1349.

Hitchhiking

Thumbing is still a time-honoured way to get a cheap ride in Finland, but you may have to wait a long time to get picked up, particularly at weekends and in the furthest reaches of Lapland where traffic can be pretty thin. Hitchhiking is prohibited on Finland's motorways; the smaller secondary routes are a better bet. As with any country in the world however, safety can never be guaranteed on the road, and this mode of transport is not recommended.

Where to Stay

Choosing a Hotel

You can pretty much depend on Finnish accommodation being clean and in good shape, but prices are high. There are bargains to be hunted out, however. Big discounts (up to 60 per cent) are available at most hotels on weekends, and in summer when they lose their business and conference trade.

Budget accommodation includes youth and family hostels, farmhouses, *gasthaus* accommodation, family villages, camping, various forms of self-catering, and so on. During the summer holidays, some student residences become Summer Hotels, opening on 1 June. The local Tourist Boards and booking centres will provide up-to-date prices, including details of weekend and summer discounts.

General information on the above is available from the **Finnish Tourist Board** in your home country, or from the head office in Helsinki (*see page 302*).

Helsinki has its own hotel booking centre at the Railway Station: **Hotel Booking Centre**, Asemaaukio 3, tel: (0)9-2288 1400; fax (0)9 175 524. E-mail: hklapj@hel.fi

Chain Hotels

Finland has many large hotel chains of its own, as well as foreign chains. Big hotel chains, such as Sokos Hotels or Cumulus, offer fairly comfortable standard services in most big towns. Some chains, such as Radisson SAS, have emerged recently to offer perhaps even more comfortable services. Most of these hotels are very reliable in providing extremely clean rooms and (their own) chain restaurants

with identical menus countrywide. Some of the best known are:

Best Western Finland
Annankatu 29A, 00100 Helsinki
Tel: (0)9-645 500.

Restel Hotel Group
PO Box 72, 00501 Helsinki
Tel: (0)9-733 5480.

Sokos Hotels (sok)
Fleminginkatu 34, 00510 Helsinki
Tel: (0)9-1881
Fax: (0)9 131 00222

Summer Hotels
Yrjänkatu 38, 00100 Helsinki.
Tel: (0)9-693 1347.

A systematic way to get discounts is to enrol in the Finncheque scheme, in which some 250 hotels participate. By spending around 200 markka on a Finncheque, you get a night's free accommodation in these hotels. The system is a co-operation between several hotel chains; further details from the Finnish Tourist Office in Helsinki (*see page 302*).

Hotel Listings

Hotels are listed in alphabetical order according to region, with the most expensive first.

HANKO

Pensionat Garbo
Raatimiehenkatu 8, 10900 Hanko.
Tel (0)19-248 7897.
This charming little house is like a museum of Hollywood superstars – each themed room features a diva from the silver screen. An unusual choice, with just 10 rooms. **££**

Villa Maija
Appelgrenintie 7, 10900 Hanko.
Tel (0)19-248 4917.
This fine 19th-century villa is one of many on this attractive street. Open all year. **££**

HELSINKI

Expensive

Grand Marina
Katajanokanlaituri 7, 00160 Helsinki.
Tel: (0)9-16661; fax: 664 764.

Price Guide

The following price categories indicate the cost of a double room in high season:
£££: £150–£200
££: £100–£150
£: £50–£100

Designed in 1911 by noted Finnish architect Lars Sonck, this hotel on the island of Katajanokka was once a warehouse. Each of the 462 rooms is exquisitely decorated and well-equipped, with specially designed accommodation for non-smokers, allergy sufferers and the disabled. Five restaurants, two conference halls and a heated garage. **£££**

Klaus Kurki
Bulevardi 2–4, 00120 Helsinki.
Tel: (0)9-618911.
Located on a handsome street just a few steps away from the Esplanadi. Early 20th-century carved granite exterior, cosy, recently decorated in Continental style. Bar, restaurant and terrace. **£££**.

Scandic Hotel Kalastajatorppa
Kalastajatorpantie 1, Helsinki.
Tel: (0)9-45811
Fax: 458 1683.
In a park about 7 km (4 miles) from the city centre bordered by the blue waters of the Gulf of Finland, this countrsyide resort hotel is spacious and ultra-modern, with 235 rooms, many with a sea view. Tennis courts, sauna, private beach and two indoor swimming pools. Business services. **£££**

Moderate

Hotel Anna
Annankatu 1, Helsinki.
Tel: (0)9-616 621
Fax: 602 664.
This quiet, comfortable hotel has 60 rooms with all the amenities, in a quiet shopping quarter in the city centre. **££**

Radisson SAS Royal
Runeberginkatu 2, 00100 Helsinki.
Tel: (0)9-69 580.
A new (1991) addition to this famed Scandinavian chain, the Helsinki SAS has sunny, open dining and bar areas and the usual good service.

About a 10-minute walk from the centre, across from the bus station. **££**

Rivoli Hotel Jardin
Kasarmikatu 40, Helsinki 00100.
Tel: (0)9-177 880
Fax: 656 988.
An intimate, charming hotel with 54 tastefully furnished rooms with all the amenities. City centre location. Breakfast buffet included. Sauna, open-air terrace. **££**

Torni
Yrjönkatu 26, 00100 Helsinki.
Tel: (0)9-131 131.
Known as the tallest building in town at 13 storeys, Torni is a gracious hotel with an old and new section. The older section is in Art Deco style, and the rooms have original features. Try for rooms overlooking the courtyard. The "new" section, with bar-lookout tower, has functional decor outside; its interior has been renovated to a high standard of comfort. **££**

Price Guide

The following price categories indicate the cost of a double room in high season:

£££: £150–£200
££: £100–£150
£: £50–£100

Inexpensive (£)

Academica
Hietaniemenkatu 14, 00100 Helsinki.
Tel: (0)9-1311 4334
Fax: 441 201.
This is a basic summer hotel which is a student quarter during the university term. Small modern rooms have their own kitchen. Family rooms and extra beds also available. Residential but central location. **£**

Eurohostel
Linnankatu 9, 00160 Helsinki.
Tel: (0)9-622 0470
Fax: 655 044.
On Katajanokka Island by the ferry terminals, this no-frills hostel is convenient for those travelling by ship, and is just a 10-minute walk from the marketplace and city centre. The 135 rooms (singles,

twins and triples) have shared facilities including kitchen. Two laundrettes, sauna and café. **£**

Stadium Hostel
Olympic Stadiu
Pohjoinen Stadiontie 3B.
Tel: (0)9-496 071.
There are several other summer hostels, but this one is open all year. About 3 km (2 miles) north of the centre, with easy access by bus and tram. **£**

IMATRA

Scandic Hotel Imatran Valtionhotelli
Torkkelinkatu 2, 55100 Imatra.
Tel: (0)5-68881.
This imposing Art Nouveau castle, next to the Imatrankoski hydro-electric power station (with daily waterfall shows in summer) is one of the most notable hotel buildings in Finland. The rooms in the main building are expensive but more attractive than the annex. **£££**

JOENSUU

Sokos Hotel Kimmel
Itäranta 1, 80100 Joensuu.
Tel: (0)13-277 2111.
The largest hotel in Joensuu, this edifice is opposite the railway station and perhaps the town's liveliest spot in the evenings. **£££**

JYVASKYLA

Hotel Yöpuu
Yliopistonkatu 23, 40100 Jyväskylä.
Tel: (0)14-333 900.
Although Jyväskylä has many large hotels, this 26-room hotel is one of the best choices, with an old-world ambiance and a fine restaurant. **£££**

KOTKA

Sokos Hotel Seurahuone
Keskuskatu 21, 48100 Kotka.
Tel: (0)5-35035.
This very central hotel has superb rooms and a fine restaurant. **£££**

KUOPIO

Scandic Hotel Kuopio
Satamakatu 1.
Tel: (0)17-195 111.
This large hotel on the waterfront is one of the finest in town. **£££**

Sokos Hotel Puijonsarvi
Minna Canthinkatu 16.
Tel: (0)17-170 111.
This chain hotel features modern architecture and clean rooms. **£££**

Hotelli-Kylpylä Rauhalahti
Katiskaniementie 8.
Tel: (0)17-473 473.
This fine spa hotel includes a hostel wing with clean apartments for budget travellers. A smoke sauna bath is open for visitors on Tuesdays and Fridays – reputedly the largest of its kind in southern Finland. A traditional dinner is also available on those evenings. **£–££**

LAPPEENRANTA

Scandic Hotel Patria
Kauppakatu 21
53100 Lappeenranta.
Tel: (0)5-677 511.
This modern hotel is situated close to the harbour and the fortress area. There are 130 rooms, and several restaurants and saunas. **£££**

OULU

Kylpylähotelli Eden
Nallikari, Oulu.
Tel: (0)8-550 4100.
This hotel offers spa facilities in the Nallikari beach area. **£££**

PUNKAHARJU

Punkaharjun Valtionhotelli
58450 Punkaharju 2.
Tel: (0)15-739 611.
This scenic region, not far from Savonlinna, offers an opportunity to stay in Finland's oldest hotel. It's a wooden Russian-style villa with lots of ambience and 24 rooms. **££**

RAUMA

Kalatorin Majatalo
Kalatori 4
Tel: (0)2-822 7111.
A small pleasant hotel in a renovated Art Deco warehouse. There are just 20 rooms and a restaurant. **££**

ROVANIEMI

Rantasipi Pohjanhovi
Pohjanpuistikko 2
96200 Rovaniemi.
Tel: (0)16 33 711
Fax: (0)16 313 997
This legendary and luxurious hotel is known for its dance and concert evenings. The hotel is pleasantly located at the Kemijoki Riverfront, with a swimming pool, nightclub, casino, and a range of travel services and outdoor activities. **£££**

SAVONLINNA

Spa Hotel Casino
PL 60, 57101 Savonlinna.
Tel: (0)15-739 5430.
This large hotel complex has very clean rooms, a large spa section and some inexpensive hostel beds available in summer. The hotel is located on an island opposite the central railway halt, access via a wooden bridge. **£££**

Perhehotelli Hospitz
Linnankatu 20, 57130 Savonlinna.
Tel: (0)15-515 661.
This cosy hotel has a superb location close to the Olavinlinna castle. It's an extremely well run family hotel with a nice garden at the waterfront. Often fully booked in summer. **££**

TURKU

Expensive
Scandic Marina Palace
Linnankatu 32, 20100 Turku.
Tel: (0)2-336 300
Fax: 251 6750.
Situated by the Aura River in a picturesque location, near the museum quarter and harbour sights. Rooms are attractive and well furnished, with all amenities. Restaurant, bar and meeting rooms. **£££**

Ateljee Hotel
Humalistonkatu 7
20100 Turku.
Tel: (0)2-233 611
Fax: 233 6699.
The building was designed by Alvar Aalto (*see page 80*) and two of the rooms contain furniture by the master. There are 230 well-equipped rooms. Many artists have taken up permanent residence and display their works here; guests can visit them in their ateliers. **££**

City Bors
Eerikinkatu 11 (across the market square), 20100 Turku.
Tel: (0)2-337 381
Fax: 231 1010.
A slightly cheaper but excellent alternative to Hamburger Bors. **££**

Hamburger Bors
Kauppiaskatu 6
20100 Turku.
Tel: (0)2-337 381
Fax: 231 1010.
Centrally located hotel, right on the Marketplace; excellent restaurants including rustic-French Fransmanni and German-style Hamburger Hof. **££**

Park Hotel
Rauhankatu 1, 20100 Turku.
Tel: (0)2-273 25555
Fax: 251 9696.
This elegantly restored Jugenstil building (1902) was once a private mansion. Each of the well-furnished rooms is different; some have a park view. **££**

Scandic Hotel Julia
Eerikinkatu 4, 20110 Turku.
Tel: (0)2-2336 311
Fax: 251 1750.
Popular hotel centrally located near the market square. Acclaimed restaurant. Attentive service and comfortable rooms. **££**

Seaport Hotel Turku
Matkustajasatama, 20100 Turku.
Tel: (0)2-2302 600
Fax: 2302 169.
One of the more imaginatively restored hotels in Finland, once a 19th-century warehouse. Its red-brick façade is in original neo-Gothic style with beautiful wooden beams inside. Views of harbour or castle. Modern bathrooms. **£**

TAMPERE

Cumulus Koskikatu
Koskikatu 5, 33100 Tampere.
Tel: (0)3-242 4111
Fax: 242 4399.
Built in 1979, the hotel's style is vibrantly modern throughout, and the bar and dining facilities are excellent. **££**

Sokos Hotel Ilves
Hatanpäänvaltatie 1
33100 Tampere.
Tel: (0)3-2626 262
Fax: 2626 263.
An 18-storey building with views over the harbour and Tammarkoski Rapids. Stylish with swimming pool, and saunas. **££**

Sokos Hotel Tammer
Satakunnankatu 13
33100 Tampere.
Tel: (0)3-262 6265
Fax: 2626 266.
The dramatically high entranceway leads into a later (1929) tribute to Finnish Art Deco. Set in a green, hilly district of the city. **££**

Victoria
Itsenäisyydenkatu 1
33100 Tampere.
Tel: (0)3-242 5111. Fax: 242 5100.
This simple, hostel-style hotel has clean, modern rooms and a lively bar and restaurant in the basement, the Tunneli. **£** (group discounts).

Hostels

Finland has a widespread network of some 115 youth and family hostels, which vary from small farmhouses, to manors, camping and special centres. They usually have family rooms (2–4 visitors) or dormitories (5–10). Some 70 of these hostels are open year-round, the remainder in summer only. Details of hostels and the Finnish Youth Hostel Cheque system are available from the **Finnish Youth Hostel Association**, Yrjönkatu 38B, 00100 Helsinki, tel: (0)9-694 0377; fax: (0)9 693 1349. E-mail: info@srm.inet.fi

Where to Eat

Finnish cuisine has broadened and improved enormously in recent years, as more foods are imported and farming and greenhouse methods are refined. Those items once unheard of above 60° north latitude can now be seen in the markets, such as Finnish-grown cucumbers and red tomatoes.

You'll also find that there are some excellent Finnish cooks who, given the right mix of fresh produce and good meats and fish, can produce a superb meal. The wild game dishes are a real treat and are usually served with exquisite mushroom and berry sauces. In summer, you are strongly recommended to try Finnish crayfish, or *ravut* (*see page 120*). However, if you eat only in cafeteria-style restaurants, you may get bored with the monotony of the offerings.

A lot of Finns eat a large hot lunch and then a smaller cold meal in the evening, although this is not to say that you can't have wonderful evening meals in Helsinki and other cities. International cuisines have also crept in slowly over the years, and you'll now find Chinese, Italian, and French-style restaurants in almost all major towns. The best Russian cuisine outside of Russia is still found all over Helsinki.

Choosing a Restaurant

It is difficult to find a really cheap meal in Finland, but you can find places where you will definitely get value for money – in other words, where portions are generous and quality is high. Fixed-price lunches are often very good deals and are usually advertised on signboards outside restaurants. Many places have English translated menus.

For on-the-run, really cheap eats, go to a *nakki* (sausage) kiosk. Hot dogs and sausages are the main fare, and you can usually get French fries and drinks as well. Other slightly more expensive quick meals can be had at any one of the ubiquitous hamburger chains like McDonalds, Hesburger or Carrols. Pizza is also popular in Finland.

Many of the hotels in the three main cities of Helsinki, Turku and Tampere, and elsewhere, have good restaurants, ranging from gourmet to wine bars and cafés, including restaurants that specialise in particular ethnic cuisines.

Restaurant Listings

Restaurants are listed in alphabetical order by region, with the most expensive first.

HELSINKI

Expensive
Havis Amanda
Unioninkatu 23.
Tel (0)9-666 882.
This very fine seafood restaurant offers seasonal fish and seafood varieties, and seldom disappoints even a connoisseur. **£££**

Kanavaranta
Kanavaranta 3E & F.
Tel: (0)9-622 2633.
Reputedly Finland's leading chefs prepare genuine Finnish treats. Try the four-course Seasonal Menu with carefully selected wines for perhaps the finest culinary experience in Finland. **£££**

Torni
Yrjönkatu 26
00100 Helsinki.
Tel: (0)9-131 131.
Hotel Torni's gourmet restaurant in this traditional hotel. Also try the Ateljee Bar on the 13th floor for light meals and drinks (outdoor seating in summer) offering the best view in Helsinki. **£££** (bar **£**)

Walhalla
Suomenlinna.
Tel: (0)9-668 552.
Open to the public in summer and the rest of the year by arrangement, the restaurant is set in the archways of the old fortress on historic Suomenlinna island (*see page 177*). It offers some of the finest Finnish cuisine in the country. Try the snow grouse or reindeer specialities. **£££**

Moderate
Kynsilaukka Garlic Restaurant
Fredrikinkatu 22.
Tel: (0)9-651 939.
The chef brings fresh market produce and high imagination to the garlic-centred dishes served here. Comfortable and friendly; small and large portions. **££**

Lappi
Annankatu 22.
Tel: (0)9-645 550.
An authentic Lapland experience is a bonus when sampling anything made of reindeer, tasty fish, salted fungi and exotic berries. Try the Lappish plate to savour a full range of northern specialities. **££**

Talon Tapaan A La Maison
Salomonkatu 19.
Tel (0)9-685 6606.
An unpretentious restaurant with a genuine Finnish menu. Reservations are essential. Finnish Symphony is a costly *hors d'oeuvre* but worth it. **££**

KUOPIO

The small *muikku* (whitefish) is a must in Kuopio, although more famous is the *kalakukko* (loaf of rye bread crust filled with fish and pork) that can be found at the market.

Musta Lammas
Satamakatu 4.
Tel: (0)17-262 3494.
A pleasant restaurant, considered Kuopio's best. The dining hall is vaulted and quite pleasant. **£££**

Vapaasatama Sampo
Kauppakatu 13.
Tel: (0)17-261 4677.
Kuopio's most famous restaurant,

formerly a "sailors' pub", this traditional restaurant serves excellent fish (*muikku* is the most popular meal) in what still seems to be a very informal pub. **££**

Wanha Satama

This rustic and lively pub-restaurant by the passenger harbour serves very tasty *muikku* fish with garlic and mashed potatoes. **££**

SAVONLINNA

The market is busy and popular in this opera town. Prices are a bit steep during the opera festival (*see page 92*), but then the market is also at its liveliest.

Majakka

Satamakatu 1
Tel: (0)15-531 456.
A popular restaurant near the market serving good fish and meat. **££**

Sillansuu

Verkkosaarenkatu 1.
Tel: (0)15- 476 0251.
This pub near the market bridge is one of the best in Finland. **££**

TAMPERE

Astor

Aleksis Kivenkatu 26.
Tel: (0)3-213 3522.
A popular spot for food and drink with live piano music every night and an even livelier crowd. Reindeer meat and a good variety of fish available. **£££**

Merirosvo

Näsinneula, Särkänniemi.
Tel: (0)3-248 8234.
This is the revolving restaurant in the Näsinnuela Observation Tower, where you dine 168 metres (635 ft) above the scenic landscape of Tampere. Fine Finnish cuisine is a speciality. **£££**

Silakka

Koskikeskus.
Tel: (0)3-214 9740.
Typical Finnish cooking with a Baltic herring buffet served daily; other fine fish meals à la carte. **££**

Eetvartti

Sumeliuksenkatu 16.
Tel: (0)3-3155 5300.

This is the restaurant of the Pirkanmaa Hotel and Restaurant School. You can dine very well on fare cooked by the students at low prices for high quality. **£**

Plevna

Itäinen katu 8.
Tel: (0)3-233 0111.
Lively pub/café and brewery, which specialises in steaks and grilled sausages. A variety of beers are brewed on the premises. **£**

Salud

Tuomiokirkonkatu 19.
Tel: (0)3-366 4460.
Salud is by nature a Spanish restaurant but at the same time Tampere's most popular place to wine and dine. **£**

TURKU

Summer in Turku is not perfect without a proper session in one of the dozen boat restaurants on Aurajoki River. Most people stop for beer, but food is also on offer.

Enkeliravintola

Kauppiaskatu 16.
Tel (0)2-231 9088.
Decorated with angels in all shapes and sizes, this very fine restaurant serves good food in a unique atmosphere. **£££**

Pinella

Porthaninpuisto.
Tel: (0)2-2517 557.
An archway-flanked building with a Victorian verandah greets you at this famous Turku restaurant. There are two dining areas, one featuring seafood and meat, the other Dutch fare. **££**

Samppalinna

Itäinen Rantakatu.
Tel: (0)2-311 165.
Continental cuisine including roast mutton and a host of specialities such as salmon soup, all served in a splendid Victorian building. **££**

VAASA

Gustav Wasa

Raastuvankatu 24.
Tel: (0)6-326 9200.
This cellar restaurant serves

Price Guide

The following price categories indicate the cost of a meal for one, without drinks:

£££:   over £25
££:   £10–£25
£:   under £10

excellent meat portions, and some fish. The pleasantly rustic dining hall was a coal-storing cellar until 1967. **£££**

Kanttarellis

Kauppapuistikko 15.
Tel: (0)6-317 0110.
This restaurant, and its bar annex Hullu Pullo are both attractions in themselves with their incredible decor. The menu has many kinds of fish and meat **££**

Drinking Notes

Alcohol is expensive in Finland due to high taxes, and beer and wine are no exceptions. The Finnish *tuoppi* is about 30 per cent larger than the British pint; a *pieni tuoppi* is about two-thirds of that quantity. If you don't specify, you will be served a large, strong (number 4 = 4.5 per cent alcohol) beer. You must say if you want the 3.5 per cent beer, known as *keski-olut*, or medium beer. Number 1 beer is the weakest (*ykkös-olut*), at just over one per cent alcohol.

Wine in Finland is imported and very costly in restaurants, but there is more choice in Alko (the state alcohol monopoly) these days. The range of prices begins with Eastern European wines (about 40 markka a bottle) and goes up precipitously.

Spirits and wine can be bought only from Alko (Stockmann's department store in Helsinki has an Alko unit on the ground floor). Medium and lower alcohol beer can be bought in supermarkets. Most restaurants serve alcohol as long as they serve food. A restaurant marked *B-oikeudet* is licensed only to serve beer and wine. Most bars and taverns are open until at least midnight in Helsinki; some stay open until 3 or 4am.

Culture

Museums

Finland is a country of small museums. The grandest in scale is the Ateneum in Helsinki, reopened in 1991 after five years of renovations (*see page 156*), which could fit neatly into London's National Gallery at least three times. Art dominates the museum scene, with the greatest variety of venues in Helsinki. In total, there is probably more contemporary art to be seen than older art.

Admission prices are generally steep, but Helsinki sells the Helsinki Card, which includes free entrance to many museums on presentation. Turku recently introduced a similar card.

Museum opening hours are almost always reduced in winter. Most museums close on Monday.

Classical Music & Opera

Most larger cities have a steady itinerary of concerts throughout the year, but music festivals abound in Finland in summer, and many of these are held in stunning settings (*see page 92*). The most famous of these are all held in July: the Savonlinna Opera Festival at Olavinlinna Castle in eastern Finland, the Kuhmo Chamber Music Festival, also in eastern Finland and the Kaustinen Folk Festival in western Finland. The festivals feature Finnish and international performers.

Finnish opera has a great following, and much of it features Finnish composers and performers.

Helsinki Events

In late summer are the Helsinki *Juhlaviikot* (festival weeks) featuring broad-ranging programmes with artists from Finland and abroad, set at different venues around the city. Information from:
Helsinki Festival Office,
Rauhankatu 7E,
00170 Helsinki
Tel: (0)9-135 4522.

Also, try the weekday evening series of concerts at the unique Temppeliaukio (Church-in-the-rock) in Töölö, Helsinki (*see page 172*).

During the rest of the year, main events are at Finlandia Concert Hall, many by the Radio Symphony Orchestra and the Helsinki Philharmonic Orchestra. The national opera (and ballet) company's new hall in Helsinki opened in 1992 (*see page 170*).

Turku Events

Turku is a lively musical city, with concerts given by the Turku City Orchestra, a series of concerts in the Sibelius Museum, and others in the Cathedral and the Castle. The Turku Musical Festival is one of the oldest in Finland and ranges from medieval music to first performances. Held in mid-August, it attracts visiting composers and international musicians.

For further information, contact the **Foundation for the Turku Music Festivals**, Uudenmaankatu 1, 20500 Turku, tel: (0)2-2511 162.

Tampere Events

Tampere has always had its share of music. Since 1975 the city has held an international choir festival each year and the Tampere Biennale, started in 1986, is a festival of new Finnish music, arranged in cooperation with the Association of Finnish Composers. For information contact:
Tampere Biennale,
Tullikamarinaukio 2
33100 Tampere
Tel: (0)3-219 6136.

Since the opening of the new Tampere Hall, interest has soared. The auditorium is one of the great concert halls of the world and the acoustics are acknowledged to be far better than those of Helsinki's Finlandia Hall. The small auditorium

Jazz and Rock

In Tampere there is an annual jazz festival called Jazz Happening. For information on dates and concerts, contact **Tampere Jazz Happening**, Tullikamarinaukio 2, 33100 Tampere, tel: (0)3-2196 136.

There is also Ruisrock on the island of Ruissalo, Finland's oldest and highly popular rock festival (*see page 92*).

is used for chamber music, and the Hall is also a conference venue. Tampere holds numerous concerts in its cathedral, churches and halls.

Theatre

Helsinki

The Finnish National Theatre and Svenska Teatern in Helsinki both enjoy long traditions of performance in, respectively, Finnish and Swedish. Unfortunately, there is no foreign-language theatre to speak of, but you may be interested in touring the theatre buildings themselves, or even going to a play you know well enough to overcome the language barrier.

The listings guides in Helsinki will list theatre events (*see page 302*). Equivalent guides in Turku and Tampere also carry listings.

Turku

Plays performed are of a high standard but rarely in languages other than Finnish or Swedish. In winter, there is the Turku City Theatre on the bank of the River Aura and the Swedish Theatre on the corner of the Marketplace – the oldest theatre in Finland still in use.

Tampere

Tampere rivals Helsinki for year-round theatrical events but, again, the difficulty is language. One exception is the Pyynikki Outdoor Summer Theatre (*see page 219*) where you can see plays from mid-June to mid-August, with synopses in English. This is particularly worthwhile if you want to enjoy the setting at the edge of the lake, Pyhäjärvi. Booking is necessary, tel: (0)3-216 0300.

The Tampere Theatre Festival in August includes many international companies who produce plays in their own languages.

Further information is available from **Tampere International Theatre Festival**, Tullikamarinaukio 2, 33100, Tampere, tel: (0)3-2228 536.

Cinema

Finns do not dub their films, and you can enjoy as good a selection of movies here as in any other European city of moderate size. **Nordia** (Yrjönkatu 36, tel: (0)9-1311 9250) in Helsinki shows a mix of commercial successes and slightly artier films, while the **Suomen Elokuva-arkisto** at the Orion Film Archive (Eerikinkatu 15–17, tel: (9)0-694 6558) has endless stocks of older films, both Finnish and foreign. **Andorra** (Eerikinkatu 11, tel: (0)9-604 873) is owned by the Kaurismäki director brothers of such films as *Drifting Clouds* (*see page 90*).

Film showings are usually at 6pm and 8.30pm. The kiosk outside the east entrance to Helsinki railway station has comprehensive listings, as do the newspapers; listings are also available at the Tourist Board. Seats are reserved at the time you buy the tickets, and box offices usually open 30–45 minutes before show time but at some cinemas may be purchased even earlier.

Tampere has a cinema centre **Finnkino Plevna** in the Finlayson area (Itäinen katu 4). In Turku most cinemas are found in the Hansa Shopping Centre (*see page 207*).

Nightlife

Pubs, Bars and Clubs

Nightlife can be a difficult thing to get the hang of in Finland. In Helsinki, you will see hordes of revellers bar-crawling their way across town into the early hours, but most are old acquaintances just getting drunk together. There are several clubs which attract the best music acts, for example the university-owned Tavastia. Occasionally a good jazz or rock act will make it to Helsinki but the city is certainly not on the itinerary of most major performers.

The official drinking age is 18 and over but some clubs may have a minimum age limit of 21. Entrance fees can be anything from free to outrageous. Nightclubs can be expensive and good dance floors are hard to find. More easily found is the casual camaraderie of the few places that attract a sprinkling of foreigners, such as the pubs O'Malley's and Vanha.

A few of the better bars and night spots in Finland's three main cities, Helsinki, Tampere and Turku, are listed as follows:

HELSINKI

Highlight Café
Frederikinkatu 42.
A sports theme pub with American-style food set in this beautifully restored former church. It is owned by Jari Kurri, a former NHL ice hockey champion.
Corona Bar
Eerinkatu 11.
Tel: (0)9-642002.
This popular spot attracts a young hip crowd who come to talk, drink beer and play pool.

Kuu
Töölönkatu 27.
Tel: (0)9-2709 0973.
An intimate, older, small bar with local jazz groups now and again. Excellent Finnish cuisine.
O'Malleys
Yrjönkatu 28.
Tel: (0)9-611 331.
Irish, mellow, small and usually crowded tavern. Some live music.
Storyville
Museokatu 8.
Tel: (0)9-408 007.
Jazz club featuring local and international musicians. A cosy spot to have a late drink. Cover charge.
Tavastia
Urho Kekkosenkatu 4.
Tel: (0)9-408 007.
This university-owned club attracts some of Helsinki's best live music. Rocking atmosphere; downstairs is a usually packed self-service bar, waiter service upstairs.
Vanhan Kellari
Vanha Yliopisto Mannerheimintie 3.
Tel: (0)9-174 357.
University students' union-owned, Vanhan, which is set in a neo-classical building, flows with the traffic of devoted beer-drinkers the year round. Occasional live music.
Zetor
Kaivopiha.
Tel: (0)9-666 966.
This "tractor-style" rock 'n' roll disco has to be seen to be believed. Experience the surrealism of the Finnish countryside.

TAMPERE

Tampere's nightlife is very evident on the main street, Hämeenkatu. Bar-hopping is very easy, although more "traditional" pubs are elsewhere, such as **Salhojankadun Pub** on Salhojan-katu, and **Ohranjyvä** at Näsilinnankatu 15. Locally brewed beer is available at **Plevna** (Itäinen katu 8) and Vanha Posti (Hämeenkatu 13A).

TURKU

Panimoravintola Koulu
Eerikinkatu 18.
Tel: (0)2-274 5757.
Just next to the market square, this old former school building has a brewery and many former class-rooms refurbished as pubs or restaurants.

Puutorin Vessa
Puutori.
Tel (0)2-233 8123.
This unusual pub was once a public toilet! After a very, very thorough cleaning, it now is the funniest theme pub in town.

Old Bank
Aurakatu 3.
Tel: (0)2-274 5700.
Once a very fine bank, this pub serves more beer varieties than any other pub in town.

Uusi Apteekki
Kaskenkatu 1.
Tel: (0)2-250 2595.
Literally "new pharmacy", this pub is set in an old chemist shop and now sells over 20 different beers.

Children

Attractions

Just a 15-minute train ride from downtown Helsinki is an ideal spot for engaging children and grown-ups: **Heureka**, the Finnish Science Centre in Vantaa-Tikkurila, has a range of permanent and temporary "hands-on" exhibitions, a planetarium and an IMAX theatre. Tel: (0)9-85799.

Further from Helsinki, the main amusement park in southern Finland is **Lystiland Children's Fun Park**, just north of Karjaa town centre. It features a miniature train tour on an enchanted forest trail.

There are several good spots in the Lakeland region for travellers with children. At **Messilä Vacation Centre** in Hollola near Lahti, there are all manner of supervised activities for children, including horse- and pony-riding. In winter, there are skiing activities (Alpine and Nordic) for children and adults.

A bit north from Hollola, towards Hartola, is the fascinating little **Musta and Valkea Ratsu Dollhouse and Puppet Theatre** on road 52 (signposted), 19230 Onkiniemi, tel: (0)3 718 6959.

In Outokumpu, north of Savonlinna, is **The Land of the Mountain Troll**, an amusement park and mineral and mining exhibition, and Mikkeli has the **Visulahti Tourist Centre**, including a dinosaur theme amusement park and wax-works. A little further from Mikkeli is an arboretum which includes a small menagerie. Contact **Mikkeli Tourism**, tel: (0)15-151 444.

Rovaniemi, near the Arctic Circle is where you will find Santa Claus' Village (*see page 139*). Rumour has it that Father Christmas stays here when he is visiting from his secret hideaway in Korvatunturi-fell. There is a post office and a shopping centre which stocks gifts from Lapland. Open daily year round.

When in the **Aland Islands**, you might want to check out the amusement park by the west harbour, the *Pommern* ship museum (at the west harbour), and Lilla Holmen bird park on the east harbour. Here you will see peacocks, ducks, and beautiful angora rabbits.

Shopping

What to Buy

Finnish Design

If people know anything at all about Finnish design, they usually think of the smooth contemporary lines associated with Finnish architecture imposed on jewellery, woodwork, clothing, glassware and sculpture. To see the best of the design, you might want to go first to the Applied Arts Museum in Helsinki.

Lapponia Aarikka and Kaleva Koru jewellery are expressly Finnish, the first being a mainly contemporary collection and the second a collection based on designs from the Finnish epic poem *Kalevala*, rendered in silver, gold, and also in more affordable brass. Aarikka also puts out some of the finer woodwork products, including chopping boards, Christmas decorations, toys and wooden jewellery.

The most impressive ceramic work is commissioned by Arabia, one of the older Finnish firms. Their factory (about 20 minutes' tram ride from downtown Helsinki) has a small museum upstairs, and first- and second-quality goods on sale downstairs. Pentik is known for its ceramics as well as beautifully crafted leather clothing.

Iittala (*see page 221*) makes beautiful glassware at their factory, from drinking glasses to candle holders. Marimekko is the quintessential Finnish clothing designer, with items made of brightly coloured fabrics for men, women and children, as well as textiles for home use.

All these companies can be found both in their own stores and department stores in most Finnish towns of any size, including Pohjoisesplanadi in Helsinki.

Shopping Areas

Helsinki

Apart from mainstream department stores and boutique shopping in Helsinki, there are several market squares that sell both fresh food and a range of other consumer goods of greatly varying quality, from second-hand clothes and records to designer jewellery, Lapp mittens, and fur hats.

Kauppatori is the main Helsinki market, followed by Hietalahdentori and Hakaniementori, all near the centre. Note that markets have extended hours in summer and are open until about 8pm, but close briefly from about 2pm.

Otherwise, the **Esplanade** is the hub of shopping delights in Helsinki. You'll find relatively few foreign retail outlets in Finland, but in recent years a few have managed to establish themselves, such as Hennes & Mauritz (H&M), Ikea, Body Shop and Benetton.

Tampere

Tampere has most of the medium-sized department stores found in Helsinki and Turku, as well as a host of smaller boutiques. A good collection is at **Kehräsaari Boutique Centre**, Laukontori 1, Keräsaari, in a converted textile mill. Visit also the **Verkaranta Arts and Crafts Centre** at Verkatehtaankatu 2, for a

good selection of handicrafts and toys. The main Tampere Market Hall is at Hämeenkatu 19, opens Monday to Saturday.

Turku

Turku has its own Stockmann's at Yliopistonkatu 22. Also on Yliopistonkatu are Pentik (No. 25), famous for ceramics, and (No. 27B) Aarikka, for handmade wooden crafts and decorations.

For crafts, look into **Sylvi Salonen**, specialising in linens and decorative crafts at Yliopistonkatu 29, or **Neoviska**, Juhana Herttuan Puisto 10 for handmade *ryijy* (rya) rugs and other textiles.

Check locally for market days at the lovely main market (the market opens in summer from 4–8pm). The **Hansa Shopping Centre** is also in Turku (*see page 207*).

Department Stores

The king of department stores in Finland is Stockmann's; it is the place Finns go to when they want to hunt down some elusive item, or some exotic gift. To the outsider it will probably seem merely a large, pleasant place to shop, but to Finns it is something of an institution; branches are also in Tampere, Turku, and Tapiola (Espoo). Stockmann's also owns the Akateeminen Kirjakauppa, Finland's best known bookstore. Another good department store to look out for throughout Finland is Sokos, with its fine food hall.

Sport

Participant Sports

Finland is known as a sporting nation, a reputation which it lives up to in every Olympic Games by producing a high number of medal winners at both summer and winter games. The devotion to training is constant; it is not unusual on a hot summer's day to see squadrons of muscular youths out on roller-skis to make sure they do not lose their touch for the coming winter.

Cycling

Bicycling is big in Finland. The countryside is ideal for cyclists, dead flat on the west coast leading to gently rolling hill areas; for suggested cycle routes, contact:
Finnish Youth Hostel Association, Yrjönkatu 38B
00100 Helsinki
Tel: (0)9-694 0377
Fax: (0)9-693 1349.

Sailing

Boating exists in all forms, and most harbours have guest marinas where one can dock for reasonable overnight fees. Canoeing is also popular in the Lakelands region.

Other sports

Orienteering, golf, hunting, fishing and tennis are a few of the other popular sports in Finland, and there are many enthusiasts of indoor sports such as badminton and squash. Basically, if there's a sport you love, no matter how popular or obscure, you will probably find co-enthusiasts in Finland.

For information on any sport in Finland, contact:
Suomen Valtakunnan Urheiluliitto (The National Sports Association), Radiokatu 20
00240 Helsinki (Ilmala)
Tel: (0)9-1581
Fax: (0)9-147 304.

Spectator Sports

There is a near endless list of spectator sports in Finland, but a shortlist of the most popular must include ski-jumping, regatta sailing and hockey.

Summer

One of the biggest sailing events of the year is the **Hanko Regatta**, which takes place in early July off Finland's south coast. **Kotka** also sponsors a yearly Tall Ships event. The biggest inland sailing regatta is on Lake Päijänne, also in July. Details are available from the **Finnish Yachting Association**, Radiokatu 20, 00093 Helsinki

Tel: (0)9-348121
Fax: (0)9-3481 2369.
Before mid-June is the **Finlandia Canoeing Relay**, held in the large Lakeland region – the venue changes annually. It lasts five days and covers over 545 km (350 miles), with day and night action.

Winter

Lahti, about 105 km (65 miles) north of Helsinki, is the best place to watch ski-jumping.

For winter spectator sports, the **Finlandia Ski Race** in mid-February is one of the top events. This 75-km (47-mile) event attracts the best Finnish skiers and ample spectator opportunities.

For information, contact:
Finlandia Ski Race Office
Urheilukeskus
15110 Lahti
Tel: (0)3-734 9811
Fax: (0)3-751 0079.
As is the case with participant sports, all general sport queries can be directed to the Suomen Valtakunnan Urheiluliitto (The National Sports Association).

Skiing in Finland

Finns are particularly famous as cross-country runners and skiers, as well as ski jumpers. You'll find facilities for any of these sports excellent; in most major urban areas there are maps of the non-auto paths set aside for such pastimes. Ask for the *Ulkoilukartta* (outdoor map) from tourist boards.

One can ski cross-country anywhere in Finland, but Lapland is a favourite spot for this very Nordic sport, as well as for downhill skiing (try to avoid school holiday weeks). Unlike Norway and even Sweden, Finland has very little in the way of mountains, except in the far north, where the Lappish hills, the highest over 1,400 metres (4,000 ft), are called *tunturi*.

There are many participant cross-country ski events as well; information is available from **Suomen Latu (Finnish Ski Trek Association)**, Fabianinkatu 7, 00130 Helsinki, tel: (0)9-170 101; fax: (0)9-663 376.

Language

Getting By

Good morning *Hyvää huomenta*
Good day *Hyvää päivää*
Good evening *Hyvää iltaa*
Today *Tänään*
Tomorrow *Huomenna*
Yesterday *Eilen*
Hello *Päivää or terve*
How do you do? *Kuinka voit*
Goodbye *Näkemiin or hei hei*
Yes *Kyllä or joo*
No *Ei*
Thank you *Kiitos*
How much does this cost?
Paljonko tämä maksaa?
It costs... *Se maksaa...*
How do I get to..? *Miten pääsen..?*
Where is...? *Missä on...?*
Right *Oikealla*
To the right *Oikealle*
Left *Vasemmalla*
To the left *Vasemmalle*
Straight on *Suoraan*
What time is it? *Paljonko kello on?*
It is (the time is) *Kello on*
Could I have your name? *Saisinko
nimesi?*
My name is... *Nimeni on...*
Do you speak English? *Puhutko
englantia?*
I only speak English *Puhun vain
englantia*
Can I help you? *Voinko auttaa
sinua?*
I do not understand *En ymmärrä*
I do not know *En tiedä*

Eating Out

Breakfast *Aamiainen*
Lunch *Lounas*
Dinner *Illallinen*
To eat *Syödä*
To drink *Juoda*
I would like to order... *Haluaisin
tilata*

Could I have the bill? *Saisko
laskun?*
Could I have the key? *Saisko
avaimen?*
Toilet *Vessa*
Gentleman *Miehet (Swedish:
Herrar)*
Ladies *Naiset (Swedish: Damer)*
Vacant *Vapaa*
Engaged *Varattu*
Entrance *Sisäänkäynti*
Exit *Uloskääynti*
No entry *Pääsy kielletty*
Open *Avoinna, Auki*
Closed *Suljettu, Kiinni*
Push *Työnnä*
Pull *Vedä*

Shopping

Clothes *Vaatteet*
Overcoat *Päällystakki*
Jacket *Takki*
Suit *Puku*
Shoes *Kengät*
Skirt *Hame*
Blouse *Pusero*
Jersey *Puuvilla or villapusero*
Handicraft *Käsityö*
Grocers *Ruoka kauppa*
Shop *Kauppa*
Food *Ruoka*
To buy *Ostaa*
Off licence *Alko*
Launderette *Pesula*
Dry cleaning *Kemiallinen pesu*
Dirty *Likainen*
Clean *Puhdas*
Stain *Tahra*
Money *Raha*

Days of the Week

Monday *Maanantai*
Tuesday *Tiistai*
Wednesday *Keskiviikko*
Thursday *Torstai*
Friday *Perjantai*
Saturday *Launantai*
Sunday *Sunnuntai*

Numbers

1 *yksi*
2 *kaksi*
3 *kolme*
4 *neljä*
5 *viisi*
6 *kuusi*

Useful Words

Chemist *Apteekki*
Hospital *Sairaala*
Doctor *Lääkäri*
Police station *Poliisilaitos*
Parking *Paikoitus*
Phrase book *Turistien sanakirja*
Dictionary *Sanakirja*
Car *Auto*
Bus, Coach *Bussi, Linja-auto*
Train *Juna*
Aircraft *Lentokone*
Cheers *Kippis, (Swedish: skål)*
To rent *Vuokrata*
For sale *Myytävänä*
Free, no charge *Ilmainen*
Room to rent *Vuokrattavana
huone*

7 *seitsemän*
8 *kahdeksan*
9 *yhdeksän*
10 *kymmenen*
11 *yksitoista*
12 *kaksitoista*
13 *kolmetoista*
14 *neljätoista*
15 *viisitoista*
16 *kuusitoista*
17 *seitsemäntoista*
18 *kahdeksantoista*
19 *yhdeksäntoista*
20 *kaksikymmentä*
30 *kolmekymmentä*
40 *neljäkymmentä*
50 *viisikymmentä*
60 *kuusikymmentä*
70 *seitsemän-kymmentä*
80 *kahdeksan-kymmentä*
90 *yhdeksänkym-mentä*
100 *sata*
200 *kaksisataa*
1,000 *tuhat*

Further Reading

General Interest

A Guide to Finnish Architecture by Kaipia & Putkonen (Otava). A fascinating town-by-town guide to individual buildings, with plenty of photos and illustrations.

Facts about Finland (Otava). The most comprehensive coverage of Finland's history and culture, by a range of Finnish authors.

Finnish Sauna, Design, Construction and Maintenance (the Finnish Building Centre). Among the many books on Finnish sauna, this one is the most practical, and is popular among home builders.

Food from Finland by Anna-Maija and Juha Tanttu (Otava). An excellent guide to Finnish food, including recipes and colourful features on raw ingredients, such as berries and fungi.

Finland – Nature's Table (Crea Video Oy). Another excellent cookbook that covers not only raw ingredients but a very colourful image of Finland's nature.

Helsinki Jugendstil Art Nouveau Promenades by Henry Moorhouse (Taide Publishing). This handy little guide is a good introduction to Helsinki's finest buildings, with illustrations and street maps.

A Short History of Finland by Singleton & Upton (Cambridge University Press). As the name suggests, this book covers Finland's history in brief, and is perhaps the best written account of the last two millennia.

The Year of the Hare by Arto Paasilinna (Peter Owen, 1996). A good example of a contemporary Finnish humorous novel.

The Egyptian by Mika Waltari (Buccaneer Books). The novel that made Finnish writer Waltari's name – a great epic of Sinuhe, the Egyptian.

Other Insight Guides

Other Insight Guides which highlight destinations in this region include The Netherlands, Russia, Norway and Sweden.

Insight Guide: Norway takes readers on a compelling journey through the Land of the Midnight Sun, from the fjords and mountains to the forests and lakes.

Sweden is one of Europe's last green lungs. Apa Publications assembled expert writers and talented photographers to produce **Insight Guide: Sweden**, which tells you what is and what is not worth seeing.

ART & PHOTO CREDITS

Cartographic Editor **Zoë Goodwin**
Production **Stuart A Everitt**
Design Consultants
Carlotta Junger, Graham Mitchener
Picture Research **Hilary Genin and Britta Jaschinski**

Index

The Insight Approach

The book you are holding is part of the world's largest range of guidebooks. Its purpose is to help you have the most valuable travel experience possible, and we try to achieve this by providing not only information about countries, regions and cities but also genuine insight into their history, culture, institutions and people.

Since the first Insight Guide – to Bali – was published in 1970, the series has been dedicated to the proposition that, with insight into a country's people and culture, visitors can both enhance their own experience and be accepted more easily by their hosts. Now, in a world where ethnic hostilities and nationalist conflicts are all too common, such attempts to increase understanding between peoples are more important than ever.

Insight Guides:
Essentials for understanding
Because a nation's past holds the key to its present, each Insight Guide kicks off with lively history chapters. These are followed by magazine-style essays on culture and daily life. This essential background information gives readers the necessary context for using the main Places section, with its comprehensive run-down on things worth seeing and doing.

Finally, a listings section contains all the information you'll need on travel, hotels, restaurants and opening times.

As far as possible, we rely on local writers and specialists to ensure that information is authoritative. The pictures, for which Insight Guides have become so celebrated, are just as important. Our photojournalistic approach aims not only to illustrate a destination but also to communicate visually and directly to readers life as it is lived by the locals. The series has grown to almost 200 titles.

Compact Guides:
The "great little guides"
As invaluable as such background information is, it isn't always fun to carry an Insight Guide through a crowded souk or up a church tower. Could we, readers asked, distil the key reference material into a slim volume for on-the-spot use?

Our response was to design Compact Guides as an entirely new series, with original text carefully cross-referenced to detailed maps and more than 200 photographs. In essence, they're miniature encyclopedias, concise and comprehensive, displaying reliable and up-to-date information in an accessible way. There are almost 100 titles.

Pocket Guides:
A local host in book form
However wide-ranging the information in a book, human beings still value the personal touch. Our editors are often asked the same questions. Where do *you* go to eat? What do *you* think is the best beach? What would *you* recommend if I have only three days? We invited our local correspondents to act as "substitute hosts" by revealing their preferred walks and trips, listing the restaurants they go to and structuring a visit into a series of timed itineraries.

The result: our Pocket Guides, complete with full-size fold-out maps. These 100-plus titles help readers plan a trip precisely, particularly if their time is short.

Exploring with Insight:
A valuable travel experience
In conjunction with co-publishers all over the world, we print in up to 10 languages, from German to Chinese, from Danish to Russian. But our aim remains simple: to enhance your travel experience by combining our expertise in guidebook publishing with the on-the-spot knowledge of our correspondents.

Table des matières